Mathematics Higher Level
Topic 10 – Option:
Discrete Mathematics
for the IB Diploma

Paul Fannon, Vesna Kadelburg,
Ben Woolley and Stephen Ward

CAMBRIDGE
UNIVERSITY PRESS

University Printing House, Cambridge CB2 8BS, United Kingdom

Cambridge University Press is part of the University of Cambridge.

It furthers the University's mission by disseminating knowledge in the pursuit of education, learning and research at the highest international levels of excellence.

www.cambridge.org
Information on this title: www.cambridge.org/9781107666948

© Cambridge University Press 2013

This publication is in copyright. Subject to statutory exception
and to the provisions of relevant collective licensing agreements,
no reproduction of any part may take place without the written
permission of Cambridge University Press.

First published 2013
Reprinted 2014

Printed in Poland by Opolgraf

A catalogue record for this publication is available from the British Library

ISBN 978-1-107-66694-8 Paperback

Cover image: Thinkstock

Cambridge University Press has no responsibility for the persistence or accuracy of URLs for external or third-party internet websites referred to in this publication, and does not guarantee that any content on such websites is, or will remain, accurate or appropriate. Information regarding prices, travel timetables and other factual information given in this work is correct at the time of first printing but Cambridge University Press does not guarantee the accuracy of such information thereafter.

....

NOTICE TO TEACHERS

Worksheets and copies of them remain in the copyright of Cambridge University Press and such copies may not be distributed or used in any way outside the purchasing institution.

Contents

How to use this book — v

Acknowledgements — viii

Introduction — 1

1 Methods of proof — 3
- **1A** Proof by contradiction — 4
- **1B** Pigeonhole principle — 6
- **1C** Strong induction — 9

2 Divisibility and prime numbers — 13
- **2A** Factors, multiples and remainders — 13
- **2B** Greatest common divisor and least common multiple — 19
- **2C** The Euclidean algorithm — 23
- **2D** Prime numbers — 26

3 Representation of integers in different bases — 33
- **3A** How many fingers do we need to count? — 33
- **3B** Changing between different bases — 35
- **3C** Arithmetic in different bases — 36

4 Linear Diophantine equations — 42
- **4A** Examples of equations with integer solutions — 42
- **4B** How many solutions are there? — 44
- **4C** Finding the general solution — 46
- **4D** Solutions subject to constraints — 47

5 Modular arithmetic — 51
- **5A** Introduction: working with remainders — 51
- **5B** Rules of modular arithmetic — 53
- **5C** Division and linear congruences — 56
- **5D** Chinese remainder theorem — 59
- **5E** Fermat's little theorem — 62

6	Graph theory	67
6A	Introduction to graphs	67
6B	Definitions	69
6C	Some important theorems	79
6D	Subgraphs and complements	85
6E	Moving around a graph	87
6F	Eulerian graphs	89
6G	Hamiltonian graphs	93

7	Algorithms on graphs	98
7A	Weighted graphs	98
7B	Minimum spanning tree: Kruskal's algorithm	102
7C	Finding the shortest path: Dijkstra's algorithm	106
7D	Travelling along all the edges: Chinese postman problem	112
7E	Visiting all the vertices: Travelling salesman problem	118

8	Recurrence relations	134
8A	Defining sequences recursively	134
8B	First order linear recurrence relations	136
8C	Second order recurrence relations	139
8D	Modelling using recurrence relations	143

9	Summary and mixed examination practice	149

Answers	158
Glossary	172
Index	177

How to use this book

Structure of the book

This book covers all the material for Topic 10 (Discrete Mathematics Option) of the Higher Level Mathematics syllabus for the International Baccalaureate course. It is largely independent of the material from the Core topics, so it can be studied at any point during the course. The only required parts of the core are proof by induction (Syllabus Topic 1.4) and sequences and series (Syllabus Topic 1.1). We have tried to include in the main text only the material that will be examinable. There are many interesting applications and ideas that go beyond the syllabus and we have tried to highlight some of these in the 'From another perspective' and 'Research explorer' boxes.

The book is split into three blocks. Chapters 2 to 5 cover number theory, chapters 6 and 7 graph theory and chapter 8 sequences and recurrence relations. The chapters within each block are best studied in the order given, but the three blocks are largely independent of each other. Chapter 1 introduces some methods of mathematical proof that are required throughout the course, and should be covered first. Chapter 9 contains a summary of all the topics and further examination practice, with many of the questions mixing several topics – a favourite trick in IB examinations.

Each chapter starts with a list of learning objectives to give you an idea about what the chapter contains. There is an introductory problem at the start of the topic that illustrates what you should be able to do after you have completed the topic. You should not expect to be able to solve the problem at the start, but you may want to think about possible strategies and what sort of new facts and methods would help you. The solution to the introductory problem is provided at the end of the topic, at the start of chapter 9.

Key point boxes

The most important ideas and formulae are emphasised in the 'KEY POINT' boxes. When the formulae are given in the Formula booklet, there will be an icon: ; if this icon is not present, then the formulae are *not* in the Formula booklet and you may need to learn them or at least know how to derive them.

Worked examples

Each worked example is split into two columns. On the right is what you should write down. Sometimes the example might include more detail then you strictly need, but it is designed to give you an idea of what is required to score full method marks in examinations. However, mathematics is about much more than examinations and remembering methods. So, on the left of the worked examples are notes that describe the thought processes and suggest which route you should use to tackle the question. We hope that these will help you with any exercise questions that differ from the worked examples. It is very deliberate that some of the questions require you to do more than repeat the methods in the worked examples. Mathematics is about thinking!

Signposts

There are several boxes that appear throughout the book.

Theory of knowledge issues

Every lesson is a Theory of knowledge lesson, but sometimes the links may not be obvious. Mathematics is frequently used as an example of certainty and truth, but this is often not the case. In these boxes we will try to highlight some of the weaknesses and ambiguities in mathematics as well as showing how mathematics links to other areas of knowledge.

From another perspective

The International Baccalaureate® encourages looking at things in different ways. As well as highlighting some international differences between mathematicians these boxes also look at other perspectives on the mathematics we are covering: historical, pragmatic and cultural.

Research explorer

As part of your course, you will be asked to write a report on a mathematical topic of your choice. It is sometimes difficult to know which topics are suitable as a basis for such reports, and so we have tried to show where a topic can act as a jumping-off point for further work. This can also give you ideas for an Extended essay. There is a lot of great mathematics out there!

Exam hint

Although we would encourage you to think of mathematics as more than just learning in order to pass an examination, there are some common errors it is useful for you to be aware of. If there is a common pitfall we will try to highlight it in these boxes. We also point out where graphical calculators can be used effectively to simplify a question or speed up your work.

Fast forward / rewind

Mathematics is all about making links. You might be interested to see how something you have just learned will be used elsewhere in the course, or you may need to go back and remind yourself of a previous topic. These boxes indicate connections with other sections of the book to help you find your way around.

How to use the questions

Calculator icon

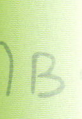

You will be allowed to use a graphical calculator in the final examination paper for this Option. Some questions can be done in a particularly clever way by using one of the graphical calculator functions. However, we recommend that you try to answer some questions without the aid of a calculator. These questions are marked with a non-calculator symbol.

The colour-coding

The questions are colour-coded to distinguish between the levels.

Black questions are drill questions. They help you practise the methods described in the book, but they are usually not structured like the questions in the examination. This does not mean they are easy, some of them are quite tough.

Each differently numbered drill question tests a different skill. Lettered subparts of a question are of increasing difficulty. Within each lettered part there may be multiple roman-numeral parts ((i), (ii),...), all of which are of a similar difficulty. Unless you want to do lots of practice we would recommend that you only do one roman-numeral part and then check your answer. If you have made a mistake then you may want to think about what went wrong before you try any more. Otherwise move on to the next lettered part.

- 🟩 Green questions are examination-style questions which should be accessible to students on the path to getting a grade 3 or 4.

- 🟦 Blue questions are harder examination-style questions. If you are aiming for a grade 5 or 6 you should be able to make significant progress through most of these.

- 🟥 Red questions are at the very top end of difficulty in the examinations. If you can do these then you are likely to be on course for a grade 7.

- ⬜ Gold questions are a type that are *not* set in the examination, but are designed to provoke thinking and discussion in order to help you to a better understanding of a particular concept.

At the end of each chapter you will see longer questions typical of the second section of International Baccalaureate® examinations. These follow the same colour-coding scheme.

Of course, these are just **guidelines**. If you are aiming for a grade 6, do not be surprised if you find a green question you cannot do. People are never equally good at all areas of the syllabus. Equally, if you can do all the red questions that does not guarantee you will get a grade 7; after all, in the examination you have to deal with time pressure and examination stress!

These questions are graded relative to our experience of the final examination, so when you first start the course you will find all the questions relatively hard, but by the end of the course they should seem more straightforward. Do not get intimidated!

We hope you find the Discrete Mathematics Option an interesting and enriching course. You might also find it quite challenging, but do not get intimidated, frequently topics only make sense after lots of revision and practice. Persevere and you will succeed.

The author team

Acknowledgements

The authors and publishers are grateful for the permissions granted to reproduce materials in either the original or adapted form. While every effort has been made, it has not always been possible to identify the sources of all the materials used, or to trace all copyright holders. If any omissions are brought to our notice, we will be happy to include the appropriate acknowledgements on reprinting.

IB exam questions © International Baccalaureate Organization. We gratefully acknowledge permission to reproduce International Baccalaureate Organization intellectual property.

Cover image: Thinkstock

Diagrams in the book were created by Ben Woolley.

Photos: Chapter 5 page 51, Edyta Pawlowska/Shutterstock

Introduction

In this Option you will learn:

- about different methods of proof used in mathematics
- about divisibility of integers, and why prime numbers are so important
- how to find integer solutions of linear equations in two variables (Diophantine equations)
- how to find a remainder when one integer is divided by another, and how to perform calculations and solve equations with remainders (modular arithmetic)
- about various properties of remainders, including the Chinese Remainder Theorem and Fermat's Little Theorem
- about a new mathematical structure called a graph, which consists of points joined by lines, and can be used to model networks
- how to solve optimisation problems on graphs, for example finding the shortest route between two points
- how to find a formula for a sequence given by a recurrence relation.

> **Introductory problem**
>
> Suppose you have a large supply of 20 cent and 30 cent stamps. In how many different ways can you make up $5 postage?

Discrete mathematics includes several branches of mathematics concerned with the study of structures which are discrete, rather than continuous. This means that they are made up of discrete (separate) objects, such as whole numbers or vertices of a cube, rather than continuous quantities such as distance or time (represented by real numbers). Some aspects of discrete mathematics, mainly the theory of whole numbers, date back to antiquity. Many of the areas started developing in the 17th century and only found substantial applications in the 20th. One of the main drivers behind recent developments in the subject is its use in computer science, as computers are fundamentally discrete machines.

Five branches of Discrete Mathematics are studied within the IB syllabus:

Number Theory is the first part of this option. It is concerned with properties of whole numbers, particularly divisibility and prime numbers. Number theory was studied by Greek mathematicians, especially around the 3rd century AD, and a little bit later by Indian and Islamic mathematicians. One of the main topics of interest was Diophantine equations – equations where we are only interested in integer solutions. We will study these in chapter 4 of this option. Number theory has held the interest of mathematicians all over the world for many centuries. This is because it is full of problems that have remained unsolved for a long time. Some examples of these problems are: the Goldbach conjecture (that every even integer greater than 2 is a sum of two primes); the twin prime conjecture (that there are infinitely many pairs of consecutive odd numbers which are both prime); and Fermat's Last Theorem (that there are no integers satisfying $x^n + y^n = z^n$ when n is greater than 2), which was first stated in 1637 but only proved in the 1990s. Prime numbers are a topic of active research because they have recently found applications in cryptography, but there are still many things we don't know about their distribution and how to find them.

Recurrence relations are equations that describe how to get from one term in a sequence to the next. Given a recurrence relation and a sufficient number of starting terms we can use these rules to build up the sequence. However, for analysing the behaviour of the sequence it is more useful to know how the value of each term depends on its position in the sequence. Finding an equation for the nth term of a sequence can be remarkably difficult and in many cases even impossible. In the final chapter of this option we will learn how to solve some types of recurrence relations. We will also use recurrence relations to solve counting problems and model financial situations involving compound interest and debt repayment.

Logic is the study of rules and principles of reasoning and structure of arguments. It is a part of both mathematics and philosophy. As well as being of philosophical interest, it is important in electronic circuit design, computer science and the study of artificial intelligence. Within the IB syllabus, logic is covered in Mathematical Studies and in Theory of Knowledge.

Graph Theory is concerned with problems that can be modelled on a network. This is when a set of points are joined by lines, possibly with a length assigned to each line. These graphs could represent road networks, molecular structures, electronic circuits or planning flowcharts, for example. One class of problems involves studying the properties of graphs, such as various ways of getting from one point to another. Another important class is optimisation problems, where graph theory is required to develop an algorithm to find, for example, the shortest possible route between two points, or the optimal sequence of operations to complete a task in the shortest possible time. This is very different from continuous optimisation problems, which are solved using calculus. Graph theory was first studied in the 18th century, but many of the developments are more recent and have applications in such diverse fields as computer science, physics, chemistry, sociology and linguistics. We will study graph theory in the second part of this option.

Group Theory is an abstract study of the underlying structure of a collection of objects, rather than objects themselves. For example, counting hours on a 12-hour clock, rotations by 30°, and remainders when numbers are divided by 12 all have the same structure, in that they repeat after 12 steps. Group theory is an example of how a single abstract mathematical concept can be applied in many concrete situations. It is important within mathematics in the theory of polynomial equations and topology (the study of certain properties of shapes), but it also has applications in physics and chemistry because it can be used to describe symmetries. Groups are covered in the Sets, Relations and Groups option.

In the first chapter of this option we will introduce various methods of proof which will be needed in subsequent chapters. Chapters 2–5 cover Number theory, chapters 6 and 7 Graph theory, and chapter 8 Recurrence relations. Chapter 9 contains a selection of examination-style questions, some of which combine material from different chapters.

1 Methods of proof

In this chapter you will learn:
- proof by contradiction
- the pigeonhole principle
- strong induction.

 Can a mathematical statement be true before it has been proved?

As we have discussed in the introduction, Discrete Mathematics deals with both the properties of large systems (such as graphs with many points and lines) and properties of natural numbers (of which there are infinitely many). In such systems it is impossible to check all possible cases, so how can we be certain about what is true? In mathematics, truth is established through proof, which is a sequence of logical steps leading from known facts or assumptions to new conclusions.

We have used proofs throughout this course to derive new results: Double-angled identities, the derivative of x^2 and the quadratic formula are some examples. Most of these were **direct proofs**, this means that we started from some results we already knew and derived new results by direct calculation. However, there are some mathematical results that cannot be proved in this way. One of the most quoted examples is the proof that $\sqrt{2}$ is an irrational number: since its decimal expansion is infinite, we cannot show that it never repeats!

An alternative approach is to try and show that $\sqrt{2}$ cannot be written as a fraction; but how can you show by direct calculation that something cannot be done? In this situation we need to use an **indirect proof**, where we find some roundabout way of showing that the statement must be true. For example, we could try to see what would happen if $\sqrt{2}$ could be written as a fraction and hope that this leads to an impossible conclusion; this is called **proof by contradiction**.

You have already met one example of indirect proof, **proof by induction**, which is used to show that a given statement is true for all integers above a certain starting value. This involves showing that the statement is true for the starting number, and that having proved it for some number we can also prove it for the next one; we can then conclude that the statement *can be proved* for all integers, even if we have only directly proved it for the first one.

If you have shown that something can be proved, rather than proving it directly, does that establish its truth?

In this chapter we look in more detail at some indirect methods for proof which will be needed later in the course.

1A Proof by contradiction

Sometimes it is difficult to show directly that something must be true, but it is much simpler to show that the opposite is impossible. For example, suppose that we have an odd square number n^2 and we want to prove that n must also be an odd number. It is not really obvious how to start. We could try taking the square root of n^2, but we don't know whether this produces an odd number (remember, this is what we are trying to prove!). However, thinking about what would happen if n was *not* an odd number allows us to do some calculations: If n was not odd it would be even, and the product of two even numbers is also even, so n^2 would be even. But we were told that n^2 was odd, so this situation is impossible! We can therefore conclude that n must be odd. This way of reasoning is very common in all branches of mathematics, and is known as **proof by contradiction**.

> Proof by contradiction is a special case of a more general form of argument, called *reductio ad absurdum*, in which a proposition is disproved by showing that its truth would lead to an impossible conclusion. This type of argument relies on the *law of excluded middle*, which states that either a proposition or its negation must be true.

> Proof by contradiction was already used by Euclid around 300 BCE. One of the most famous examples was his proof that there are infinitely many prime numbers (see Worked example 2.15). Although it has been a widely used tool in mathematics since then, its validity has been disputed by some, most notably by the 20th century Dutch mathematician and philosopher L.E.J. Brouwer.

KEY POINT 1.1

Proof by contradiction

You can prove that a statement is true by showing that if the opposite was true, it would contradict some of your assumptions (or something else we already know to be true).

One of the most cited examples of proof by contradiction is the proof that $\sqrt{2}$ is an irrational number. Remember that the definition of an irrational number is that it cannot be written in the form $\frac{p}{q}$, where p and q are integers. It is difficult (if not impossible) to express the fact that a number is not of a certain form using an equation. Here proof by contradiction, where we start by assuming that $\sqrt{2}$ is of the form $\frac{p}{q}$, is a really useful tool.

Worked example 1.1

Prove that $\sqrt{2}$ cannot be written in the form $\frac{p}{q}$, where $p, q \in \mathbb{Z}$.

Try proof by contradiction: Start by writing $\sqrt{2}$ as a fraction and show that this leads to impossible consequences	Suppose that $\sqrt{2} = \frac{p}{q}$ with $p, q \in \mathbb{Z}$,
The same fraction can be written in several ways (e.g. $\frac{1}{2} = \frac{3}{6} = \frac{5}{10}$) so we should specify which one we are using	and that the fraction is in its simplest form so that p and q have no common factors.

continued...

> We can now do some calculations
>
> Then $\dfrac{p^2}{q^2} = 2$ (squaring both sides), so $p^2 = 2q^2$.
>
> Looking for common factors is useful in solving problems involving integers
>
> This means that p^2 is even, so p must also be even: $p = 2r$
> Then
> $(2r)^2 = 2q^2$
> $\Rightarrow 4r^2 = 2q^2$
> $\Rightarrow 2r^2 = q^2$
> so q^2 is even and therefore q is also even.
>
> We have reached a contradiction, as we assumed that p and q had no common factors
>
> Hence p and q have common factor 2, which is a contradiction.
> So $\sqrt{2}$ cannot be written as $\dfrac{p}{q}$.

We will use proof by contradiction to prove several results in this option. The exercise below is intended to give you some practice in writing up this type of proof, but does not represent typical examination questions.

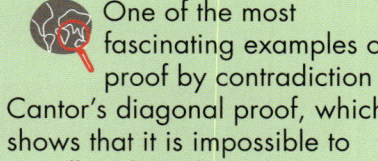

One of the most fascinating examples of proof by contradiction is Cantor's diagonal proof, which shows that it is impossible to put all real numbers into an (infinite) list.

Exercise 1A

1. Prove that if n^2 is an even integer than n is also an even integer.

2. Show that there are no positive integers x and y such that $x^2 - y^2 = 1$.

3. Prove that $\log_2 5$ is an irrational number.

4. Prove that there is no largest even integer.

5. The mean age of five students is 18. Show that at least one of them must be at least 18 years old.

6. Show that the sum of a rational and an irrational number is irrational.

7. Prove the converse of Pythagoras' Theorem: If a, b, c are the sides of a triangle and $a^2 + b^2 = c^2$, then $\hat{C} = 90°$.

1 Methods of proof

8. (a) Use your calculator to show that the equation $x^3 + x + 1 = 0$ has one real root, and find this root correct to 3 significant figures.
   (b) Prove that this root is irrational.

1B Pigeonhole principle

If you have a group of 367 people, you can be certain that two of them share a birthday. This is because there are at most 366 days in a year, so if each person had a different birthday this would account for at most 366 people. This simple observation can be a surprisingly powerful tool in solving seemingly very difficult problems. It is traditionally stated in the following form:

> The pigeonhole principle is also known as Dirichlet's principle, after the 19th century German mathematician Gustav Lejeune Dirichlet.

KEY POINT 1.2

Pigeonhole principle

If $n + 1$ pigeons are placed in n pigeonholes, then there is a pigeonhole which contains at least two pigeons.

Worked example 1.2

You are given 11 different real numbers between 1 and 100 inclusive. Use the pigeonhole principle to show that two of those numbers differ by at most 10.

Since we have 11 numbers, to use the pigeonhole principle we need 10 'pigeonholes'

Divide the interval [1, 100] into 10 equal intervals:
1–10, 11–20, …, 91–100

Since there are 11 numbers, two of them must be in the same interval (by the pigeonhole principle).

What is the largest possible difference between two numbers in the same interval?

These two numbers differ by at the most 10.

Notice that we could also have proved the above claim by contradiction.

Put the 11 numbers in order, $x_1 < x_2 < \ldots < x_{11}$, and suppose that each pair of consecutive numbers differ by more than 10. Then, as $x_1 \geq 1$, it follows that $x_2 > x_1 + 10 \geq 11$, $x_3 > x_2 + 10 \geq 21$, and so on, ending with $x_{11} > 101$, which contradicts the assumption that all the numbers are between 1 and 100. Hence there must be two of the numbers which differ by at most 10.

The pigeonhole principle itself can be proved by contradiction. A more general form of the principle is:

KEY POINT 1.3

General pigeonhole principle

If $kn + 1$ objects are divided into n groups (some of which may be empty) then there is a group which contains at least $k + 1$ objects.

Worked example 1.3

Prove the general pigeonhole principle stated above.

We don't know anything about how the objects are split into groups, so a direct proof seems unlikely. So try a proof by contradiction	Suppose that the statement is false, so each of the n groups contains at most k objects.
	Then the total number of objects can be at most kn. This contradicts the assumption about the number of objects. Hence at least one of the groups must contain at least $k + 1$ objects.

Not all statements that can be proved using the pigeonhole principle can easily be proved by contradiction. The next example uses the general pigeonhole principle.

Worked example 1.4

Nineteen points are drawn inside a square of side 3 cm. Use the pigeonhole principle to show that it is possible to find three points that form a triangle with an area less than 1 cm².

We want one of the 'pigeonholes' to contain a triangle, so we need to define 9 'pigeonholes' (since $2 \times 9 = 18$)	The square can be split into nine squares of side 1 cm. Since $19 = 2 \times 9 + 1$, by the pigeonhole principle there is one of these squares which contains at least three of the points.
What is the largest possible area of a triangle which is inside a square of side 1 cm?	These three points form a triangle with area less than the area of the square, which is 1 cm².

It is not obvious that we could prove the above statement by contradiction. We can try assuming that all the triangles have an area more than 1 and try to show that the total area is too large, but since some of the triangles overlap it is difficult to say anything about their total area. This last example illustrates the power of the pigeonhole principle in proving statements which would be difficult to prove using any other method.

1 Methods of proof   **7**

The pigeonhole principle is an example of a *non-constructive existence proof*. In the last example we found that a triangle with the required property exists, but not how to find it. Some mathematicians dispute the validity of such proofs. Is it useful to know that something exists if we don't know how to find it? Can an object be said to exist if there is no known method of finding or constructing it?

 We will use the pigeonhole principle to prove some theorems about graphs, see Worked example 6.1.

Exercise 1B

1. A bag contains sweets of five different colours. How many sweets do you need to pick to be certain that you have three of the same colour? Prove your result using the pigeonhole principle.

2. Prove that among any 8 positive integers there are two whose difference is divisible by 7.

3. Prove that if you pick five different integers between 1 and 8 (inclusive) then two of them must add up to 9.

4. Show that if 9 people are seated in a row of 12 chairs, there must be three consecutive occupied chairs.

5. Show that among 91 positive integers it is possible to find 10 whose sum ends in a 0.

6. There are n people at the party and some of them are friends.
   (a) Explain why it is impossible that there is both a person who is friends with everyone and a person who has no friends at the party.
   (b) Show that there are two people who have the same number of friends.

7. Five points are drawn on the surface of an orange. Prove that it is possible to cut the orange in half in such a way that at least four of the points are on the same hemisphere (any points lying along the cut count as being on both hemispheres).

8. Each point in the plane is coloured either red or blue. Show that there are two points of the same colour which are exactly 1 cm apart.

9. 51 points are selected inside a square of side 1 m. Show that it is possible to find three of those points which lie inside a circle of radius $\frac{1}{7}$ m.

10. Each side and diagonal of a regular hexagon is coloured either red or blue. Show that there is a triangle with all three sides of the same colour.

The result in question 10 is a special case of Ramsey's theorem, which deals with colouring of graphs. It is often stated in the following form: In any group of six people, there are either three who all know each other, or three none of whom know each other.

8 Topic 10 – Option: Discrete mathematics

1C Strong induction

You will have learnt that some statements about positive integers can be proved using the Principle of mathematical induction. The key idea in inductive proofs is that if we know that the statement is true for a certain positive integer, we can use this to show that it is true for the next integer. This relies on establishing a connection between the statement for n and the statement for $n + 1$.

However, sometimes the statement for n depends on more than one previous value. One familiar example is the Fibonacci sequence, defined by $F_n = F_{n-1} + F_{n-2}$ with starting values $F_1 = F_2 = 1$. If we want to prove something about F_n we need information about both F_{n-1} and F_{n-2}.

For example, let us prove that $F_n < 2^n$ for all n. First of all, the formula $F_n = F_{n-1} + F_{n-2}$ only applies for $n \geq 3$, so we need to start by checking the two starting values: $F_1 = 1 < 2^1$ and $F_2 = 1 < 2^2$. Now suppose that we have checked that the statement is true for all terms up to and including F_{k-1} for some k. Since $F_k = F_{k-1} + F_{k-2}$, we need to use the result for two previous terms. As we are assuming that we have checked the statement up to and including F_{k-1}, we can use the fact that $F_{k-1} < 2^{k-1}$ and $F_{k-2} < 2^{k-2}$. Then:

$$F_k = F_{k-1} + F_{k-2}$$
$$< 2^{k-1} + 2^{k-2}$$
$$= 2^{k-2}(2+1)$$
$$< 2^{k-2} \times 4 = 2^k$$

This shows that $F_k < 2^k$, so the statement is also true for $n = k$.

Thus we have shown that:

- The statement $F_n < 2^n$ is true for $n = 1$ and $n = 2$.
- If the statement is true for all $n < k$ then we can show that it is also true for $n = k$.

It follows that the statement $F_n < 2^n$ is true for all positive integers n, as we can reach any n by repeating the steps above: Use the statements for $n = 1$ and $n = 2$ to prove it when $n = 3$, then use the statements for $n = 2$ and $n = 3$ to prove it for $n = 4$, and so on.

This variant of proof by induction, where in the inductive step we need to use several previous values rather than just one, is called **strong induction**.

KEY POINT 1.4

Strong induction

Suppose that we have a statement (or rule) about a positive integer n. If we can show that:

(a) the statement is true for some number of **base cases**, and

(b) *assuming* that the statement is true for all $n < k$, we can show that it is also true for $n = k$ (this is called the **inductive step**)

then the statement is true for all positive integers n.

Note that the number of base cases needed depends on how many previous terms are required to calculate the next term in the sequence. In our example above, each term was found by using two previous terms, so we needed two base values.

Sometimes the inductive step requires some of the previous terms, but we don't necessarily know which ones. We then really need to know that the statement is true for *all* previous values of n. This is where the method of strong induction is particularly useful.

Worked example 1.5

Use strong induction to show that every positive integer n can be written in the form

$$n = 2^p c_p + 2^{p-1} c_{p-1} + \ldots + 2 c_1 + c_0$$

where $p \in \mathbb{N}$ and each c_i is either 0 or 1.

It is not immediately obvious how many base cases we need, so look at the inductive step first	Inductive step: Suppose that we have proved the statement for all $n < k$, and look at $n = k$.
There is no obvious connection between $n = k$ and any particular previous terms. However, as the required expression involves powers of 2, we may be able to establish a connection between k and $\dfrac{k}{2}$	Consider two separate cases: k can be either even or odd.
If k is even we can relate k to $\dfrac{k}{2}$	If k is even, then $\dfrac{k}{2}$ is an integer less than k, so we know that the statement is true for $n = \dfrac{k}{2}$: $$\dfrac{k}{2} = 2^p c_p + 2^{p-1} c_{p-1} + \ldots + 2 c_1 + c_0$$ for some p and $c_i = 0$ or 1.
Multiply this by 2 to get k	Then $k = 2^{p+1} c_p + 2^p c_{p-1} + \ldots + 2^2 c_1 + 2 c_0$ which is also of the required form.

10 Topic 10 – Option: Discrete mathematics

continued...

> If k is odd, we can relate k to $\frac{k-1}{2}$.

If k is odd, $\frac{k-1}{2}$ is an integer less than k, so we know that the statement is true for $n = \frac{k-1}{2}$:

$$\frac{k-1}{2} = 2^p c_p + 2^{p-1} c_{p-1} + \ldots + 2c_1 + c_0$$

for some p and $c_i = 0$ or 1.

> To get k we need to double and add 1

Then
$$k = 2(2^p c_p + 2^{p-1} c_{p-1} + \ldots + 2c_1 + c_0) + 1$$
$$= 2^{p+1} c_p + 2^p c_{p-1} + \ldots + 2^2 c_1 + 2c_0 + 1$$

which is also of the correct form.

Therefore the statement is true for $n = k$.

> Remember that we have not done a base case yet: we can get to $n = 2$ and $n = 3$ by using $n = 1$, so we only need one base case

Base case:
When $n = 1$, take $p = 0$ and $c_0 = 1$ to get the required form.

> Always write a conclusion

Conclusion:
The statement is true for $n = 1$, and if it is true for all $n < k$ then we can show that it is also true for $n = k$. Hence the statement is true for all integers $n \geq 1$ by strong induction.

To prove the statement for each value of k in the above example, we used one of the previous values. The value used depended on k; so to prove the statement for $n = 10$ and $n = 11$ we used $n = 5$ and to prove it for $n = 31$ we used $n = 15$. This is why we needed to assume that the statement was true for *all* previous values of n.

 The form from the previous example is called the binary form, or base 2 representation of n. It is a special case of a number base, which we will investigate in more detail in chapter 3.

Exercise 1C

In this exercise, n is a natural number.

1. Given that $a_0 = 2, a_1 = 5$ and $a_{n+2} = 5a_{n+1} - 6a_n$, show that $a_n = 2^n + 3^n$.

2. A sequence is defined by $a_{n+3} = 3a_{n+2} - 3a_{n+1} + a_n$ with $a_1 = 0, a_2 = 1, a_3 = 4$. Prove that for all n, $a_n = (n-1)^2$.

3. The sequence x_n is defined by $x_1 = 1, x_2 = 2$ and $x_n = (n-1)(x_{n-1} + x_{n-2})$. Show that $x_n = n!$

4. Fermat numbers are defined by $F_n = 2^{2^n} + 1$ for $n \geq 1$. Prove that all Fermat numbers except for the first one end in a 7.

5. The sequence G_n is defined by $G_1 = 1, G_2 = 2, G_3 = 3$ and $G_{n+3} = G_{n+2} + G_{n+1} + G_n$. Show that for all $n \geq 1$, $G_n < 2^n$.

6. Show that any amount of postage greater than or equal to 12 cents can be made using only 4 cent and 5 cent stamps.

7. Show that for all integers $n \geq 2$, the number $\cos\left(\dfrac{\pi}{2^n}\right)$ is irrational.

8. Let $u_0 = 1$ and $u_n = u_{n-1} + u_{n-2} + \ldots + u_2 + u_1 + 2u_0$ for $n \geq 1$. Show that $u_n = 2^n$ for all $n \in \mathbb{N}$.

9. Show that n straight lines divide the plane into at most 2^n regions.

Fermat studied the numbers from question 4 in the 17th century and believed that they were all prime. (He only checked the first four!) It was only 100 years later that Euler proved that F_5 is in fact divisible by 641. It is not known whether any other Fermat numbers are prime.

2 Divisibility and prime numbers

In this chapter you will learn:

- about factors and multiples, including the greatest common divisor and the least common multiple
- a method for finding the greatest common divisor of two large numbers (the Euclidean algorithm)
- various useful properties of factors and multiples
- why prime numbers are so important.

Whole numbers can always be added, subtracted and multiplied and the result is a whole number. The only basic operation that does not always result in a whole number is division. For this reason, looking at factors is an important tool in solving problems in number theory. Some of the material in this chapter will be familiar to you already, but some of the more abstract results may be new. You are expected to be able to prove many of these results. The proofs are also examples of techniques you will need to use in later chapters.

2A Factors, multiples and remainders

Much of number theory is concerned with finding factors or multiples of numbers, or looking at remainders when numbers cannot be divided exactly. In this section we review some of the basic terminology and properties relevant to division and the divisibility of whole numbers. Throughout this chapter, by 'number' we mean a whole number (integer).

Consider two numbers, a and b. If there is a number k such that $b = ka$ we can write $a \mid b$ and say that:

a divides b,
or b is divisible by a,
or a is a factor of b,
or b is a multiple of a.

Note that $a \neq 0$ as we cannot divide by zero, but that $b = 0$ is possible and in fact $a \mid 0$ for all a.

KEY POINT 2.1

Some basic properties of divisibility:
- If $a \mid b$ and $a \mid c$ then $a \mid (b \pm c)$.
- If $a \mid b$ then $a \mid (bc)$ for any number c.

Note that 1 is a factor of every number, and that every number is a factor of itself. When talking about factors, we will always specify whether we want to include 1 and the number itself.

We can always find numbers k and r such that:
$$b = ka + r \text{ and } 0 \leq r < a$$

We call k the **quotient** and r the **remainder** when b is divided by a. Note that $r = 0$ if and only if $a \mid b$, and in that case we can write $b = ka$.

In chapter 4 we will examine other rules for working with remainders, called modular arithmetic.

The process of finding k and r is called the **division algorithm**. Although it seems very simple, writing b as $ka + r$ or ka is surprisingly useful when proving other results.

As division can be a long process, it is useful to have ways of deciding whether one number divides another without having to perform the division. For divisibility by many small numbers there are **divisibility tests** which use the digits of the number to be divided.

KEY POINT 2.2

Divisibility tests using last digits:

- A number is divisible by 2 if its last digit is even.
- A number is divisible by 5 if its last digit is 0 or 5.
- A number is divisible by 10 if its last digit is 0.
- A number is divisible by 4 if the number formed by its last two digits is divisible by 4.
- A number is divisible by 8 if the number formed by its last three digits is divisible by 8.

Divisibility test using all the digits:

- A number is divisible by 3 if the sum of its digits is divisible by 3.
- A number is divisible by 9 if the sum of its digits is divisible by 9.
- A number is divisible by 11 if the alternating sum of its digits is divisible by 11. (So if the number has digits $a_1, a_2, a_3 \ldots$ we calculate the sum $a_1 - a_2 + a_3 - \ldots$)

In chapter 3 you will prove divisibility tests for numbers written in bases other than 10.

We will now prove some of the divisibility tests listed above. You could be asked to reproduce those proofs in an exam but, more importantly, they are examples of types of proof used in number theory, and you will be asked to produce proofs with similar structure and using similar techniques.

In order to derive those proofs we need a way of expressing a number using its digits.

KEY POINT 2.3

If N is a k-digit number with digits $a_k, a_{k-1} \ldots a_2, a_1, a_0$ then:

$$N = 10^k a_k + 10^{k-1} a_{k-1} + \ldots + 10^2 a_2 + 10 a_1 + a_0.$$

We use shorthand $N = (a_k a_{k-1} \ldots a_2 a_1 a_0)$.

Worked example 2.1

Prove that a number is divisible by 4 if and only if the number formed by its last two digits is divisible by 4.

This is an 'if and only if' statement so we have two things to prove. Knowing something about the last two digits gives us a way to start, so first prove 'if the number formed by the last two digits is divisible by 4, then the whole number is divisible by 4'

(i) Let N be a number such that the number formed by its last two digits is divisible by 4. Prove that N is divisible by 4.

As the statement is about digits of N, it makes sense to write $N = (a_k a_{k-1} \ldots a_2 a_1 a_0)$

Separate the last two digits

Let $N = 10^k a_k + 10^{k-1} a_{k-1} + \ldots + 10^2 a_2 + 10 a_1 + a_0$

We are told that the last 2 digits $(a_1 a_0)$, that is $10a_1 + a_0$, is divisible by 4. This means that we can write it as $4M$ for some number M (it's not important what M is)

$= \left(10^k a_k + 10^{k-1} a_{k-1} + \ldots + 10^2 a_2\right) + (10 a_1 + a_0)$

$= \left(10^k a_k + 10^{k-1} a_{k-1} + \ldots + 10^2 a_2\right) + 4M$

When proving divisibility, it is usually a good idea to take out common factors. All the terms in the first bracket have a factor of 100

$= 100 \left(10^{k-2} a_k + 10^{k-3} a_{k-1} + \ldots + a_2\right) + 4M$

But 100 is divisible by 4, so both terms are divisible by 4

As $4 \mid 100$, both parts are divisible by 4, so N is divisible by 4.

We now need to prove the other direction. It is a good idea to try and reverse the previous proof (and only look for an alternative strategy if this doesn't work)

(ii) Let N be a number which is divisible by 4. Prove that the number formed by its last two digits is divisible by 4.

So we write N in terms of its digits and separate the last two digits

Let
$N = 10^k a_k + 10^{k-1} a_{k-1} + \ldots + 10^2 a_2 + 10 a_1 + a_0$
$= \left(10^k a_k + 10^{k-1} a_{k-1} + \ldots + 10^2 a_2\right) + (10 a_1 + a_0)$
$= 100 \left(10^{k-2} a_k + 10^{k-3} a_{k-1} + \ldots + a_2\right) + (10 a_1 + a_0)$

We can see that the first part is divisible by 4. We have also assumed that N is divisible by 4. If $4 \mid (b+c)$ and $4 \mid b$ then it must be that $4 \mid c$

As $4 \mid N$ and $4 \mid 100$, it follows that $4 \mid (10a_1 + a_0)$.

2 Divisibility and prime numbers

> **EXAM HINT**
> To prove a statement of the form 'A if and only if B' you need to produce two separate proofs: if A then B, and if B then A. Often (but not always) the two different directions use similar techniques.

The proofs for divisibility by 3, 9 and 11 use the following results, which follow from the Factor Theorem.

KEY POINT 2.4

> For any integer power n, $a^n - b^n$ has a factor $(a-b)$.
>
> For any *odd* power n, $a^n + b^n$ has a factor $(a+b)$.

Worked example 2.2

Prove that if a number is divisible by 9 then the sum of its digits is divisible by 9.

It seems sensible to write the number in terms of its digits and then separate the sum of the digits

Let
$N = 10^k a_k + 10^{k-1} a_{k-1} + \ldots + 10^2 a_2 + 10 a_1 + a_0$
Then
$N = (a_k + a_{k-1} + \ldots + a_1 + a_0) + (10^k - 1) a_k + (10^{k-1} - 1) a_{k-1} + \ldots$
$+ (10^2 - 1) a_2 + (10 - 1) a_1$

All the brackets after the first one are of the form $(10^p - 1)$, so we can use the result from Key point 2.4 with $a = 10, b = 1$

Each term of the form $(10^p - 1)$ has a factor of $(10-1) = 9$, so all terms after the first bracket are divisible by 9.

But we are told that N is divisible by 9, so the first bracket must also be divisible by 9

As N is divisible by 9, $(a_k + a_{k-1} + \ldots + a_1 + a_0)$ must also be divisible by 9.

You can use the same technique to show that if the sum of the digits is divisible by 9 then the number is divisible by 9. The proofs for divisibility by 3 and 11 follow a similar argument.

We can combine these basic divisibility tests to check for divisibility by other numbers. In doing so, we use the following result, which we will prove in the next section.

KEY POINT 2.5

See the end of the next section for the proof of this result.

> If $a \mid N$ and $b \mid N$, and if a and b have no common factors (other than 1), then $(ab) \mid N$.

Worked example 2.3

Find the possible values of digits p and q such that the five-digit number ($386pq$) is divisible by 18.

As $18 = 2 \times 9$, for divisibility by 18 it is sufficient that the number is divisible by both 2 and 9	We need $386pq$ to be divisible by 2 and by 9.
We know the divisibility tests for 2 and for 9	Divisibility by 2: q is an even digit Divisibility by 9: $3+8+6+p+q = 9k$ $\Leftrightarrow 17+p+q = 9k$
As p and q are digits, they are both between 0 and 9, which limits the possibilities	But $0 \leq p+q \leq 18$, so $p+q = 1$ or 10.
We can now combine this with the fact that q is even	If $p+q = 1$: $\qquad q=0, p=1$ If $p+q = 10$: $\qquad q=2, p=8$ $\qquad q=4, p=6$ $\qquad q=6, p=4$ $\qquad q=8, p=2$

As well as showing that a specific number is divisible by something, we can sometimes prove that a whole class of numbers is divisible by a given number. Two main methods used in such proofs are:

- factorising, in particular the difference of two squares and the results of Key point 2.4
- proof by induction.

The following example illustrates the use of factorising:

Worked example 2.4

If n is an odd integer, prove that $n^2 - 1$ is divisible by 8.

We can factorise $n^2 - 1$ using the difference of two squares	$n^2 - 1 = (n-1)(n+1)$
Since $8 = 2 \times 4$, hopefully we can show that one of the factors is divisible by 2 and the other one by 4. Remember that n is odd, and that every other even number is divisible by 4	$(n-1)$ and $(n+1)$ are two consecutive even integers, so they are both divisible by 2, and one of them is divisible by 4. Hence their product is divisible by $2 \times 4 = 8$, as required.

2 Divisibility and prime numbers

The next example shows a proof by induction. You have already seen such questions in the core course, but they can also be asked in this option.

Worked example 2.5

Prove by induction that for every positive integer n, $2^{n+2} + 3^{2n+1}$ is divisible by 7.

We follow the standard format of proof by induction, so start by checking the case $n = 1$

When $n = 1$:
$2^3 + 3^3 = 35 = 5 \times 7$
So it is true for $n = 1$.

If a number is divisible by 7, it can be written as $7a$ for some integer a. This may be useful in a later calculation

Assume it is true for $n = k$: Then
$2^{k+2} + 3^{2k+1} = 7a$ $\quad$ (*)
for some integer a.

Then for $n = k + 1$:
$2^{n+2} + 3^{2n+1} = 2^{k+3} + 3^{2k+3}$

Relate to the expression for $n = k$

$= 2 \times 2^{k+2} + 9 \times 3^{2k+1}$

We need to use the assumption for $n = k$. The easiest way is to express one of the terms using equation (*)

$= 2 \times (7a - 3^{2k+1}) + 9 \times 3^{2k+1}$ using (*)
$= 14a + 7 \times 3^{2k+1}$

Both terms are divisible by 7, so the whole expression is divisible by 7.
Hence it is true for $n = k + 1$.

Remember to write the conclusion

As the expression is divisible by 7 when $n = 1$, and if it divisible by 7 for $n = k$ then it is also divisible by 7 for $n = k + 1$, it follows that the expression is divisible by 7 for all $n \in \mathbb{Z}^+$ by the Principle of Mathematical Induction.

Exercise 2A

1. Check whether each of these numbers is divisible by 3, 4 and 11:
   (a) (i) 333 444 (ii) 33 334 444
   (b) (i) 515 151 (ii) 5 151 515
   (c) (i) 123 456 (ii) 8 765 432
   (d) (i) 515 152 (ii) 747 472

2. Find the missing digits so that the given number is divisible by 36:
   (a) (i) $(32a4b)$ (ii) $(11a65b)$
   (b) (i) $(613ab)$ (ii) $(2213ab)$

3. Find digits a and b so that the number $(2006ab)$ is divisible by 33. *[7 marks]*

4. Show that the number 19581958…….1958 (400 digits) is divisible by 22 but not by 44. *[6 marks]*

5. Given two positive integers p, q such that $p \mid q$, show that $p^k \mid q^k$ for every positive integer k. *[5 marks]*

6. Show that for all values of n the number $n^4 + 12n^2 + 35$ has at least two factors (other than 1 and itself). *[3 marks]*

7. Prove by induction that $5^n - 1$ is divisible by 4 for all values of n. *[6 marks]*

8. (a) Explain why every positive integer can be written in one of the following four forms: $4k$, $4k \pm 1$, $4k + 2$.

   (b) Hence prove that a square number takes the form $4k$ or $4k + 1$.

   (c) Prove that a square number can only be of the form $8k$, $8k + 1$ or $8k + 4$. *[8 marks]*

9. Find all three digit numbers which have the hundreds and the units digits equal and which are divisible by 15. *[5 marks]*

10. For which values of n is the number $\underbrace{111\cdots11}_{n \text{ digits}}$ divisible by
    (a) 9?
    (b) 11? *[4 marks]*

11. Number N is given in terms of its digits as:
    $N = 10^k a_k + 10^{k-1} a_{k-1} + \ldots + 10^2 a_2 + 10 a_1 + a_0$
    Show that N is divisible by 11 if and only if
    $a_k - a_{k-1} + a_{k-2} - \ldots + (-1)^k a_0$
    is divisible by 11. *[8 marks]*

12. Prove by induction that $7^n + 4^n + 1$ is divisible by 6 for all $n \in \mathbb{Z}^+$. *[8 marks]*

2B Greatest common divisor and least common multiple

In the previous section we used the result from Key point 2.5, which only applies when two numbers do not have any common factors. For many results in number theory it is important to know the common factors of two numbers.

> **EXAM HINT**
> The gcd is also called the highest common factor, or hcf, but the IB uses notation gcd (a, b).

 See Euclidean algorithm in Section 2C.

> **EXAM HINT**
> Your calculator can find the greatest common divisor, which is useful for checking your answers.

The **greatest common divisor (gcd)** of a and b is the largest number d which divides both a and b. We write $d = \gcd(a,b)$. For example, $\gcd(4,6) = 2$ and $\gcd(12,35) = 1$. Two numbers are called **relatively prime** (or **coprime**) if their gcd is 1 (so they have no common factors other than 1). For example, 12 and 35 are relatively prime.

One way to find $\gcd(a,b)$ is to list all the factors of a and b. A slightly more efficient way is to list only the prime factors. For example, $36 = 2 \times 2 \times 3 \times 3$ and $90 = 2 \times 3 \times 3 \times 5$, so $\gcd(36,90) = 2 \times 3 \times 3 = 18$. Finding prime factors can be difficult, so in the next section we will see an alternative method, which is of more use with larger numbers.

The greatest common divisor has some important properties which you can use to prove other results. The proofs of these properties themselves have been required on examination papers in the past, so we will show one of the proofs here. You should try to understand the thought processes and strategies involved in theses proofs, as they can be applied to proving other results.

Worked example 2.6

Prove that if $\gcd(a,b) = d$ then $\gcd\left(\dfrac{a}{d}, \dfrac{b}{d}\right) = 1$.

It is a good idea to write some sort of equation relating a, b and d. As d divides both a and b we can write $a = md$ and $b = nd$	We can write $a = md$ and $b = nd$. Then we need to show that $\gcd(m,n) = 1$.
Give gcd(m, n) a name and try to find out something about it, using definitions of m and n	Suppose $\gcd(m,n) = f$. Then $m = pf$ and $n = qf$, so $a = pfd$ and $b = qfd$.
This shows that both a and b have fd as a factor. But we know that the largest common factor of a and b is d	This means that fd divides both a and b. However, the largest number that divides both a and b is d, so $fd \leq d$.
Remember that $f = \gcd(m, n)$, and we wanted to know that this is 1	Hence $f \leq 1$. But f is a positive integer, so $f = 1$, as required.

The above example says that if we divide two numbers by their greatest common divisor, the resulting numbers are relatively prime.

There are two further important properties which tell us what happens to the gcd when we subtract two numbers. All three results are summarised below:

KEY POINT 2.6

If $\gcd(a,b) = d$ then:
- $\gcd\left(\dfrac{a}{d}, \dfrac{b}{d}\right) = 1$
- $\gcd(a, a-b) = d$
- $\gcd(b, a-qb) = d$ for any $q \in \mathbb{Z}$

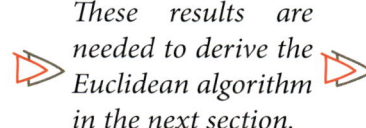

These results are needed to derive the Euclidean algorithm in the next section.

Let us return to the result in Key point 2.5: if a and b both divide N and if $\gcd(a,b) = 1$, then ab also divides N. For example, 6 and 5 both divide 600 so 30 ($= 6 \times 5$) also divides 600. However, 6 and 4 both divide 36, but 24 ($= 6 \times 4$) does not. So the condition that $\gcd(a,b) = 1$ is necessary for the result to apply. Notice that 12 does divide 36, and 12 is the smallest number which is divisible by both 4 and 6.

This leads us to another important concept. The **least common multiple** (lcm) of a and b is the smallest number l such that both a and b divide l. We write $l = \mathrm{lcm}(a,b)$. For example, $\mathrm{lcm}(4,6) = 12$ and $\mathrm{lcm}(5,6) = 30$. The above example suggests the following extension of Key point 2.5.

KEY POINT 2.7

If $a \mid N$ and $b \mid N$ then $\mathrm{lcm}(ab) \mid N$.

To prove this result we need to look in more detail at the properties of and relationship between lcm and gcd.

We can find the lcm by listing multiples of a and b until we find a number which is in both lists. A slightly better method is to use prime factors. For example $18 = 2 \times 3 \times 3$ and $120 = 2 \times 2 \times 2 \times 3 \times 5$, so every multiple of both 18 and 120 must be divisible by 2^3, 3^2 and 5. Hence $\mathrm{lcm}(18, 120) = 2^3 \times 3^2 \times 5 = 360$. A convenient way to see what's going on is to draw a Venn diagram showing prime factors of the two numbers.

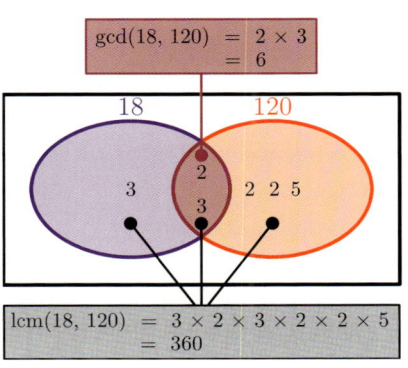

The common prime factors are those in the intersection of the two sets, so $\gcd(18, 120) = 2 \times 3 = 6$.

Any common multiple must contain all the factors which appear in at least one of the numbers, so the lcm is the product of all the prime factors in the union of the two sets, $\mathrm{lcm}(18, 120) = 2^3 \times 3^2 \times 5 = 360$. Notice that $6 \times 360 = 2160$ and $18 \times 120 = 2160$. This is one example of a very important result.

KEY POINT 2.8

$$\gcd(a,b) \times \text{lcm}(a,b) = ab$$

Once we have found $\gcd(a,b)$, this result can be used to find the lcm. The proof of this result has often appeared on examination papers, and it is also an example of a more complex number theory proof you may be asked to produce.

Worked example 2.7

Prove that $\gcd(a,b) \times \text{lcm}(a,b) = ab$.

We can write $a = md$ and $b = nd$ with $\gcd(m,n) = 1$	Let $d = \gcd(a,b)$. Then $a = md$ and $b = nd$ with $\gcd(m,n) = 1$.
We know two things about $\text{lcm}(a,b)$: it is a multiple of both a and b, and it is the smallest such multiple. How can we express the first fact?	Let S be any multiple of both a and b. Then $S = ka$ and $b \mid S$, so $\dfrac{ka}{b}$ is a whole number. Then $\dfrac{kmd}{nd}$ is a whole number, so $\dfrac{km}{n}$ is a whole number.
How can n divide km? Remember that m and n have no common factors. We are trying to get an expression in terms of a, b and d	As $\gcd(m,n) = 1$, n must divide k; so $k = qn$ for some q. Hence $S = ka = qna = qmnd = q\dfrac{ab}{d}$
Now we use the fact that $\text{lcm}(a,b)$ is the smallest possible value of S. The smallest possible value of q is 1	As $\text{lcm}(a,b)$ is the smallest possible value of S, it corresponds to $q = 1$. Hence $\text{lcm}(a,b) = \dfrac{ab}{d}$ so $\text{lcm}(a,b) \times \gcd(a,b) = ab$.

We can now prove the result of Key point 2.7.

Worked example 2.8

Prove that if $a \mid N$ and $b \mid N$ then $\text{lcm}(a,b) \mid N$.

We almost proved this in Worked example 2.7, as we have shown that any common multiple of a and b can be written as $S = q\dfrac{ab}{d}$ for some q.	From the previous proof, $N = q\dfrac{ab}{d}$. But $\dfrac{ab}{d} = \text{lcm}(a,b)$, so $\text{lcm}(a,b)$ divides N.

Topic 10 – Option: Discrete mathematics

In the special case when *a* and *b* are relatively prime, we get the result from Key point 2.5.

KEY POINT 2.9

If *a* and *b* are relatively prime then:
- $\text{lcm}(a,b) = ab$.
- If $a \mid N$ and $b \mid N$ then $ab \mid N$.

Exercise 2B

1. Find the greatest common divisor and the least common multiple for the following pairs of numbers:
   (a) (i) 36 and 68   (ii) 35 and 42
   (b) (i) 225 and 180   (ii) 360 and 135
   (c) (i) 56 and 81   (ii) 49 and 85
   (d) (i) 28 and 56   (ii) 35 and 105
   (e) (i) 64 and 72   (ii) 27 and 18
   (f) (i) $6p^2q$ and $9pq^3$ where p and q are prime numbers
       (ii) $25pq^2$ and $15pq$ where p and q are prime numbers

2. Verify that the results in Key points 2.6 and 2.8 are true for the following pairs of numbers:
   (a) (i) 68 and 32   (ii) 56 and 21
   (b) (i) 120 and 60   (ii) 100 and 50
   (c) (i) 35 and 16   (ii) 42 and 25

3. Let $l = \text{lcm}(a,b)$ and write $l = pa$ and $l = qb$. Prove that $\gcd(p,q) = 1$. [7 marks]

4. If $\gcd(a,b) = 1$ prove that $\gcd(a+b, a-b)$ is either 1 or 2. [6 marks]

5. Prove that if $a \mid (bc)$ and $\gcd(a,b) = 1$ then $a \mid c$. [5 marks]

6. If $d = \gcd(a,b)$ and f is any other common divisor of a and b, prove that $f \mid d$. [5 marks]

2C The Euclidean algorithm

In this section we describe another method for finding the greatest common divisor of two numbers, one which is useful for large numbers when prime factorisation is not feasible.

The Euclidean algorithm appears in Euclid's *Elements*, but it is believed that it had been known at least a century earlier. It was later discovered independently in both India and China by astronomers trying to solve equations needed to make accurate calendars.

KEY POINT 2.10

The **Euclidean algorithm** for finding $\gcd(a, b)$ with $a > b$:

- Find the remainder when a is divided by b. Call this r_1.
- Find the remainder when b is divided by r_1. Call this r_2.
- Find the remainder when r_1 is divided by r_2. Call this r_3.
- Continue this process, at each stage finding the remainder when r_n is divided by r_{n+1}.
- The last non-zero remainder is $\gcd(a, b)$.

The method becomes much clearer when illustrated with an example.

Worked example 2.9

Use the Euclidean algorithm to find $\gcd(102, 72)$.

Start by finding the quotient and remainder when 102 is divided by 72

$102 = 1 \times 72 + 30$

For the next step we are dividing 72 by 30. Continue until there is no remainder

$72 = 2 \times 30 + 12$
$30 = 2 \times 12 + 6$
$12 = 2 \times 6 + 0$

The gcd is the remainder on the penultimate line

$\therefore \gcd(102, 72) = 6$

This method works because of the result from Key point 2.6, which says that:

$\gcd(a, b) = \gcd(b, a - qb)$.

But we can choose a value of q so that $a - qb$ is the remainder when a is divided by b, which we called r_1. So we have:

$\gcd(a, b) = \gcd(b, r_1)$

An identical argument provides:

$\gcd(b, r_1) = \gcd(r_1, r_2)$

And this continues in the same pattern. We can connect these statements together so that, in Worked example 2.9 we have

$\gcd(102, 72) = \gcd(72, 30) = \gcd(30, 12) = \gcd(12, 6) = 6$.

As well as finding the greatest common divisor of two numbers, the Euclidean algorithm can be used to prove the following important result.

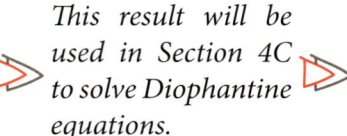

This result will be used in Section 4C to solve Diophantine equations.

KEY POINT 2.11

There exist integers m and n such that $ma + nb = \gcd(a, b)$.

The Euclidean algorithm provides a way of finding m and n, as illustrated in the next example.

Worked example 2.10

Find integers m and n such that $102m + 72n = 6$.

> From the previous example, we can rearrange the first line to express 30 in terms of 102 and 72, then rearrange the second line to express 12 in terms of 72 and 30, and so on. As we want an expression for 6 in terms of 102 and 72, we work back from the penultimate line

$$6 = 30 - 2 \times 12$$
$$= 30 - 2 \times (72 - 2 \times 30)$$
$$= -2 \times 72 + 5 \times 30$$
$$= -2 \times 72 + 5 \times (102 - 1 \times 72)$$
$$= 5 \times 102 - 7 \times 72$$

$$\therefore m = 5, n = -7$$

Note that this is not the only pair of such integers; for example, $m = -19, n = 27$ is another possibility. In fact, we will see in chapter 3 that there are infinitely many pairs of such numbers.

Exercise 2C

1. Use the Euclidean algorithm to find $\gcd(a,b)$ in the following cases:
   (a) $a = 35, b = 12$
   (b) $a = 122, b = 39$
   (c) $a = 63, b = 42$
   (d) $a = 320, b = 80$
   (e) $a = 462, b = 200$

2. For each pair of numbers from the previous question, find integers m and n such that $ma + nb = \gcd(a,b)$.

3. (a) Use the Euclidean algorithm to show that $\gcd(86, 45) = 1$.
   (b) Find a pair of integers x and y such that
       $86x + 45y = 1$. [7 marks]

4. Let $\gcd(48, 30) = d$. Find two integers, p and q, such that $48p + 30q = d$. [6 marks]

5. Use the Euclidean algorithm to show that $3k + 1$ and $13k + 4$ are always relatively prime. [4 marks]

6. Given two positive coprime integers a and b, show that it is possible to find two consecutive positive integers such that one is a multiple of a and the other a multiple of b. [4 marks]

2D Prime numbers

A **prime number** has *exactly two factors*, 1 and itself. Remember that 1 is not a prime number, as it has only one factor. Numbers which are not prime are called **composite**. Note that 2 is the only even prime number, all other prime numbers are odd.

When it comes to division, prime numbers have some interesting properties which distinguish them from composite numbers. One of the most important ones is **Euclid's lemma**, which states that if a prime divides a product of two numbers, then it must divide at least one of those numbers. For example, $600 = 15 \times 40$ and we know that $3 \mid 600$, so 3 must divide either 15 or 40. Composite numbers do not have this property: For example, $6 \mid 600$ but it does not divide either 15 or 40. There are two more related results.

> Euclid's lemma appears in the *Elements*, a collection of mathematical results written by Euclid of Alexandria around 300BCE. Although best known for the first formal treatment of geometry, the *Elements* also contain many important number theory results. With over a thousand editions published to date, it is believed to be the second most published book after the Bible.

KEY POINT 2.12

(i) If p is a prime and $p \mid mn$ then $p \mid m$ or $p \mid n$.

(ii) If p is prime and $p \mid c^2$ then $p \mid c$ and $p^2 \mid c^2$.

(iii) If a and b are relatively prime and $ab = c^2$, then both a and b are square numbers.

You will be expected to use these results to produce other proofs, as in the following example.

Worked example 2.12

Show that it is impossible to find positive numbers n and c such that $n^2 - c^2 = n$.

If we put all terms with n on one side of an equation, we may be able to factorise it

$n^2 - c^2 = n$
$\Leftrightarrow n^2 - n = c^2$
$\Leftrightarrow n(n-1) = c^2$

We have a result about $ab = c^2$, but we need to check that the two numbers are relatively prime. Two consecutive numbers cannot have any common factors

n and $n-1$ are consecutive numbers, so they are relatively prime. Hence both n and $n-1$ are square numbers.
But there aren't two consecutive square numbers, so such n and c do not exist.

Prime numbers are 'building blocks' of arithmetic, as all other numbers can be made by multiplying together some prime numbers. For example, $360 = 2^3 \times 3^2 \times 5$; this is called **prime factorisation**. Every whole number has a unique prime factorisation, and this result is so important that it is given a name.

KEY POINT 2.13

Fundamental Theorem of Arithmetic

There is exactly one way to write a given number $N > 1$ in the form:

$$N = p_1 p_2 \ldots p_k$$

where $p_1 \leq p_2 \leq \ldots \leq p_k$ are prime numbers.

We order the prime factors $p_1 \leq p_2 \leq \ldots \leq p_k$ for convenience, so that there is no danger of thinking, for example, that $3 \times 5 \times 3$ and $3 \times 3 \times 5$ are two different factorisations. Some of the p values can be the same, and we usually write the prime factorisation in a shortened form $N = p_1^{\alpha_1} p_2^{\alpha_2} \ldots p_m^{\alpha_m}$.

It is important to note that the Fundamental Theorem of Arithmetic really states two things:

1. Every positive integer greater than 1 can be written as a product of prime numbers.

2. There is only one way to do this.

You can prove this theorem using a combination of facts and methods of proof you already know. The first statement can be proved using strong induction.

> **EXAM HINT**
>
> The syllabus explicitly mentions proving the Fundamental Theorem of Arithmetic as an example of strong induction.

Worked example 2.13

Prove that every positive integer greater than 1 is either prime, or can be written as a product of two or more prime numbers.

This is a statement which should be true for all positive integers, so it may be possible to prove by induction. As it is not possible to get from n to $n+1$ using a multiplication by a prime number, we may need to use strong induction	Proof by strong induction. The statement is true for $n = 2$, as 2 is a prime number. Assume that the statement is true for all $n < k$ for some k, i.e. every integer smaller than k can be written as a product of primes. Now look at k: It is either prime, or it is composite.
Consider the two cases separately	1. If k is prime, the statement is true for $n = k$. 2. If k is composite, by definition this means that k has a factor other than 1 and k; call this factor a. Then we can write $k = ab$.
We have related k to two numbers smaller than it, so we can apply the inductive hypothesis	But $a, b < k$, so both a and b can be written as products of primes. Multiplying them together we get k written as a product of primes. Hence the statement is true for $n = k$.
We should write a conclusion	So the statement is true for $n = 2$ and if it is true for all $n < k$ we can prove that it is also true for $n = k$; it is therefore true for all $n \geq 2$ by strong induction.

Proof by contradiction was introduced in Section 1A.

The second part of the Fundamental Theorem of Arithmetic is a little more difficult to prove, and we need to use Euclid's lemma from Key point 2.12 combined with proof by contradiction.

Worked example 2.14

Show that prime factorisation is unique, that is: any given integer $N \geq 2$ can be written as a product of primes in only one way.

We have already proved that N can be written as a product of primes. Now see what happens if two such factorisations were possible. This means that we are using proof by contradiction	Proof by contradiction. Suppose that N has two different prime factorisations: $N = p_1 p_2 \ldots p_k$ and $N = q_1 q_2 \ldots q_m$ with $p_1 \leq p_2 \leq \ldots \leq p_k$ and $q_1 \leq q_2 \leq \ldots q_m$.
If there are some common factors in the two factorisations, we should cancel them so they don't get in the way	So $p_1 p_2 \ldots p_k = q_1 q_2 \ldots q_m$ If there are some common factors on both sides we can divide by them and then none of the remaining p's are equal to any of the remaining q's.
If two sides are equal, any number that divides one side must also divide the other. This is where it's important that p_1 is a prime, and Euclid's lemma comes in	Now consider p_1. As it divides the left hand side of the equation, it must also divide the right hand side. By Euclid's lemma, p_1 must divide one of the q's. But q's are all prime, so p_1 must be equal to one of the q's.
We have now reached a contradiction	This is a contradiction, as we have assumed that p's and q's are all different. Hence it is impossible for N to have two different prime factorisations.

As prime numbers are so important, it would be nice to have an easy way of finding them. Unfortunately, the only way to check whether a number is prime is to try dividing it by all primes smaller than it. (In fact, you only need to divide by all primes $\leq \sqrt{n}$; can you see why?)

Primes have a very irregular distribution: there are pairs of consecutive odd numbers which are prime, and there are also long sequences of consecutive composite numbers. The second of these claims can be proved relatively easily (see question 7 below). However, although numerical experiments suggest that there are infinitely many pairs of consecutive odd primes, this result (known as the Twin prime conjecture) has not yet been proved. It is problems like this, with relatively simple statements but elusive proofs, which have kept mathematicians fascinated by prime numbers for centuries.

> Although we cannot predict exactly how large the next prime number will be, there is an approximation to how many primes there are up to a given size. This result is called the Prime Number Theorem, and it requires understanding of limits of functions and integration.

Topic 10 – Option: Discrete mathematics

We do know that there are infinitely many prime numbers. The first proof of this is attributed to the Greek mathematician Euclid, and is another example of proof by contradiction.

Worked example 2.15

Prove that there are infinitely many prime numbers.

What would happen if there were only finitely many prime number? We assume that is the case and see whether it leads to an impossible conclusion

Suppose there are finitely many prime numbers: $p_1, p_2, \ldots, p_k$.

How do we characterise a prime number?

This means that every integer greater than 1 is either equal to one of the p_i values or it is divisible by at least one of them.

Try to find a number which does not satisfy either of the above conditions. How can we make a number that is obviously not divisible by any of the p_i's?

Consider the number
$N = p_1 p_2 \ldots p_k + 1$
Clearly $N \neq p_i$, as it is larger than all of them. Also, N gives remainder 1 when divided by each p_i, so it is not divisible by any of them. But this situation is impossible.

We have reached an impossible situation, so we have made an incorrect assumption somewhere

Hence our assumption that there are finitely many primes was incorrect, and so there are infinitely many prime numbers.

For many centuries mathematicians have been interested in prime numbers, mainly because of the challenges presented by proving their properties. But recently prime numbers have become extremely important in many modern fields such as computer science, cryptography and banking. Because their distribution is so unpredictable and checking whether a number is prime is very time-consuming, primes are used in data encryption. This encryption is vital to keeping personal data secure when it is transmitted electronically, for example over the Internet.

It is also possible to prove that there are infinitely many prime numbers of various types. For example, there are infinitely many prime numbers which give remainder 1 when divided by 4. Another interesting result is the recently proved Green-Tao theorem, which states that you can find an arithmetic sequence of any given length such that all of its terms are prime.

If you would like to see some examples of use of prime numbers, find out about public key cryptography.

Exercise 2D

1. Find the prime factorisation of the following numbers:
   (a) (i) 120   (ii) 200
   (b) (i) 172   (ii) 138
   (c) (i) 155   (ii) 235

2. (a) Write 846 as a product of primes.
   (b) What is the smallest number that 846 must be multiplied by to get:
      (i) a square number?
      (ii) a cube number? [6 marks]

3. Prove that a prime number can only give remainder 1 or 5 when divided by 6. [5 marks]

4. (a) Show that $5 \mid a$ if and only if $5 \mid a^2$.
   (b) Show that if $3 \mid b$ then $9 \mid b^2$. [7 marks]

5. Show that if n is an even number greater than 2 then $2^n - 1$ cannot be prime. [4 marks]

6. Show that there is no prime number p for which $2p+1$ is a square number. [6 marks]

7. (a) Show that $10!+2$ is divisible by 2 and that $10!+3$ is divisible by 3.
   (b) Show that the numbers $10!+2, 10!+3, \ldots, 10!+10$ are all composite.
   (c) Show that there are 100 consecutive composite numbers.

8. This question leads you through one proof that $\sqrt{2}$ is an irrational number.
   (a) Any rational number can be written in the form $\frac{p}{q}$ where $\gcd(p,q) = 1$. Show that if $\sqrt{2} = \frac{p}{q}$ then $4 \mid p^2$.
   (b) By writing $p = 4k$, show that $4 \mid q^2$.
   (c) Deduce that p and q have a common factor, and hence that $\sqrt{2}$ cannot be written as a ratio of two coprime integers.

Summary

- If a divides b then $b = ka$ for some integer k. We write $a \mid b$.
- The **division algorithm** states that for any pair of numbers a and b we can find k and $0 \leq r < a$ such that $b = ka + r$.
- If N is a k-digit number with digits $a_k, a_{k-1} \ldots a_2, a_1, a_0$ then:
$$N = 10^k a_k + 10^{k-1} a_{k-1} + \ldots + 10^2 a_2 + 10 a_1 + a_0$$
- In proving theorems about divisibility we often use factorising and proof by induction.
- For any integer power n, $a^n - b^n$ has a factor $(a - b)$.

  For any *odd* power n, $a^n + b^n$ has a factor $(a + b)$.
- If $a \mid N$ and $b \mid N$, and if a and b have no common factors (other than 1), then $(ab) \mid N$.
- The **greatest common divisor**, $\gcd(a,b)$, is the largest number which divides both a and b.
- The **least common multiple**, $\text{lcm}(a,b)$, is the smallest number which both a and b divide.
- $\gcd(a,b) \times \text{lcm}(a,b) = ab$
- You need to know how to prove and use the following results:
  - if $\gcd(a,b) = d$ then $\gcd\left(\dfrac{a}{d}, \dfrac{b}{d}\right) = 1$
  - $\gcd(a,b) = \gcd(a, a-b)$
  - if q is any integer then $\gcd(a,b) = \gcd(b, a - bq)$
  - if $a \mid N$ and $b \mid N$ then $\text{lcm}(a,b) \mid N$.
- $\gcd(a,b)$ can be found using the **Euclidean algorithm**:

  Write $a = qb + r$

  Replace a by b and b by r, and repeat

  Stop when $r = 0$

  $\gcd(a,b)$ is the previous value of r.
- It is always possible to find two numbers, m and n, such that $am + bm = \gcd(a,b)$. This can be done by reversing the Euclidean algorithm.
- If p is a prime and $p \mid mn$ then $p \mid m$ or $p \mid n$.

  If p is prime and $p \mid c^2$ then $p \mid c$ and $p^2 \mid c^2$.

  If a and b are relatively prime and $ab = c^2$, then both a and b are square numbers.
- The **Fundamental Theorem of Arithmetic** states that every integer has a unique prime factorisation. To prove it, you need to use strong induction and proof by contradiction.

Mixed examination practice 2

1. Find all possible pairs of digits a and b such that the four digit number $(4a1b)$ is divisible by 12. *[7 marks]*

2. (a) Use the Euclidean algorithm to show that 68 and 345 are relatively prime.
   (b) Find integers m and n such that $345m + 68n = 1$. *[7 marks]*

3. Use Euclidean algorithm to show that $\gcd(11k+7, 5k+3) = 1$ for all values of k. *[4 marks]*

4. (a) Write $a^4 - b^4$ as a product of three factors.
   (b) Show that, if a and b are both odd numbers, then $a^4 - b^4$ is divisible by 8. *[5 marks]*

5. (a) Show that if $d \mid n$ then $(3^d - 1) \mid (3^n - 1)$.
   (b) Hence show that $3^{12} - 1$ is divisible by 26. *[6 marks]*

6. Show that if $\gcd(a,b) = d$ then $\gcd(qa, qb) = qd$. *[4 marks]*

7. If $\gcd(a,b) = 1$, prove that $\gcd(a, bc) = \gcd(a, c)$. *[4 marks]*

8. (a) Prove that the product of two consecutive integers is always divisible by 2.
   (b) Prove that the product of three consecutive integers is always divisible by 6.
   (c) Show that if n is odd, $n^3 - n$ is divisible by 24. *[9 marks]*

9. Let a and b be two positive integers.
   (a) Show that $\gcd(a, b) \times \operatorname{lcm}(a, b) = ab$
   (b) Show that $\gcd(a, a + b) = \gcd(a, b)$ *[13 marks]*

   (© IB Organization 2005)

3 Representation of integers in different bases

In this chapter you will learn:

- how to represent integers in bases other than 10
- how to perform arithmetic in those bases
- about divisibility tests in different bases.

You may know that computer scientists use binary numbers. This is a way of writing numbers using only two digits, 0 and 1. They also use hexadecimal, a system with 16 digits. Throughout history different cultures have used different number systems. In this chapter we will learn how to write numbers and perform arithmetic in different bases.

3A How many fingers do we need to count?

We use the decimal system to write numbers: this means that when we write the number 635, the 5 represents five units, the 3 represents three tens (30) and the 6 represents six hundreds (600). So 635 means $5 + 30 + 600$. This is an example of a number system which uses place value, so that the digits have different meanings depending on their position in the number.

People have not always written numbers in this way. For example, in roman numerals V stands for 5 units, and there are different symbols for 50 and 500. One advantage of the place value system is that it is easy to perform written arithmetic, because we can work with individual digits rather than with entire numbers.

In our number system, as we move from right to left each place is worth ten times more than the previous one. We say that our number system has **base 10** and it has ten digits, 0 to 9. This system probably developed because we use our fingers for counting, so moving onto the next digit in the number corresponds to using another pair of hands to count. It is reasonable to imagine that creatures with eight fingers would write their numbers in base 8.

Just as in the decimal system, we use ten digits (0 to 9), in base n we need n digits, 0 to $n - 1$. This means that we can write numbers 1 to $n - 1$ using just one digit. The number n is written as 10, because the '1' on the left is worth n units. For example in base 8, only eight digits are needed: 0 to 7. The number 8

Throughout history different cultures have used number systems with different bases, with bases 12, 20 and 60 being most common. Although we now use the decimal system for most purposes, the duodecimal (base 12) system is still present in measuring time: 12 months in a year and 24 hours in a day. More recently, bases 2, 8 and 16 have been used when working with computers. Base 2, or binary number system, uses only two digits (0 and 1), which correspond to the two states (on and off) of electronic switches. Bases 8 (octal) and 16 (hexadecimal) are used because they are related to base 2 (for example, a group of four binary digits corresponds to one hexadecimal digit).

is then written 10, number 9 is 11, and so on. Base 8 number 63 corresponds to our number 51, because $3 + (6 \times 8) = 51$. The highest two-digit number in base 8 is 77, which is 63 in the decimal system (because $7 + 7 \times 8 = 63$). To write numbers larger than this in base 8 we need three digits, so 100 represents number 64. As we move from right to left, each place is worth eight times more than the previous one, so the base eight number 254 represents our number 172 (4 units, 5 eights and 2 sixty-fours: $4 + 5 \times 8 + 2 \times 8^2 = 172$).

To avoid confusion when talking about numbers in different bases, it is conventional to write the number in brackets with the base in the subscript. So $(63)_8 = (51)_{10}$, $(77)_8 = (63)_{10}$ and $(172)_{10} = (254)_8$.

When reading out the numbers in bases other then 10 we say them digit by digit, so for example $(63)_8$ would be read as 'six-three', not 'sixty-three'.

When we write numbers in bases greater than 10 we use letters to represent the extra digits. For example, in the hexadecimal system the letter B stands for 'digit' 11, so the hexadecimal number $(3B)_{16}$ represents the decimal number $(59)_{10}$ (as $11 + 3 \times 16 = 59$).

Worked example 3.1

Write $(1632)_7$ in base 10.

It is easiest to work from right to left, as we start with units
The units digit is 2
The second place represents sevens; there are 3 of them
The third place represents forty-nines (7^2); there are 6 of them
The next place represents $7^3 = 343$

$(1632)_7 = 2 + 3 \times 7 + 6 \times 7^2 + 1 \times 7^3$
$= (660)_{10}$

Exercise 3A

1. Write down all the digits needed to write numbers in:
   (a) (i) base 6 (ii) base 4
   (b) (i) base 12 (ii) base 15

2. Write the following numbers in base 10:
   (a) (i) $(23)_8$ (ii) $(62)_8$
   (b) (i) $(471)_8$ (ii) $(266)_8$
   (c) (i) $(286)_{16}$ (ii) $(591)_{16}$
   (d) (i) $(4A)_{16}$ (ii) $(C7)_{16}$
   (e) (i) $(DA6)_{16}$ (ii) $(1B4)_{16}$
   (f) (i) $(B25)_{12}$ (ii) $(1BB)_{12}$

3. What is the largest base 10 number that can be written as a three-digit number in base 5? *[3 marks]*

4. How many numbers require 3 digits when written in base 12, but 4 digits when written in base 9? *[5 marks]*

3B Changing between different bases

To convert from any base to base 10 we just need to remember that in base n the place values are powers of n.

To convert from base 10 to another base, n, we need to write the number in the form $a_1 + a_2 \times n + a_3 \times n^2 + a_4 \times n^3 \ldots$ where $a_1, a_2, a_3 \ldots$ are digits between 0 and $n-1$.

The next example illustrates how to do this.

◁ *For an example of conversion to base 10 see Worked example 3.1.* ◁

◁ *We showed in Worked example 1.5 that every integer can be written in base 2. We can show that any integer can be converted into any base, using a similar proof.* ◁

Worked example 3.2

Write $(862)_{10}$ in base 7.

Write out powers of 7	Powers of 7: 1, 7, 49, 343, 2401
The largest power of 7 that goes into 862 is 343. There are **two** 343s in 862, so the first digit is 2. There is 176 remaining	$862 \div 343 = 2$, remainder 176
There are **three** 49s in 196 so the 2nd digit is 3	$176 \div 49 = 3$, remainder 29
How many 7's go into 29? The next digit is 4	$29 \div 7 = 4$, remainder 1
There is 1 unit left, so the units digits is 1	$1 \div 1 = 1$
We now just write down the digits, from left to right	$\therefore (862)_{10} = (2341)_7$

KEY POINT 3.1

To convert a base 10 number into base n:

- Find the largest power of n that goes into the number. The quotient is the first digit.
- Divide the remainder by the previous power of n to find the next digit.
- Repeat until division by 1 has been done.

To convert from one base to any other base, it is easiest to go via base 10.

Worked example 3.3

Convert $(9A1)_{11}$ to base 5.

First convert to base 10

$(9A1)_{11} = 1 + 10 \times 11 + 9 \times 11^2 = (1200)_{10}$

Write out powers of 5 up to 1200

Powers of 5: 1, 5, 25, 125, 625

Start with the largest power of 5 below 1200, and do the divisions

$1200 \div 625 = 1$, remainder 575
$575 \div 125 = 4$, remainder 75
$75 \div 25 = 3$, remainder 0

Although we have remainder 0, we continue and divide by 5 and 1

$0 \div 5 = 0$, remainder 0
$0 \div 1 = 0$

Read off the digits

$\therefore (9A1)_{11} = (14300)_5$

Exercise 3B

1. Write the following base 10 numbers in the given base:
   (a) (i) 62 in base 2   (ii) 186 in base 3
   (b) (i) 183 in base 7   (ii) 212 in base 5
   (c) (i) 821 in base 11   (ii) 601 in base 15
   (d) (i) 1199 in base 16   (ii) 4632 in base 20

2. Convert the following numbers to the given base:
   (a) (i) $(11001)_2$ to base 3   (ii) $(210012)_3$ to base 2
   (b) (i) $(5A1)_{16}$ to base 2   (ii) $(DB3)_{15}$ to base 3
   (c) (i) $(314421)_5$ to base 15   (ii) $(30132)_4$ to base 16
   (d) (i) $(A5A)_{12}$ to base 16   (ii) $(F0F)_{16}$ to base 14

3. Given that $9^6 = 531\,441$, write 531 440 in base 9. *[3 marks]*

3C Arithmetic in different bases

As we have already mentioned, one big advantage of a place value system is that it is easy to perform written arithmetic. However large the numbers are, we are always working with individual digits. Think how you add in base 10: you add pairs of digits, and if the answer exceeds 9 you 'carry' to the next position. We can use the same process to add in any other base. For example, working in base 7 you 'carry' when the answer exceeds 6. When working in a base larger than 10, we may need to 'translate' letters into numbers when calculating.

Worked example 3.4

Calculate $(3A8)_{16} + (C19)_{16}$.

First add the units digits (Calculate this in base 10)	$8 + 9 = 17$
Is the answer larger than 15?	$= 15 + 2$ write 2, carry 1
Add the next pair of digits, plus the one carried from above. Remember that A represents number 10	$10 + 1 + 1 = 12$
12 is C in base 16	write C
Add the next pair of digits. C stands for number 12	$3 + 12 = 15$
15 is F in base 16	write F $\therefore (3A8)_{16} + (C19)_{16} = (FC2)_{16}$

You can also set out your answer in the traditional column format.

Worked example 3.5

Calculate $(62)_7 \times (35)_7$.

$2 \times 5 = 10 = 7 + 3$, so write 3, carry 1. $6 \times 5 + 1 = 31 = (43)_7$	$\begin{array}{r} 6\ 2 \\ \times\ \ 3\ 5 \\ \hline 4\ 3\ 3 \\ {}_1 \end{array}$
Write 0 as we are multiplying by the 'sevens' digit	$2\ 4\ 6\ 0$
$3 \times 2 = 6$ $6 \times 3 = 18 = (24)_7$	
Add $(433)_7 + (2460)_7$ as in the previous example	$\begin{array}{r} 3\ 2\ 2\ 3 \\ {}_1\ {}_1 \end{array}$
	$\therefore (62)_7 \times (35)_7 = (3223)_7$

> **EXAM HINT**
>
> It is a good idea to check your answer by converting to base 10. You may also be able to use your calculator to work in some common bases, but you must show your full working and only use the calculator to check your answer.

In chapter 2 we saw that looking at digits of a number can often tell us something about its factors. For example, a base 10 number which ends in 0 is divisible by 10. We can derive similar divisibility tests for other bases. As well as using these tests, you can be asked to prove them.

Worked example 3.6

Show that if a base 15 number ends in 0, 5 or A then it is divisible by 5.

Let the digits be $a_1, a_2, a_3 \ldots$, with a_1 being the units digit

$$(\ldots a_3 a_2 a_1)_{15} = a_1 + a_2 \times 15 + a_3 \times 15^2 + \ldots$$

All terms except for the first are divisible by 15

$$= 15(a_2 + 15 \times a_3 + \ldots) + a_1$$

Look at the first part and the last digit separately

The first part is always divisible by 5. If a_1 is 0, 5 or A (which stands for 10), then it is also divisible by 5, which makes the whole number divisible by 5.

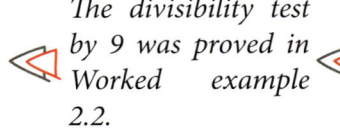

The divisibility test by 9 was proved in Worked example 2.2.

The next example shows a result which is analogous to the base 10 test for divisibility by 9. The proof follows the same strategy.

Worked example 3.7

Show that if a base 7 number is divisible by 6, then the sum of its digits is also divisible by 6.

Write out the number using digits

$$(a_n a_{n-1} \ldots a_3 a_2 a_1)_7 = a_1 + a_2 \times 7 + a_3 \times 7^2 + \ldots + a_n \times 7^{n-1}$$

If this is divisible by 6, we should be able to take out a factor of 6. We also want the sum of its digits, so separate the expression into $a_1 + a_2 + \ldots a_n$ and the rest

$$= (a_1 + a_2 + a_3 + \ldots a_n) + [a_2(7-1) + a_3(7^2-1) + \ldots + a_n(7^{n-1}-1)]$$

The terms of the form $7^k - 1$ can be factorised as $(7-1)(\ldots)$, so they all have a factor of 6

$$= (a_1 + a_2 + a_3 + \ldots a_n) + [a_2 \times 6 + a_3 \times 6(\ldots) + \ldots + a_n \times 6(\ldots)]$$

We want to show that the sum of the digits, which is the first bracket, is divisible by 6

As the terms in the square bracket are all divisible by 6, if the whole number is also divisible by 6, then the sum of the digits is divisible by 6.

The last Worked example illustrates a divisibility test that applies in all bases.

KEY POINT 3.2

> A base n number is divisible by $n - 1$ if and only if the sum of its digits is divisible by $n - 1$.

You are often asked to prove particular cases of this divisibility test.

Exercise 3C

1. Do the following calculations in the given base. Check your answers by converting to base 10.
   (a) (i) $(324)_6 + (115)_6$ (ii) $(152)_6 + (214)_6$
   (b) (i) $(6A2)_{12} + (BB1)_{12}$ (ii) $(A61)_{12} + (13B)_{12}$

2. Do the following calculations in the given base. Check your answers by converting to base 10.
   (a) (i) $(22)_7 \times (16)_7$ (ii) $(51)_7 \times (35)_7$
   (b) (i) $(2C)_{16} \times (41)_{16}$ (ii) $(53)_{16} \times (A8)_{16}$

3. (a) If a base 7 number ends in 0, what must it be divisible by?
   (b) If a base 12 number ends in 0, which numbers is it divisible by?
   (c) In base 6, what is the criterion for a number to be divisible by $(36)_{10}$?

4. (a) Find the possible values of digit k so that the number $(3A5k)_{14}$ is divisible by 7.
   (b) What is the criterion for a base 14 number to be divisible by 13?
   (c) Find the possible values of digits k and m so that the number $(3Amk)_{14}$ is divisible by $(91)_{10}$.   [8 marks]

5. (a) Show that if the last digit of a base 15 number is 0, 3, 6, 9 or C, then the number is divisible by 3.
   (b) Show that for a base 15 number, if the number formed by the last two digits is divisible by 9, then the whole number is divisible by 9.   [8 marks]

3 Representation of integers in different bases   **39**

Summary

- To represent an integer in base n we use digits 0 to $n-1$. The place values are $1, n, n^2, n^3$, etc.
$$(a_k a_{k-1} \ldots a_3 a_2 a_1)_n = a_1 + a_2 n + a_3 n^2 + \ldots + a_k n^{k-1}$$
- To convert from **base 10** to base n, divide the number by powers of n, starting with the largest.
- We can perform written addition and multiplication in any base, using the same column method as in base 10.
- Divisibility criteria in base n are similar to those for base 10:
    - For divisibility by factors of n look at the last digit.
    - A base n number is divisible by $n-1$ if and only if the sum of its digits is divisible by $n-1$.

Mixed examination practice 3

1. (a) Write $(136)_8$ in base 10.
   (b) Convert $(1439)_{10}$ to base 16.
   [7 marks]

2. (a) Convert $(AB2F)_{16}$ to binary.
   (b) Convert $(110001)_2$ to base 7.
   [8 marks]

3. (a) Write the number 41 012 in base 8.
   (b) Prove that if a number is divisible by 7 then the sum of its base 8 digits is also divisible by 7.
   (c) Use your answers to parts (a) and (b) to show that 41 012 is not divisible by 7.
   [11 marks]

4. (a) Convert the number 84 from base 10 to base 5.
   (b) Working in base 5, square your answer to part (a).
   (c) Convert your answer to part (b) to a base 10 number.
   [9 marks]

5. (a) Show that if a number is divisible by 3 then in its representation in base 6 the last digit is 0 or 3.
   (b) In base 6, write down a criterion for the number to be divisible by 5.
   (c) Given that $(2a104b)_6$ is divisible by 15 find the possible values of a and b.
   [12 marks]

6. (a) Convert the base 9 number 8415 to a decimal number.
   (b) Prove that a base 9 number is divisible by 4 if the sum of its digits is divisible by 4.
   [8 marks]

7. The positive integer N is expressed in base b as $(a_k a_{k-1} \ldots a_1 a_0)_b$.
   (a) Show that N is divisible by b if and only if $a_0 = 0$.
   (b) Show that N is divisible by b^2 if and only if $a_0 = a_1 = 0$.
   [10 marks]

8. The positive integer N is expressed in base p as $(a_n a_{n-1} \ldots a_1 a_0)_p$.
   (a) Show that when p = 2, N is even if and only if its last digit is 0.
   (b) Show that when p = 3, N is even if and only if the sum of its digits is even.
   [11 marks]
   (© IB Organization 2008)

In this chapter you will learn:

- how to tell whether a linear equation in two variables has integer solutions
- how to find one solution of such an equation
- that given one solution, it is possible to construct infinitely many other solutions.

4 Linear Diophantine equations

Many practical problems involve solving equations which need only integer solutions. Such equations are called Diophantine equations. In this chapter we will learn how to solve linear Diophantine equations in two variables using some of the results we met in chapter 2.

4A Examples of equations with integer solutions

Can you solve the equation $2x + 3y = 5$?

If x and y are real numbers, then for every x we can find y which satisfies the equation. So there are infinitely many solutions of the form $\left(x, \dfrac{5-2x}{3}\right)$. However, if we require x and y to be integers then $y = \dfrac{5-2x}{3}$ will only be an integer for some values of x. We can find several solutions by inspection, for example $(1,1), (4,-1), (-2,3)$. There are still infinitely many solution pairs, but not all integer values of x will make y an integer; we can only use the values of x for which $5-2x$ is divisible by 3. A bit of experimenting shows that x has to be one more than a multiple of 3. We can therefore write that all of the solutions are of the form $(3k+1, 1-2k)$ for some integer k.

The above is an example of a linear **Diophantine equation**; a linear equation in several variables where we only seek integer solutions.

You will meet only linear Diophantine equations in this course, but there are other types. It is often impossible to find all the solutions, but it may be possible to prove whether or not solutions exist, and if they do, whether there are infinitely many of them.

For example, we can show that the equation $x^2 - y^2 = 122$ has no integer solutions as follows. The expression on the left factorises as $(x-y)(x+y)$. The two factors differ by $2y$, which is an even number, so they must be either both even or both odd. As their product is even, they must both be even. But

Topic 10 – Option: Discrete mathematics

the product of two even numbers is divisible by 4, which 122 is not. Hence such numbers x and y cannot exist. Looking at factors and remainders is very useful when solving Diophantine equations.

> **Worked example 4.1**
>
> Show that the equation $15x - 35y = 17$ has no integer solutions.
>
> *Looking for factors is often useful: if two terms of this equation are divisible by a number, then the third term must be divisible by the same number*
>
> 15 and 35 are both divisible by 5.
> Hence $15x - 35y$ must be divisible by 5 for all x and y.
> 17 is not divisible by 5, so $15x - 35y$ cannot equal 17.

A well known example of a Diophantine equation is $x^2 + y^2 = z^2$. This has infinitely many solutions, known as Pythagorean triples. On the other hand, the equation $x^n + y^n = z^n$ with $n \geq 3$ has no integer solutions. This is a famous result called Fermat's Last Theorem.

> In 1637, Fermat famously claimed, in a margin of a book, that he had a proof for his theorem. Many mathematicians over the centuries tried to find a proof, but this was only accomplished in 1995 by Andrew Wiles, building on new theories developed by several mathematicians over preceding decades. Although the result itself has not found any applications so far, the new theories developed during the search for the proof have turned out to be extremely interesting and useful.

Exercise 4A

1. Explain why the equation $6x + 9y = 137$ has no integer solutions.

    [3 marks]

2. (a) Find one integer solution of the equation $15x - 12y = 18$.
   (b) Show that every pair of numbers of the form $x = 2 + 4k$, $y = 1 + 5k$ is a solution of the above equation.

    [4 marks]

3. (a) Show that $x = 1 + 3k$ and $y = 1 - 11k$ satisfy the equation $11x + 3y = 14$ for all integers k.
   (b) Show that only one of those solutions has both x and y positive.

    [5 marks]

4. Darya has 15 pieces of paper. She selects several of those pieces and cuts them into 10 pieces each. She then selects some of the new small pieces and cuts them into 10 pieces each. She says that she now has 2007 pieces of paper. Show that she must have counted incorrectly.

    [6 marks]

5. (a) Show that for every pair of relatively prime positive integers m and n with $m > n$, the numbers $x = m^2 - n^2$, $y = 2mn$ and $z = m^2 + n^2$ satisfy the equation $x^2 + y^2 = z^2$. (This is a method for generating infinitely many Pythagorean triples).

   (b) Show that if a, b and c form a Pythagorean triple, then so do ka, kb and kc for any integer k.

4B How many solutions are there?

We now look at techniques for solving linear Diophantine equations in two variables. Before we search for solutions, we need to find out whether any exist. It turns out that there is a very simple criterion for deciding this.

KEY POINT 4.1

- The Diophantine equation $ax + by = c$ has no solutions if $\gcd(a,b)$ does not divide c.
- If $\gcd(a,b) | c$, the equation has infinitely many solutions.

The first part of this result is straightforward: If both terms on the left hand side are divisible by a number, then that number has to divide the right hand side as well.

In Section 4C we will see that all solutions can be found starting from just one particular solution.

The second part really says two things: that whenever $\gcd(a,b) | c$ we can find a solution; and that if there is one solution then there are in fact infinitely many. We will first see how to find one solution, and will return to the question of infinitely many solutions in the next section.

To find one solution we can use the Euclidean algorithm from the previous section. We saw there that there are numbers m and n such that $am + bn = \gcd(a,b)$. So if $c = \gcd(a,b)$, then m and n are solutions of the equation $ax + by = c$.

> Diophantine equations have been studied throughout history and all over the world. The earliest known record is probably in Diophantus' *Arithmetica* from the 3rd century BCE. They were also studied by Sun Tzu in the 3rd century AD and Brahmagupta in the 7th century.

If $c \neq d$ but $d | c$, then $c = kd$ for some integer k. So the equation is equivalent to $ax + by = kd$. Since $am + bn = d$, it follows that $a(km) + b(kn) = kd$, so $x = km$ and $y = kn$ are solutions of the equation $ax + by = c$.

Worked example 4.2

(a) Find x and y such that $27x + 15y = 3$.

(b) Hence find one integer solution of the equation $27x + 15y = 21$.

Check whether gcd (27, 15) divides the RHS

(a) $\gcd(27, 15) = 3$, so we can find a solution by Euclidean algorithm.

Apply Euclidean algorithm

$27 = 1 \times 15 + 12$
$15 = 1 \times 12 + 3$
$12 = 4 \times 3 + 0$

Reverse the steps to write $3 = 27x + 15y$

$3 = 15 - 1 \times 12$
$= 15 - 1 \times (27 - 1 \times 15)$
$= -1 \times 27 + 2 \times 15$
So $x = -1, y = 2$

As $21 = 3 \times 7$, we can use the answer from the previous part and multiply the whole equation by 7

(b) $27(-1) + 15(2) = 3$
Multiply by 7: $27(-7) + 15(14) = 21$
So $x = -7, y = 14$

In the next section we will see how to find all the solutions of linear Diophantine equations.

Exercise 4B

1. Which of these equations have integer solutions?
   (a) $7x + 8y = 29$ (b) $3x + 6y = 17$
   (c) $15x + 27y = 3$ (d) $15x + 27y = 30$
   (e) $15x + 27y = 35$ (f) $21x + 37y = 1$

2. Use the Euclidean algorithm to find one solution of the following Diophantine equations:
   (a) (i) $45x + 20y = 5$ (ii) $66x + 42y = 6$
   (b) (i) $102x + 72y = 6$ (ii) $165x + 105y = 15$

3. Find one solution of the following Diophantine equations:
   (a) (i) $66x + 20y = 12$ (ii) $45x + 20y = 25$
   (b) (i) $81x + 36y = 27$ (ii) $100x + 35y = 15$

4. (a) Find $\gcd(45, 129)$.
   (b) Hence explain why the equation $45x + 129y = 28$ has no integer solutions. *[5 marks]*

5. (a) Find $\gcd(132, 78)$.

   (b) For which values of c does the equation $132x + 78y = c$ have integer solutions?

   (c) Find one solution for $c = 6$. [10 marks]

6. (a) For which values of λ does the equation $\lambda x + 5y = 7$ have integer solutions?

   (b) Find one solution for $\lambda = 14$. [8 marks]

4C Finding the general solution

In the previous section we saw how to find one solution of the equation $ax + by = c$ when $\gcd(a,b)$ divides c. For example, we found that the equation $27x + 15y = 3$ has a solution $x = -1, y = 2$. This is called a **particular solution**. But there are other solutions, for example $x = 4, y = -7$. How can we find all such solutions?

In the above equation, if x is increased by a certain amount, y needs to be decreased for the expression on the left to keep the same value. So let $x = -1 + P$, $y = 2 - Q$. Then:

$$27(-1+P) + 15(2-Q) = 3$$
$$\Leftrightarrow -27 + 27P + 30 - 15Q = 3$$
$$\Leftrightarrow 27P - 15Q = 0$$
$$\Leftrightarrow 27P = 15Q$$
$$\Leftrightarrow 9P = 5Q$$

The last equation is satisfied by $P = 5k$ and $Q = 9k$ for any integer k. Hence the original equation has solutions of the form

$$x = -1 + 5k, \, y = 2 - 2k \text{ for } k \in \mathbb{Z}.$$

Note that on the last line of the above derivation we divided by 3 which is $\gcd(27, 15)$. This gives us the general form for all solutions of a linear Diophantine equation.

KEY POINT 4.2

If (x_1, y_1) is one solution of the equation $ax + by = c$ and $d = \gcd(a, b)$ then all the other solutions are given by:

$$x = x_1 + \frac{kb}{d}, \, y = y_1 - \frac{ka}{d} \quad \text{for } k \in \mathbb{Z}$$

This is called the **general solution** of the Diophantine equation.

We now have a complete method for solving linear Diophantine equations.

Worked example 4.3

Use the result from Worked example 4.2 to find the general solution of the equation $27x + 15y = 21$.

We have found one solution already

One solution is $x = -7$, $y = 14$

To find the general solution we need gcd(a, b)

$\gcd(27, 15) = 3$

We can now use the formula

$x = -7 + \dfrac{15k}{3} = -7 + 5k$

$y = 14 - \dfrac{27k}{3} = 14 - 9k$

Exercise 4C

1. Find the general solution of the following Diophantine equations:
   (a) (i) $45x + 20y = 5$ (ii) $66x + 42y = 6$
   (b) (i) $102x + 72y = 6$ (ii) $165x + 105y = 15$
   (c) (i) $66x + 20y = 12$ (ii) $45x + 20y = 25$
   (d) (i) $81x + 36y = 27$ (ii) $100x + 35y = 15$

2. (a) Use the Euclidean algorithm to find $\gcd(162, 78)$.
   (b) Find the general solution of the equation $162x - 78y = 12$. [11 marks]

3. (a) Show that 55 and 38 are relatively prime.
   (b) Find a pair of integers m, n such that $55m - 38n = 1$.
   (c) Find a general solution of the Diophantine equation $55x - 38y = 1$. [11 marks]

4. Find all pairs of points with integer coordinates in the x–y plane which lie on the line $3x + 5y = 13$. [8 marks]

4D Solutions subject to constraints

Sometimes a Diophantine equation is set in a context where there are some restrictions on the types of solutions allowed. One of the most common constraints is requiring all the solutions to be positive.

Worked example 4.4

Show that the equation $75x + 45y = 300$ has only one solution with both x and y positive.

Notice that we can divide the whole equation by 15 to make the numbers smaller

$5x + 3y = 20$

We can find the general solution in terms of k and then look for the values of k for which $x, y > 0$. In this case, we can find one solution by inspection. (If you don't see it, use the Euclidean algorithm)

Particular solution:
$x = 1, y = 5$

General solution:
$\gcd(27, 15) = 1$
$x = 1 + 3k, y = 3 - 5k$

Use the condition $x > 0, y > 0$

$x > 0 \Rightarrow 3k > -1 \Rightarrow k \geq 0$

$y > 0 \Rightarrow 5 > 5k \Rightarrow k < 1$

$\therefore k = 1$, so there is only one positive solution $(x = 1, y = 5)$.

Exercise 4D

1. (a) Find one pair of integers x, y such that $5x + 8y = 42$.
   (b) Find all the solutions of the equation $5x + 8y = 42$ with x, y positive integers. *[11 marks]*

2. (a) Find $\gcd(62, 74)$.
   (b) Find the general solution of the equation $62x - 74y = 2$.
   (c) Hence show that the above equation has infinitely many solutions with both x and y positive. *[13 marks]*

3. (a) Find the general solution of the Diophantine equation $132x + 78y = 6$.
   (b) Find all the solutions with $|x| < 20$. *[14 marks]*

4. (a) You have a pair of scales with an unlimited supply of 12 g and 9 g weights. What weights of objects can you measure using these?
   (b) Could you measure more different weights if all the 12 g weights are replaced by 13 g ones?
   (c) If you are only allowed to put the weights on one side of the scales, how does that affect your answer to part (b)?

Summary

- The **Diophantine equation** $ax + by = c$ has integer solutions if and only if $d = \gcd(a,b)$ divides c.
- One solution (**particular solution**) can be found by reversing the Euclidean algorithm to find m, n such that $am + bn = d$; then one solution is $x_1 = \dfrac{c}{d}m$, $y_1 = \dfrac{c}{d}n$.
- The **general solution** is $x = x_1 + \dfrac{kb}{d}$, $y = y_1 - \dfrac{ka}{d}$ for $k \in \mathbb{Z}$.
- Sometimes there are constraints on the solution so that only some values of k are allowed.

Mixed examination practice 4

1. (a) Use the Euclidean algorithm to show that 27 and 59 are relatively prime.
   (b) Find integers m and n such that $59m + 27n = 1$.
   (c) Find the general solution of the Diophantine equation $59x + 27y = 20$. *[13 marks]*

2. Use the Euclidean Algorithm to find the greatest common divisor of 7854 and 3315. Hence state the number of solutions to the diophantine equation $7854x + 3315y = 41$ and justify your answer. *[7 marks]*
   (© IB Organization 2008)

3. (a) Find $\gcd(45, 111)$.
   (b) Hence explain why the equation $45x + 111y = 17$ has no integer solutions.
   (c) Find the general solution of the equation $45x + 111y = 15$ with $x, y \in \mathbb{Z}$. *[13 marks]*

4. (a) For which values of λ does the equation $\lambda x + 3y = 5$ have integer solutions?
   (b) Find the general solution for $\lambda = 4$. *[9 marks]*

5. (a) Find a pair of integers m, n such that $5m + 3n = 17$
   (b) Hence find a general solution of the equation $5x + 3y = 17$ with x, y integers.
   (c) Find the two solutions which minimise $|x| + |y|$. *[13 marks]*

6. Show that there are no positive integers p and q such that $102p + 72q = 1800$. *[11 marks]*

5 Modular arithmetic

In this chapter you will learn:

- rules for working with remainders, called modular arithmetic
- how to solve equations involving remainders, called linear congruences
- how to solve simultaneous congruences
- a shortcut for calculating powers in modular arithmetic.

Can you find the last digit of 333^{333} without evaluating the number? A little thought leads us to realise that this is really a question about divisibility and remainders: What is the remainder when 333^{333} is divided by 10? In this section we will investigate rules for working with remainders that enable us to answer questions like this one.

5A Introduction: working with remainders

Look at the clock: what time will it show after 12 hours? What about after 7 hours? After 19 hours?

After how many hours will the clock show 5 o'clock? There are infinitely many answers: 2, 14, 26,… We could say that, as far as the clock is concerned, all these numbers are the same.

When you divide 38 by 12 the remainder is 2. What other numbers give remainder 2 when divided by 12? Again, there are infinitely many answers: 2, 14, 26, 50,… As far as division by 12 is concerned, all these numbers are the same. We say that they are **congruent modulo 12**.

If a number gives remainder 2 when divided by 12, what remainder does twice that number give? Trying some examples suggests that the remainder is always 4. Similarly, three times the number gives remainder 6. In the next section we will prove that similar rules hold in general, but first let us look at a few more results concerning division by 12. We will need the following result:

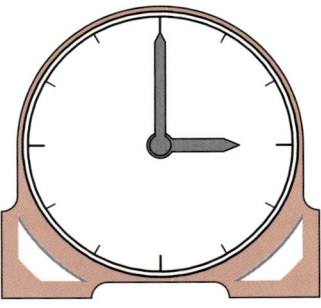

> If you are studying Further Maths, you will also meet congruence as an example of equivalence classes in the Sets, Relations and Groups option.

KEY POINT 5.1

If a number n gives remainder r when divided by d then $n = kd + r$ for some number k.

◁ *This is just the division algorithm we met in Section 2A.* ◁

Worked example 5.1

(a) If x gives remainder 6 and y gives the remainder 3 when divided by 12, find the remainders when the following are divided by 12.

  (i) $x + y$ (ii) $x - y$ (iii) xy

(b) Find an example to show that $\dfrac{x}{y}$ does not give remainder 2.

Write the numbers in the form from Key point 5.1 and then do the calculations

(a) Write $x = 12k + 6, y = 12m + 3$

Write the resulting expression in the form $12q + r$ and identify the remainder

(i) $x + y = (12k + 6) + (12m + 3)$
$\qquad = 12(k + m) + 9$
Hence $x + y$ gives remainder 9.

(ii) $x - y = (12k + 6) - (12m + 3)$
$\qquad = 12(k - m) + 3$
Hence $x - y$ gives remainder 3.

(iii) $xy = (12k + 6)(12m + 3)$
$\qquad = 144km + 36k + 72m + 18$
$\qquad = 12(12km + 3k + 6m) + 18$

We want the remainder to be smaller than 12

$\qquad = 12(12km + 3k + 6m + 1) + 6$
Hence xy gives remainder 6

The result is not always a whole number and even when it is, we can find several different remainders

(b) If $x = 486$ and $y = 27$, then $\dfrac{x}{y} = 18$ which gives remainder 6.

The above example suggests that we can add, subtract and multiply remainders, but we need to be careful when dividing them. In the next section we will prove these assertions in general, and investigate under what circumstances we can perform division with remainders.

Exercise 5A

In questions 1 to 4 try to produce proofs similar to those in Worked example 5.1.

1. (a) (i) If x gives remainder 5 when divided by 12, what remainder does $2x$ give?

    (ii) If x gives remainder 2 when divided by 12, what remainder does $3x$ give?

    (b) (i) If x gives remainder 5 when divided by 13, what reminder does $4x$ give?

    (ii) If x gives remainder 7 when divided by 13, what remainder does $4x$ give?

Topic 10 – Option: Discrete mathematics

(c) (i) If y gives remainder 4 when divided by 12, what remainder does y^3 give?

(ii) if y gives remainder 2 when divided by 12, what remainder does y^4 give?

2. (a) If a number gives remainder 1 when divided by 9, what remainder does it give when divided by 3?

(b) If a number gives remainder 3 when divided by 15, what remainder does it give when divided by 5?

(c) If a number gives remainder 4 when divided by 12, what remainder does it give when divided by 3?

(d) If a number gives remainder 4 when divided by 12, what remainder does it give when divided by 4?

3. (a) If a number gives remainder 1 when divided by 3, what remainders can it give when divided by 9?

(b) If a number gives remainder 3 when divided by 5, what remainders can it give when divided by 15?

4. (a) If a gives remainder 4 when divided by 15 and b gives remainder 5 when divided by 15, what remainder does $a + b$ give?

(b) If m gives remainder 4 when divided by 13 and n gives remainder 8 when divided by 13, what remainder does mn give?

5. (a) If x gives remainder 2 when divided by 3 and y gives remainder 1 when divided by 3, what can you say about $x + y$?

(b) Describe all numbers which give remainder 1 when divided by both 2 and 3. *[4 marks]*

5B Rules of modular arithmetic

We start by introducing some new notation and terminology for **modular arithmetic**.

We say that a is *congruent* to b modulo m if $m \mid (a - b)$. This is written as $a \equiv b \pmod{m}$. The definition has several implications.

KEY POINT 5.2

If $a \equiv b \pmod{m}$ then:

- a and b give the same remainder when divided by m
- we can write $a = km + b$

The first fact is usually used to check whether two numbers are congruent modulo m, and the second fact is often used in proofs. Note that if $a < b$, then k needs to be negative, but this is not a problem.

Worked example 5.2

Show that if $a \equiv b \pmod{m}$ and $c \equiv d \pmod{m}$ then $a + c \equiv b + d \pmod{m}$.

We need to write equations connecting a and b, and c and d. Use the second point above

Write $a = km + b$, $c = lm + d$.
Then
$$a + c = (km + b) + (lm + d)$$
$$= (k + l)m + (b + d)$$

We have written $a + c$ in the form $Nm + (b + d)$, so use the second point above again

Hence
$a + c \equiv b + d \pmod{m}$

Similar proofs can be produced for other rules of modular arithmetic, summarised here.

KEY POINT 5.3

If $a \equiv b \pmod{m}$ and $c \equiv d \pmod{m}$ then:

- $ka \equiv kb \pmod{m}$ for all $k \in \mathbb{Z}$
- $a + c \equiv b + d \pmod{m}$
- $a - c \equiv b - d \pmod{m}$
- $ac \equiv bd \pmod{m}$
- $a^n \equiv b^n \pmod{m}$ for all $n \in \mathbb{N}$.

With practice, doing modular arithmetic is just as quick as doing normal arithmetic, and in some sense even easier, because we are working with smaller numbers. For example, if $x \equiv 5 \pmod{6}$ then $3x \equiv 15 \equiv 3 \pmod{6}$ so $(3x)^2 \equiv 9 \equiv 3 \pmod{6}$. In calculations with multiple steps like this, we should always 'reduce' to the smallest possible remainder after each step, so we are never calculating with numbers larger than m.

It is sometimes convenient to use negative remainders, if this produces smaller numbers. For example: $98 \equiv -2 \pmod{100}$, so $98^2 \equiv (-2)^2 \equiv 4 \pmod{100}$.

> **Worked example 5.3**
>
> Find the remainder when 2^{30} is divided by 13.
>
> *Start by evaluating small powers, and then look at the smallest possible remainder*
>
> $2^3 \equiv 8 \pmod{13}$
>
> *Square both sides*
>
> $2^6 \equiv 64 \equiv 12 \equiv -1 \pmod{13}$
>
> *To get power 30, raise to the power 5*
>
> $(2^6)^5 \equiv (-1)^5 \equiv -1 \equiv 12 \pmod{13}$
>
> $\therefore 2^{30}$ gives remainder 12.

If you look at remainders when a number is raised to a power you will find that they eventually start to repeat. For example:

$4^1 \equiv 4 \pmod{10}$

$4^2 \equiv 6 \pmod{10}$

$4^3 \equiv 4 \pmod{10}$

$4^4 \equiv 6 \pmod{10}$

So all even powers of four give a remainder of six when divided by ten and all odd powers of four give a remainder of four. If we were asked to find the last digit of 4^{312} (which is equivalent to finding the remainder when dividing by ten) we could then immediately write down the answer: six.

Exercise 5B

1. Find the following remainders:
   (a) (i) $5^{13} \pmod 7$ (ii) $4^{19} \pmod 7$
   (b) (i) $6^{15} \pmod{12}$ (ii) $5^{22} \pmod{25}$
   (c) (i) $35^{131} \pmod{11}$ (ii) $29^{223} \pmod{11}$

2. Find the following remainders:
   (a) (i) $3^{16} + 7 \pmod 5$ (ii) $2^{12} + 3 \pmod 7$
   (b) (i) $4^7 - 22 \pmod 7$ (ii) $6^6 - 37 \pmod 5$
   (c) (i) $5^{32} + 3^{23} \pmod 6$ (ii) $7^{53} - 6^{53} \pmod 4$
   (d) (i) $6 \times 5^{18} \pmod 7$ (ii) $8 \times 3^{21} \pmod 5$

3. Find the last digit of 2222^{3333}.   *[4 marks]*

4. Find the remainder when $55^{44} + 44^{55}$ is divided by 7.   *[7 marks]*

5 Modular arithmetic

5. Given that x is a whole number such that 2^x has last digit 4, find the last digit of $2^{3x}+1$. *[4 marks]*

6. Given that $(a+b)^5 \equiv 2 \pmod 5$ show that $(a+b) \equiv 2 \pmod 5$. *[4 marks]*

5C Division and linear congruences

So far we have used addition, subtraction, multiplication and powers in congruences. To be able to solve equations we also need to be able to divide. However, we have already seen examples where dividing both sides by the same number does not work. For example, $15 \equiv 3 \pmod{12}$ but $5 \not\equiv 1 \pmod{12}$. In this section we will see that there are some situations where the division is possible.

Suppose that we want to divide both sides of $a \equiv b \pmod m$ by d. To start with, both sides have to be divisible by d, as we can only work with whole numbers. For example, starting from $48 \equiv 3 \pmod{15}$ we cannot divide both sides by 2. However, $3 \equiv 18 \pmod{15}$, so we can replace 3 by 18 on the right hand side to get $48 \equiv 18 \pmod{15}$. This can be divided by 2 to give $24 \equiv 9 \pmod{15}$, which is correct.

The above calculation illustrates an important difference between congruences and equations.

KEY POINT 5.4

If $a \equiv b \pmod m$ then $a \equiv b \pm m \pmod m$

In other words, we can add or subtract a multiple of m to just one side of the congruence.

We can use this to make both sides divisible by d if they are not already. It turns out that we can divide by any number which is coprime with m.

KEY POINT 5.5

Division rule 1

If $a \equiv b \pmod m$, d divides both a and b and $\gcd(d,m)=1$,

then $\dfrac{a}{d} \equiv \dfrac{b}{d} \pmod m$.

This rule says that, for example:

if $5x \equiv 15 \pmod{24}$ then $x \equiv 3 \pmod{24}$ as 5 is coprime with 24.

When d and m have some common factors we have to change the modulus when dividing. For example, we saw that

$15 \equiv 3 \pmod{12}$ but $5 \not\equiv 1 \pmod{12}$, so we cannot just divide both sides by 3. However, $5 \equiv 1 \pmod 4$, so the division seems to work if m is also divided by 3.

KEY POINT 5.6

Division rule 2

If $a \equiv b \pmod m$ and d divides a, b and m, then:

$$\frac{a}{d} \equiv \frac{b}{d} \pmod{\frac{m}{d}}$$

Division rule 3

If $a \equiv b \pmod m$ and d divides both a and b, then:

$$\frac{a}{d} \equiv \frac{b}{d} \left(\bmod \frac{m}{\gcd(d,m)}\right)$$

For example, if $6x \equiv 6 \pmod{15}$ we can divide both sides by 6. But $\gcd(6,15) = 3$, so we also have to divide the modulus by 3. Hence $x \equiv 1 \pmod 5$.

We can see why this works if we rewrite the congruence as equations:

If $6x \equiv 6 \pmod{15}$ then $6x = 15k + 6$.

At this stage we can only divide both sides by 3:

$2x = 5k + 2$

As $2x$ and 2 are both even k must also be even, so write $k = 2n$ to get:

$2x = 10n + 2$

Now we can divide by 2:

$x = 5n + 1$

and hence $x \equiv 1 \pmod 5$.

We can now solve **linear congruences**; that is find the values of x for which $ax \equiv b \pmod m$. The method is similar to solving linear equations, although some of the rules are different.

KEY POINT 5.7

If $ax \equiv b \pmod m$ then:

- we can divide both sides by d if we also divide m by $\gcd(m,d)$
- we can add a multiple of m to *only one side*.

Worked example 5.4

Find the values of x such that:

(a) $2x \equiv 7 \pmod{5}$ (b) $6x + 5 \equiv 8 \pmod{9}$
(c) $11x \equiv 5 \pmod{8}$ (d) $25x \equiv 10 \pmod{30}$

We need to divide both sides by 2, but 7 is not divisible by 2. We can add 5 to the right hand side

(a) $2x \equiv 7 \pmod{5}$
$\Leftrightarrow 2x \equiv 12 \pmod{5}$

$\gcd(2,5) = 1$, so we can now divide by 2

$\Leftrightarrow x \equiv 6 \pmod{5}$

It is customary to reduce to the smallest positive remainder

$\Leftrightarrow x \equiv 1 \pmod{5}$

This means that x can be any number which gives remainder 1 when divided by 5, i.e. $x = 1, 6, 11, \ldots$ or $-4, -9, \ldots$

Start by isolating x on one side

(b) $6x + 5 \equiv 8 \pmod{9}$
$\Leftrightarrow 6x \equiv 3 \pmod{9}$

We need to divide by 6, so add 9 to the right hand side so it is divisible by 6

$\Leftrightarrow 6x \equiv 12 \pmod{9}$

Divide both sides by 6 $\gcd(6,9) = 3$, so divide the modulus by 3

$\Leftrightarrow x \equiv 2 \pmod{3}$

We could keep adding to the RHS until it is divisible by 11. Alternatively, as $8x$ is always a multiple of 8, we can subtract $8x$ from the left

(c) $11x \equiv 5 \pmod{8}$
$\Leftrightarrow 3x \equiv 5 \pmod{8}$
$\Leftrightarrow 3x \equiv 13 \equiv 21 \pmod{8}$
$\Leftrightarrow x \equiv 7 \pmod{8}$

We don't have to divide by 25 in one go. Both sides are divisible by 5, and we must remember to divide the modulus by 5

(d) $25x \equiv 10 \pmod{30}$
$5x \equiv 2 \pmod{6}$

We can now divide by 5 again

$5x \equiv 8 \equiv 14 \equiv 20 \pmod{6}$
$x \equiv 4 \pmod{6}$

In all of these examples there are infinitely many numbers x which satisfy the congruence. However, they all give the same remainder when divided by the final modulus. In the first example the solution is unique modulo 5, and in the second example it is unique modulo 3. Note that in the second example, the solution is not unique modulo 9 (which was the original modulus): x could give remainder 1, 4 or 7 when divided by 9.

Linear congruences do not always have a solution as shown in the next example.

Worked example 5.5

Solve $3x \equiv 5 \pmod{12}$.

In order to divide both sides by 3 we need to keep adding 12 to the right hand side until it is divisible by 3

$3x \equiv 5 \equiv 17 \equiv 29 \equiv 41 \equiv \ldots \pmod{12}$

It seems we can never make it divisible by 3. This is because we are adding 12, which is a multiple of 3, to 5, which is not

$5 + 12k$ can never be a multiple of 3 because 5 is not a multiple of 3. So there are no solutions.

Exercise 5C

1. Solve the following linear congruences:
   (a) (i) $3x \equiv 7 \pmod{11}$ (ii) $4x \equiv 9 \pmod{15}$
   (b) (i) $15x \equiv 7 \pmod{11}$ (ii) $11x \equiv 7 \pmod{9}$
   (c) (i) $5x \equiv 30 \pmod{15}$ (ii) $3x \equiv 18 \pmod{9}$
   (d) (i) $12x + 2 \equiv 4x + 7 \pmod{9}$ (ii) $11x - 2 \equiv 3x + 5 \pmod{9}$
   (e) (i) $21x \equiv 18 \pmod{9}$ (ii) $15x \equiv 60 \pmod{24}$

2. Solve the linear congruence $5x \equiv 7 \pmod{13}$. *[4 marks]*

3. Solve the linear congruence $3x \equiv 12 \pmod{21}$ giving your answer in the form $x \equiv a \pmod{m}$. *[4 marks]*

4. (a) Explain why the linear congruence $6x \equiv 4 \pmod 9$ has no solutions.
   (b) Solve $6x \equiv 3 \pmod 9$.
   (c) List all the solutions of the equation in (b) which satisfy $|x| < 10$. *[8 marks]*

5. (a) Solve the linear congruence $6x \equiv 3 \pmod{15}$, giving your answers in the form $x \equiv a \pmod{15}$.
   (b) How many solutions modulo 63 does the linear congruence $21x \equiv 147 \pmod{63}$ have? Justify your answer. *[7 marks]*

6. Given that $3x + y \equiv 21 \pmod 5$ and $x - y \equiv 7 \pmod 5$ find the smallest positive value of a such that $x \equiv a \pmod 5$. *[8 marks]*

5D Chinese remainder theorem

Consider the following problem: find all numbers which give remainder 2 when divided by 3 and remainder 3 when divided by 5. In the language of congruences from the previous section, we are trying to solve simultaneous congruences:

5 Modular arithmetic

$$\begin{cases} x \equiv 2 \pmod{3} \\ x \equiv 3 \pmod{5} \end{cases}$$

We can list solutions for each congruence separately and see which ones appear in both lists. To keep things simple, let us just list the positive solutions.

$x \equiv 2 \pmod{3}$: $x = 2, 5, 8, 11, 14, 17, 20, 23, \ldots$

$x \equiv 3 \pmod{5}$: $x = 3, 8, 13, 18, 23, 28, \ldots$

So far we have found two solutions: 8 and 23. We can see that to get any number in the first list we need to add a multiple of 3 and for any number in the second list a multiple of 5. Hence to get another number which is in both lists we need to add a multiple of 15. This means that every solution is of the form $8 + 15k$, in other words $x \equiv 8 \pmod{15}$. Although there are infinitely many numbers that satisfy this congruence, the solution is unique modulo 15.

This is an example of the following general result:

KEY POINT 5.8

Chinese remainder theorem

If m_1 and m_2 are coprime then the simultaneous congruences

$$x \equiv a \pmod{m_1}, \quad x \equiv b \pmod{m_2}$$

have a unique solution $\pmod{m_1 m_2}$.

> The Chinese remainder theorem was first written down by the Chinese mathematician Sun Tzu in the 3rd century CE and republished by Qin Jiushao in 1247. Its first applications were in solving Diophantine equations, but it has also found uses in public key cryptography in the 20th century.

The result generalises to any number of congruences, as long as the moduli are pairwise coprime (so any two are relatively prime).

Worked example 5.6

Given the system of linear congruences:

$$\begin{cases} x \equiv 2 \pmod{5} \\ x \equiv 3 \pmod{7} \\ x \equiv 5 \pmod{13} \end{cases}$$

(a) Find one number x which satisfies all three congruences.

(b) Hence write down the solution of the system in the form $x \equiv a \pmod{m}$.

We can solve the first two equations first. It is a good idea to start with the two smallest moduli

(a) $x \equiv 2 \pmod 5$: $2, 7, 12, 17, \ldots$
$x \equiv 3 \pmod 7$: $3, 10, 17, \ldots$
So $x \equiv 17 \pmod{35}$

We now make a list for the third equation and compare to all the numbers which are $17 \pmod{35}$

$x \equiv 1 \pmod{13}$:
$5, 18, 31, 44, 57, 70, 83, 96, 109, 122$
$x \equiv 17 \pmod{35}$: $17, 52, 87, 122$

This answer is unique modulo 35×13

(b) $\therefore x \equiv 122 \pmod{455}$

As numbers get larger, finding a solution by inspection becomes more time-consuming. An alternative is to rewrite the congruence as a Diophantine equation. We will illustrate this method by an example.

The method for finding a solution of Diophantine equations was given in Section 4B.

Worked example 5.7

Solve the simultaneous congruences $x \equiv 12 \pmod{32}$, $x \equiv 21 \pmod{31}$.

As 31 and 32 are relatively prime, the solution is unique modulo $31 \times 32 = 992$. We just need to find one solution

By Chinese remainder theorem, the solution is
$x \equiv c \pmod{992}$

Write each congruence as an equation for x

We can write:
$x = 32a + 12$
$x = 31b + 21$ } (*)

Hence $32a + 12 = 31b + 21$
$\Leftrightarrow 32a - 31b = 9$

This is a Diophantine equation, so we know how to find one solution

$\gcd(32, 31) = 1$, and $1 = 32 - 31$
So $9 = 32 \times 9 - 31 \times 9$
$\therefore a = 9, b = 9$

We can now find x from (*). Both equations for x should give us the same solution (we should check!) This is the solution mod(992)

From (*), $x = 300$.
$\therefore x \equiv 300 \pmod{992}$

Exercise 5D

1. Solve the following simultaneous congruences:
   (a) (i) $x \equiv 3 \pmod 5$, $x \equiv 4 \pmod 7$

   (ii) $x \equiv 2 \pmod{11}$, $x \equiv 4 \pmod 5$

   (b) (i) $x \equiv 0 \pmod 2$, $x \equiv 2 \pmod 5$, $x \equiv 4 \pmod 7$

   (ii) $x \equiv 0 \pmod 3$, $x \equiv 1 \pmod 4$, $x \equiv 1 \pmod 5$

2. By first solving an appropriate Diophantine equation, solve the following simultaneous congruences:
   (a) (i) $x \equiv 6 \pmod{19}$, $x \equiv 6 \pmod{11}$

   (ii) $x \equiv 6 \pmod{13}$, $x \equiv 3 \pmod{22}$

   (b) (i) $x \equiv 15 \pmod{31}$, $x \equiv 2 \pmod{30}$

   (ii) $x \equiv 4 \pmod{17}$, $x \equiv 9 \pmod{24}$

3. Solve this system of congruences:
$$\begin{cases} x \equiv 2 \pmod 3 \\ x \equiv 5 \pmod 7 \end{cases}$$ [6 marks]

4. Solve this system of linear congruences:
$x \equiv 2 \pmod 3$, $x \equiv 0 \pmod 5$, $x \equiv 6 \pmod 7$ [8 marks]

5. (a) Find the smallest positive value of x such that $5x \equiv 1 \pmod 7$.

   (b) Hence solve the system of linear congruences
   $5x \equiv 1 \pmod 7$, $x \equiv 3 \pmod 5$ [7 marks]

6. Solve these simultaneous linear congruences:
   $3x \equiv 2 \pmod 5$
   $5x \equiv 2 \pmod 3$ [8 marks]

7. Solve the system of linear congruences:
   $x \equiv 3 \pmod{17}$, $x \equiv 21 \pmod{31}$. [10 marks]

8. (a) Prove that the system of linear congruences:
   $x \equiv 2 \pmod 6$, $x \equiv 4 \pmod 9$ has no solutions.

   (b) (i) Find the general solution of the Diophantine equation:
   $6m - 9n = 3$.

   (ii) Hence solve the system of congruences:
   $x \equiv 2 \pmod 6$, $x \equiv 5 \pmod 9$. [10 marks]

5E Fermat's little theorem

We have already answered questions such as: find the remainder when 5^{17} is divided by 7. We start by evaluating small powers and see if we can spot a pattern:

$$5^2 \equiv 25 \equiv 4 \pmod 7$$
$$5^3 \equiv 5 \times 4 \equiv 6 \equiv -1 \pmod 7$$

We can get close to the power 17 by raising this to the power of 5:

$$5^{15} \equiv (-1)^5 \equiv -1 \pmod 7$$
$$5^{15} \times 5^2 \equiv -1 \times 4 \equiv -4 \equiv 3 \pmod 7$$

Hence 5^{17} gives remainder 3 when divided by 7.

Our strategy in these problems is to keep evaluating powers until we get remainder 1 or −1 and then 'jump' to a multiple close to the required power. But how do we know that this will ever happen? For example, looking at powers of 3 modulo 12, we find that:

$3^1 \equiv 3 \pmod{12}$, $3^2 \equiv 9 \pmod{12}$, $3^3 \equiv 27 \equiv 3 \pmod{12}$,
$3^4 \equiv 3 \times 3 \equiv 9 \pmod{12}$

It seems that the remainders alternate between 3 and 9, so we will never get remainder 1. In this case, it seems that all odd powers give remainder 3 and all even powers remainder 9.

In all the examples we have seen so far the remainders of powers follow a periodic pattern. When we are looking at remainders modulo a prime, the following result tells us how many powers we need to find before they start to repeat.

KEY POINT 5.9

Fermat's little theorem

If p is a prime and a is any integer then $a^p \equiv a \pmod{p}$.

This is equivalent to saying that $p \mid (a^p - a)$.

We can extract even more information when a is not a multiple of p: as a and p are relatively prime we can divide both sides of the congruence by a to get the following special case of Fermat's little theorem.

KEY POINT 5.10

If p is a prime and a is not a multiple of p then $a^{p-1} \equiv 1 \pmod{p}$.

The proof of Fermat's little theorem uses ideas from Group Theory, a branch of Discrete Mathematics studied in Option 8, Sets, Relations and Groups.

We now have a good strategy for finding remainders.

Worked example 5.8

Find the remainder when 28^{28} is divided by 13.

Fermat's little theorem is useful because we can jump to quite a high power	Fermat's little theorem $\Rightarrow 28^{12} \equiv 1 \pmod{13}$
We can square this to get power 24	$\Rightarrow 28^{24} \equiv 1^2 \equiv 1 \pmod{13}$
We now just need to multiply by 28^4 $28 \equiv 2 \pmod{13}$	$\Rightarrow 28^{28} \equiv 28^4 \equiv 2^4 \equiv 16 \equiv 3 \pmod{13}$ ∴ 28^{28} gives remainder 3 when divided by 13.

When we are looking at divisibility by a composite number, Fermat's little theorem may need to be used several times in the same question.

Worked example 5.9

Prove that for all integers n, $n^7 - n$ is divisible by 42.

We first factorise 42 to see which primes we need to look at	$42 = 2 \times 3 \times 7$

continued . . .

> Because there is n^7 in the question, we can use Fermat's little theorem for divisibility by 7

Divisibility by 7:
By Fermat's little theorem,
$n^7 \equiv n \pmod 7$
So $7 \mid (n^7 - n)$.

> Now look at divisibility by 3: Fermat's little theorem can only be used to get to n^3, but we can then apply other rules of congruences

Divisibility by 3:
By Fermat's little theorem,
$n^3 \equiv n \pmod 3$
$\Rightarrow n^6 \equiv n^2 \pmod 3$ (square both sides)
$\Rightarrow n^7 \equiv n^3 \pmod 3$ (multiply by n)
$\Rightarrow n^7 \equiv n \pmod 3$ (from the first line)
So $3 \mid (n^7 - n)$.

> Similar strategy works for divisibility by 2

Divisibility by 2:
By Fermat's little theorem,
$n^2 \equiv n \pmod 2$
$\Rightarrow n^6 \equiv n^3 \pmod 2$ (cube both sides)
$\Rightarrow n^7 \equiv n^4 \pmod 2$ (multiply by n)
But $n^4 \equiv (n^2)^2 \equiv n^2 \equiv n \pmod 2$
So $2 \mid (n^7 - n)$.

> We have proved divisibility by 2, 3 and 7

Therefore $n^7 - n$ is divisible by 2, 3 and 7 and hence by 42.

It is worth noting alternative approaches here. First, the divisibility by 2 could have been proved by simply noting that an even number to any power is even and an odd number to any power is odd; hence n^7 and n are either both even or both odd, so their difference is even. Secondly, we could have proved divisibility by 2 and 3 together by factorising:

$$n^7 - n = n(n^6 - 1)$$
$$= n(n^3 - 1)(n^3 + 1)$$
$$= n(n-1)(n^2 + n + 1)(n+1)(n^2 - n + 1)$$

n, $n-1$ and $n+1$ are three consecutive integers, so at least one of them is even and at least one of them is divisible by 3. Hence their product is divisible by 6.

Exercise 5E

1. Find the following remainders:
   (a) (i) $3^{42} \pmod{41}$ (ii) $5^{39} \pmod{37}$
   (b) (i) $4^{11} \pmod{11}$ (ii) $5^{17} \pmod{17}$
   (c) (i) $7^{24} \pmod{13}$ (ii) $5^{18} \pmod 7$
   (d) (i) $5^{25} \pmod 3$ (ii) $12^{31} \pmod{11}$

2. Find the remainder when 35^{32} is divided by 11. [5 marks]

3. (a) Prove that $x^{25} \equiv x \pmod{13}$.
   (b) Hence solve $x^{25} \equiv 5 \pmod{13}$.
   (c) Explain why the linear congruence $x^{12} \equiv 5 \pmod{13}$ has no solution. [8 marks]

4. Let a and b be two whole numbers such that $a + b$ is divisible by 17. Show that $a^{17} + b^{17}$ is also divisible by 17. [3 marks]

5. Given that p is a prime number show that $p \mid (ab^p - a^p b)$ for all positive integers a, b. [6 marks]

6. Let p be a prime number greater than 2 and let x and y be such that $p \mid (x^p + y^p)$. Show that $p^2 \mid x^p + y^p$. [7 marks]

Summary

- $a \equiv b \pmod{m}$ means that:
  - $m \mid (a - b)$
  - a and b give the same remainder when divided by m
  - we can write $a = b + km$.
- We can add, subtract and multiply congruences, and raise both sides to the same power.
- We can add or subtract a multiple of m from just one side of a congruence.
- There are special rules for division:
  - if $a \equiv b \pmod{m}$ and d divides a, b and m, then $\frac{a}{d} \equiv \frac{b}{d} \pmod{\frac{m}{d}}$
  - if $a \equiv b \pmod{m}$ and d divides both a and b, then $\frac{a}{d} \equiv \frac{b}{d} \left(\mod \frac{m}{\gcd(d,m)} \right)$.
- The **Chinese remainder theorem** says that if m_1 and m_2 are coprime then the system of linear congruences $x \equiv a \pmod{m_1}$, $x \equiv b \pmod{m_2}$ has a unique solution $\pmod{m_1 m_2}$. This solution can be found either by inspection or by solving a Diophantine equation.
- **Fermat's little theorem** says that if p is a prime then for all a, $a^p \equiv a \pmod{p}$. A consequence is that if p is prime which does not divide a then $a^{p-1} \equiv 1 \pmod{p}$.

Mixed examination practice 5

1. Use Fermat's little theorem to find the remainder when 14^{112} is divided by 11. [5 marks]

2. Find the last digit of 4^{32}. [3 marks]

3. Solve the linear congruence $3x \equiv 5 \pmod{11}$. [6 marks]

4. Find the last digit of 5^{60} when written in base 13. [6 marks]

5. Show that $2222^{5555} + 5555^{2222}$ is divisible by 7. [6 marks]

6. (a) Find $\gcd(32, 12)$. [6 marks]
   (b) Solve the linear congruence $12x \equiv 36 \pmod{32}$. [4 marks]

7. Consider the equation $x^{12} + 1 = 7y$, where $x, y \in \mathbb{Z}^+$.
Using Fermat's little theorem, show that this equation has no solution. [9 marks]
(© IB Organization 2007)

8. (a) Find the remainder when 4^5 is divided by 25.
   (b) Hence show that $4^{10n+2} \equiv 16 \pmod{25}$.
   (c) Find the last two digits in the base 5 expansion of 4^{42}. [7 marks]

9. Solve the system of linear congruences $x \equiv 2 \pmod{13}$, $x \equiv 3 \pmod{5}$. [4 marks]

10. Solve the simultaneous congruences:
$x \equiv 0 \pmod{2}$, $x \equiv 2 \pmod{5}$, $x \equiv 14 \pmod{17}$. [7 marks]

11. Use Fermat's little theorem to show that $7^{120} - 1$ is divisible by 143. [5 marks]

12. (a) Show that 5^{36} gives remainder 13 when divided by 17.
   (b) Find the remainder when 5^{36} is divided by 13.
   (c) By solving simultaneous congruences, find the remainder when 5^{36} is divided by 221. [8 marks]

13. (a) Let p be a prime and $\gcd(a, p) = 1$. Use Fermat's little theorem to show that $x \equiv a^{p-2}b \pmod{p}$ is a solution of the linear congruence $ax \equiv b \pmod{p}$.
   (b) Hence solve the system of linear congruences $2x \equiv 1 \pmod{31}$, $6x \equiv 5 \pmod{11}$. [7 marks]

14. Find all the solutions of the linear congruence $120x \equiv 110 \pmod{65}$, giving your answers in the form $x \equiv k \pmod{65}$. [5 marks]

15. (a) State Fermat's little theorem.
   (b) Prove that, if $p \geq 3$ is a prime then $\sum_{k=1}^{p-1} k^p \equiv 0 \pmod{p}$. [4 marks]

6 Graph theory

In this chapter you will learn:

- that many different types of real-life problems can be solved using graphs
- about main features of a graph and different ways of representing a graph
- how to recognise some special types of graphs
- how to prove some important theorems about the number of vertices and edges in a graph
- about different ways of moving around a graph.

What do social networks, molecular structures, traffic flow and the syntax of a language have in common? One answer is that they can all be studied using graphs, mathematical structures which are normally represented as a set of points joined by lines. Graphs seem an abstract mathematical concept but they have many applications in a wide variety of unexpected places. In this chapter we will look at basic mathematical properties of graphs, and in the next we will apply them to finding optimal routes around a network.

6A Introduction to graphs

In this section we will introduce some typical problems that can be solved using graphs. You should attempt to find a solution, but don't be disappointed if you can't; the problems are intended to illustrate the sort of difficulties that started the development of graph theory. They should help you understand the need for the precise definitions and theorems that are introduced in this chapter and for the algorithms we develop in the next.

The table below shows the cost of direct flights between ten cities.

cost($)	Athens	Beijing	Cairo	Dubai	Frankfurt	Johannesburg	London	New York	Moscow	Sydney
Athens	-	-	213	96	52	-	65	-	-	-
Beijing	-	-	-	412	450	526	-	486	350	225
Cairo	213	-	-	320	186	250	212	386	-	-
Dubai	96	412	320	-	250	315	234	-	312	524
Frankfurt	52	450	186	250	-	-	36	312	387	-
Johannesburg	-	526	250	315	-	-	325	-	-	216
London	65	-	212	234	36	325	-	215	428	-
New York	-	486	386	-	312	-	215	-	-	243
Moscow	-	350	-	312	387	-	428	-	-	-
Sydney	-	225	-	524	-	216	-	243	-	-

1. Can you find the cheapest combination of flights to get from Athens to Sydney?

2. Can you find the cheapest combination of flights to visit each city at least once and return to the starting city?

To answer the first question, it is tempting to try one of two approaches. We can either try the route with fewest legs, which in this case is Athens-Dubai-Sydney or we can try the one in which the initial flight is the least expensive, which would be

There is an efficient method for solving this problem, called Dijkstra's Algorithm. We will meet it in section 7C.

This is called the Travelling Salesman problem and we will investigate its solution in Section 7E.

Athens-Frankfurt-New York-Sydney. However, more testing reveals that neither of these is the cheapest. The best possible route is in fact Athens-London-Johannesburg-Sydney. It is not clear that this is the cheapest without checking lots of possibilities. You can imagine that if we had 100 cities instead of 10, the problem would be impossible to solve in a reasonable time.

The second problem is even more difficult. It is not even obvious that the best route should visit each city exactly once, as sometimes the direct route between the two cities is not the cheapest one. Even checking all the routes in which each city appears just once does not seem to be an easy task. It turns out that usually the only way to solve this type of problem is to check all possible routes, and generally this is not feasible. However, there are some clever ways to estimate the cost of the cheapest route.

The information from the table can be represented as a diagram in which points (representing cities) are joined by lines (representing direct routes). Such a diagram is called a **graph**. Where these types of problems are used in practical applications, the graphs can consist of hundreds of points or lines. An example similar to our problem is a satellite navigation system, which tries to find the shortest route between two places and has a choice of many different roads and junctions. It is impossible for a human to solve such a problem in a reasonable time, so we need to program a computer to do this.

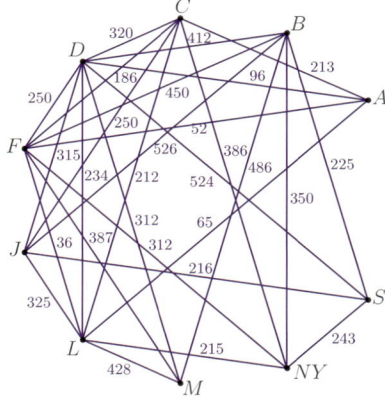

Would you say that if we program a computer to try all possible routes, we can be certain that we have found the best possible solution? Is this the same as proving it mathematically?

Using a computer introduces a new set of problems. We need to program the computer to solve all problems of this type, not just one particular one. This means that we need to have a method, called an **algorithm**, which always finds the best possible solution. Such an algorithm has to have a well-defined sequence of steps, and cannot take shortcuts based on 'guessing' or 'experience'. It must also be efficient so that it can perform the task in a reasonable time. Checking all possible routes is not practical, and the time it takes increases rapidly with the size of the graph. A typical computer can perform around 3 billion operations per second; checking all possible routes for our second problem would take around a millisecond, but if we increase the number of cities to 15 it would take around 5 minutes and with 20 cities this goes up to 500 years – not very practical if you are waiting at the travel agent!

Here is a different problem: Is it possible to draw this shape without lifting your pen off the paper and without going over any lines more than once?

This problem was first studied by Leonhard Euler in 1836, and is usually regarded as the first published result of graph theory.

After trying for a while you may decide that it is impossible. This is equivalent to saying, for example, that the shape cannot be made out of a single piece of wire. Can you explain why? What feature of the shape would need to change for it to become possible?

Later we will prove that the key feature for this problem is the number of lines coming out of each point. This is one of the important features of graphs that we will study in the rest of this chapter.

> This problem is related to Eulerian graphs, which we will meet in Section 6F of this chapter.

6B Definitions

In order to solve problems with graphs it is useful to introduce some new terminology. In this section we will define various concepts associated with graphs.

A graph consists of **vertices** connected by **edges**. Two vertices are called **adjacent** if they are joined by an edge. Two edges are called adjacent if they have a common vertex. When we draw a graph, the position of the vertices and the shape of the edges are not relevant; the only thing that matters is which vertices are adjacent. So the two diagrams below represent the same graph. The edges may intersect at points other than vertices, so it is important to label the vertices clearly.

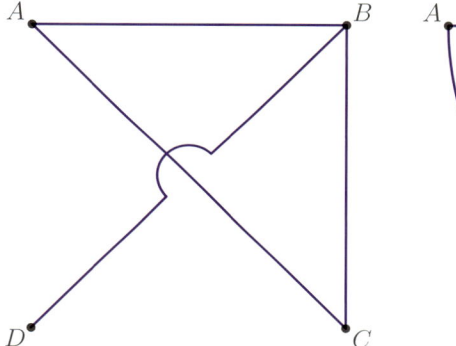
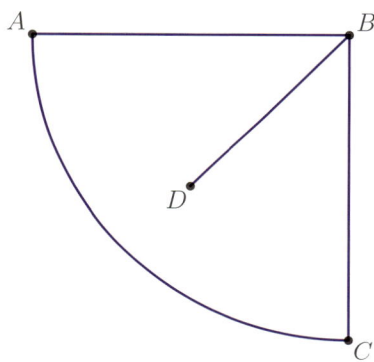

The vertices of the graph are usually labelled by capital letters. So the graphs above have vertices A, B, C and D and edges AB, AC, BC and BD.

Sometimes we need to show a situation where we can only move in one direction between vertices, for example when modelling a road network with one-way roads. In such cases we can put arrows on the edges to indicate the allowed direction. The resulting graph is called a **directed graph**, or **digraph**. In Graph 1, it is possible to get from D to A but not from A to D, while both directions between A and B are allowed.

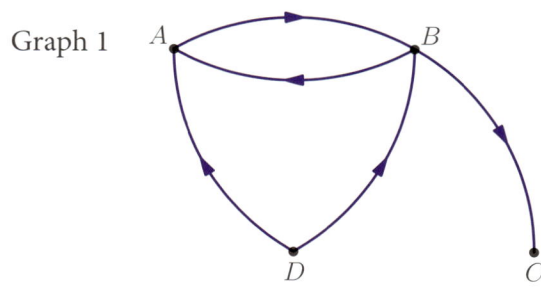

Graph 1

> Graph theory is a relatively new branch of mathematics, with its beginnings in the 18th century and many important developments in the early 20th century. Because many of its findings were motivated by applications it has had contributions from many different communities: mathematicians, computer scientists, chemists and even linguists. For these reasons some of the terminology is not yet firmly standardised, so you may find slightly different definitions in other books. For example, vertices and edges are also called nodes and arcs. The terminology we use here is what will be used in your IB examination.

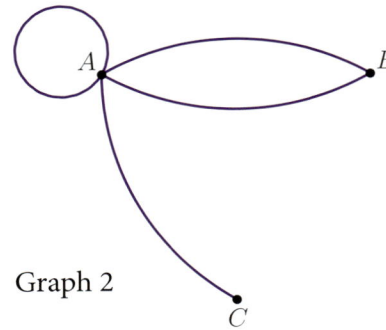

Graph 2

In a **simple graph** no vertex is joined to itself (no **loops**) and there are no multiple edges between vertices. So Graph 2 shown alongside, is not simple. Some theorems of graph theory only apply to simple graphs, so it is important to note this when learning them. A graph in which there are some multiple edges is sometimes called a **multigraph**.

When a graph has many vertices and edges it can be complicated to draw. In such cases it is more convenient to represent it by an **adjacency table**. This table shows the number of edges joining each pair of vertices. For example, the adjacency table for Graph 1 is:

		to			
		A	B	C	D
from	A	0	1	0	0
	B	1	0	1	0
	C	0	0	0	0
	D	1	1	0	0

> **EXAM HINT**
> You should not assume that a graph is simple unless this is explicitly stated.

and the table for Graph 2 is:

	A	B	C
A	1	2	1
B	2	0	0
C	1	0	0

KEY POINT 6.1

- For a simple graph, all entries on the leading diagonal (top left to bottom right) are zeros, and all other entries are either 0 or 1.
- The adjacency table of an undirected graph is symmetrical about the leading diagonal.

The number of edges coming out of a vertex is called the **degree** of that vertex. For example, in Graph 2:

$$\deg(A) = 5, \deg(B) = 2, \deg(C) = 1.$$

Note that when calculating the degree, we count the edge joining A to A twice, as each edge has to have two ends. However, in the adjacency table the number in the (A, A) cell is 1, because there is only one edge joining A to itself. The list of degrees of all the vertices of the graph is called its **degree sequence**. It is usually given in descending order; for example, Graph 2 has degree sequence 5, 2, 1.

KEY POINT 6.2

The degree of a vertex is equal to the sum of the numbers in the row or column of the adjacency table corresponding to that vertex. If there is an edge connecting a vertex to itself that edge needs to be added twice.

Topic 10 – Option: Discrete mathematics

In the next section we will prove several theorems about the number of edges and vertices of different types of graphs. They will show that there are restrictions on what the degree sequence of a graph can be. Here we show just one interesting result about the degree sequence of a simple graph.

You may want to review the pigeonhole principle from Section 1B before reading the next Worked example.

Worked example 6.1

Show that in a simple graph there are always two vertices with the same degree.

This sounds like the type of problem we solved using the pigeonhole principle. The vertices can be 'pigeons', and the possible values of the degree 'pigeonholes'

Suppose the graph has n vertices. As the graph is simple, the smallest possible degree of a vertex is 0 and the largest one is $n-1$.

There seem to be n pigeonholes! But can they all appear in the same graph?

If there is a vertex with degree 0, then no other vertex is connected to it, so the largest possible degree is $n-2$. So there are in fact only $n-1$ possible values for the degrees: either 0 to $n-2$, or 1 to $n-1$. Hence, by the pigeonhole principle, two of the vertices must have the same degree.

This result can be expressed in various different ways in different contexts. For example, in each group of people there are two who have the same number of friends in the group; or in a football league, at each point in the season there are two teams that have played the same number of games.

One of the main applications of graphs is modelling situations where we need to move between vertices. It is therefore important to know whether it is possible to get from one vertex to another. A graph is called *connected* if every two vertices are connected (directly or indirectly); in other words, there is a path between every two vertices. This means that the graph cannot be split into two parts. Most of the results in this course deal with **connected graphs**.

We will look at various types of paths in more detail in Section 6F of this chapter. For the moment we just use the term to mean a route between two vertices.

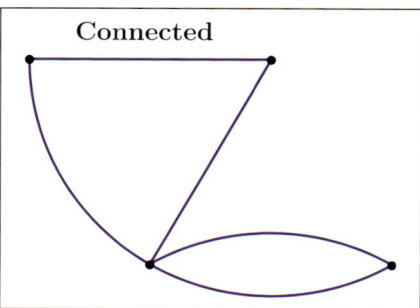
Connected

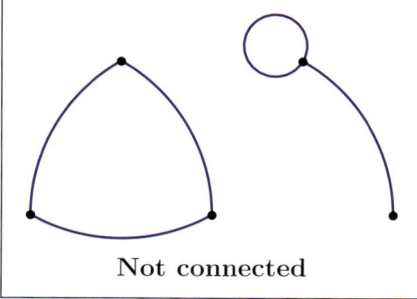
Not connected

There are some special types of graphs which you need to know.

A **complete graph** is a graph where every pair of vertices are joined by an edge. A symbol for a complete graph with n vertices is κ_n.

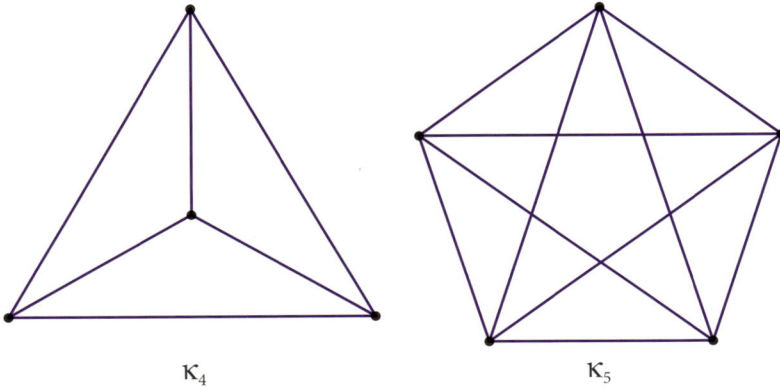

κ_4 κ_5

EXAM HINT

You may be asked to give explanations and proofs for most of the results in this chapter.

KEY POINT 6.3

The number of edges in κ_n is $\binom{n}{2}$.

This is because there is an edge corresponding to every pair of vertices, and selecting two vertices from n can be done in $\binom{n}{2}$ ways.

A **bipartite graph** is a graph whose vertices can be split into two groups, X and Y, such that edges only join vertices in X to those in Y, and there are no edges joining vertices in the same group. If every vertex in X is joined to every vertex in Y the graph is called a **complete bipartite graph** and denoted $\kappa_{r,s}$, where r and s are the number of vertices in groups X and Y, respectively.

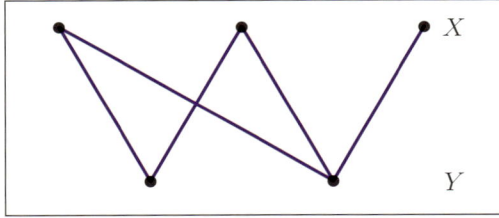

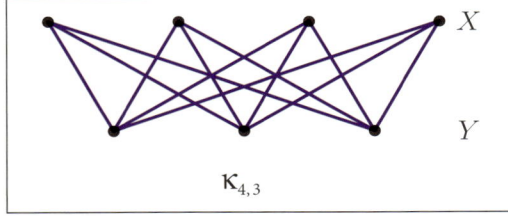

$\kappa_{4,3}$

Worked example 6.2

Show that the number of edges in $\kappa_{r,s}$ is rs.

How many edges start from each vertex in X? | There are s edges from each vertex in X.

How many vertices are there in X? | There are r vertices in X.

So there are rs edges in the graph.

72 Topic 10 – Option: Discrete mathematics

A **tree** is a connected graph in which there are no closed paths (**cycles**), i.e. it is not possible to find a sequence of distinct edges which returns to the starting vertex.

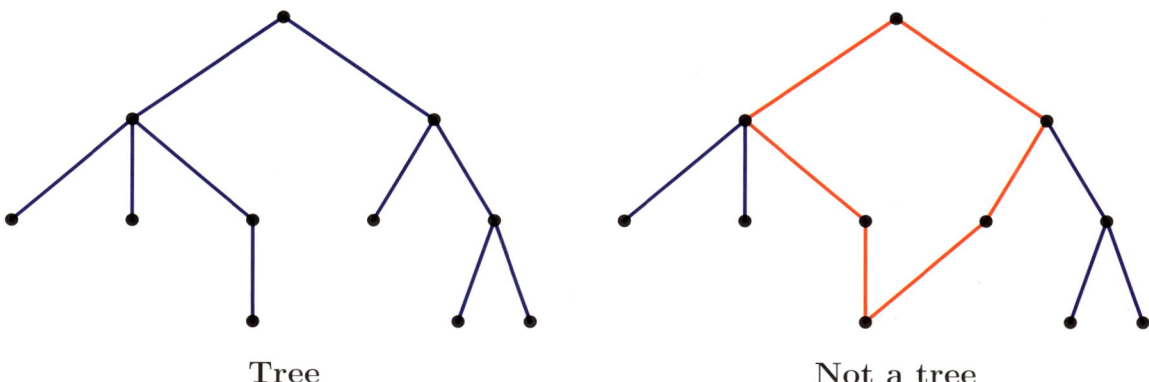

Tree   Not a tree

KEY POINT 6.4

A tree with n vertices has $n - 1$ edges.

Note that this is the smallest possible number of edges needed to make a graph with n vertices connected, so if any one edge of a tree is removed the graph is no longer connected.

You need to be able to prove the above result about the number of edges of a tree. The proof uses strong induction and is given in the next example. Proof by induction is common in graph theory because we can think of 'building up' any graph by adding vertices and edges one at a time.

Worked example 6.3

Use strong induction to prove that a tree with n vertices has $n - 1$ edges.

Prove the base case. We will check later that $n = 1$ is the only base case needed

When $n = 1$:
The tree with one vertex has no edges, so the statement is true for $n = 1$.

Assume the statement is true for all $n \leq k$. Now let $n = k$ and look at a tree with k vertices.

6 Graph theory   **73**

> continued...
>
> **It is tempting to try and take out one vertex and one edge to get a tree with $k-1$ vertices and $k-2$ edges. However, this vertex would need to be from the 'end' of the tree, and it is not easy to identify such a vertex. But since we can use strong induction, we can take out any edge to split the tree into two smaller trees (we need to explain why this is the case)**

Take out any edge.
This splits the graph into two separate trees: If the remaining graph was still connected there would be another path between the endpoints of the removed edge; but putting the removed edge back would then form a cycle, which is impossible.
Let the numbers of vertices of the two new trees be a and b.

> **We have not removed any vertices**

Then $a + b = k$.

> **We can apply the inductive hypothesis**

Both a and b are less than k, so the inductive hypothesis applies: The two trees have $a - 1$ and $b - 1$ edges.
Hence the number of edges of the original tree was
$(a-1)+(b-1)+1 = (a+b)-1 = k-1$
So the statement is true for $n = k$.

> **We should always write a conclusion. Note that we only need $n = 1$ as the base case, as when $n = 2$ we can split the graph into two graphs with one vertex each**

The statement is true for $n = 1$, and if it is true for all $n < k$ we can prove that it is also true for $n = k$. Hence the statement is true for all n by strong induction.

We will prove this result in the next section.

Another important type of graph is a **planar graph**. This is any graph that can be drawn in the plane so that the edges do not cross. Not every graph is planar; for example it is impossible to draw $K_{3,3}$ without any edges crossing.

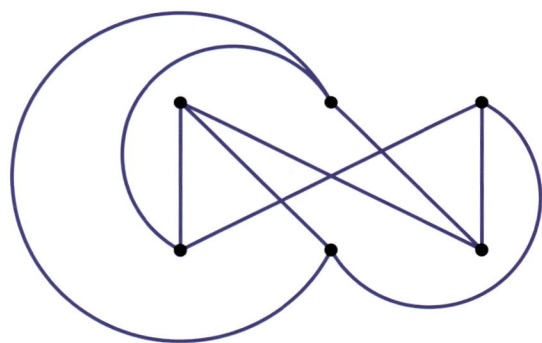

This type of path is called a Hamiltonian cycle, and we will study it in more detail in Section 6G.

A planar graph may be drawn with edges crossing, or given by its adjacency table. To redraw the graph in its planar form, one good strategy is to look for a closed path which includes all vertices of the graph, draw this path first, and then fit other edges around it. Note, however, that such a closed path does not always exist.

Worked example 6.4

Graph G is given by the following adjacency table.

	A	B	C	D	E
A	0	1	1	1	1
B	1	0	1	1	1
C	1	1	0	1	1
D	1	1	1	0	0
E	1	1	1	0	0

Draw G in planar form.

First draw G with vertices in alphabetical order and find a closed path which includes all the vertices

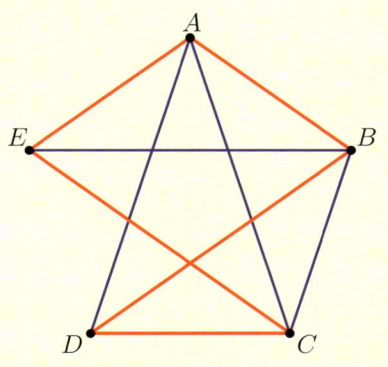

Hamiltonian cycle: ABDCEA

Redraw G so that this path forms a pentagon
Then fit in the other edges. Put as many as you can inside the pentagon, and then the others round the outside

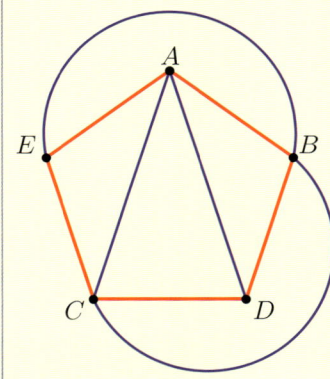

Exercise 6B

1. For each of the graphs shown below state the number of vertices and the number of edges.

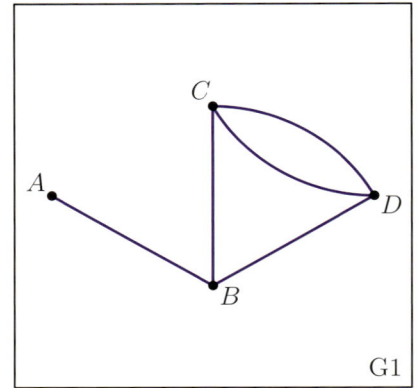
G1

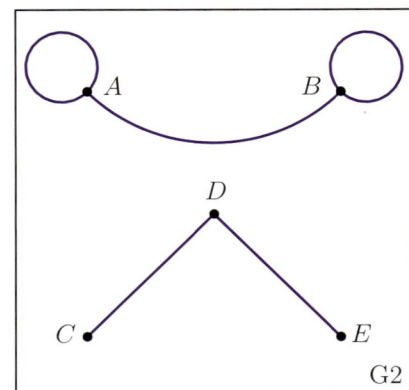
G2

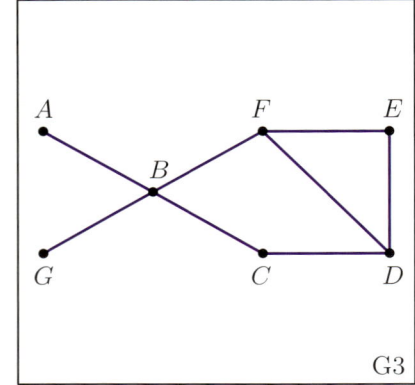
G3

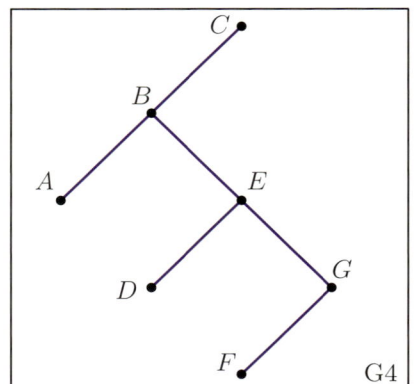
G4

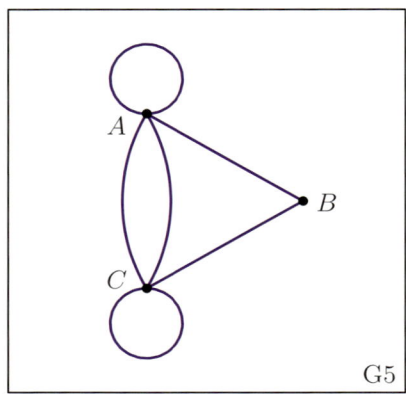
G5

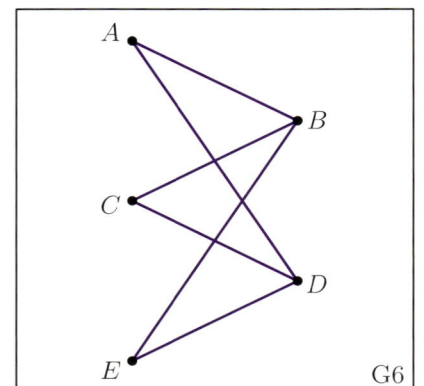
G6

2. For each of the graphs above list the degrees of the vertices.

3. Copy and complete the table to classify the graphs above. Use ticks to mark correct options.

	G1	G2	G3	G4	G5	G6
Connected						
Simple						
Complete						
Tree						
Bipartite						

4. Represent each of the graphs above in an adjacency table.

5. Draw the graphs represented by the following adjacency tables:

(a) (i)

	A	B	C	D
A	1	2	0	1
B	2	0	1	2
C	0	1	0	0
D	1	2	0	0

(ii)

	A	B	C	D
A	0	0	2	1
B	0	1	1	0
C	2	1	0	2
D	1	0	2	1

(b) (i)

	A	B	C	D
A	0	1	1	0
B	1	0	1	1
C	1	1	0	0
D	0	1	0	0

(ii)

	A	B	C	D
A	0	1	0	1
B	1	0	0	1
C	0	0	0	1
D	1	1	1	0

(c) (i)

	A	B	C	D	E
A	0	1	1	0	1
B	1	1	0	2	0
C	1	0	1	1	0
D	0	2	1	0	2
E	1	0	1	2	0

(ii)

	A	B	C	D	E
A	1	1	0	0	2
B	1	0	1	1	0
C	0	1	2	0	1
D	0	1	0	1	2
E	2	0	1	2	0

6. Without drawing the graphs, write down the degree of each vertex for the graphs with the following adjacency tables:

(a) (i)

	A	B	C	D	E
A	0	1	1	0	0
B	1	0	0	1	1
C	1	0	0	1	1
D	0	1	1	0	0
E	0	1	1	0	0

(ii)

	A	B	C	D
A	0	1	1	1
B	1	0	0	1
C	1	0	0	1
D	1	1	1	0

(b) (i)

	A	B	C	D	E
A	0	1	1	0	2
B	1	2	0	0	2
C	1	0	1	0	0
D	0	0	0	2	3
E	2	2	0	3	0

(ii)

	A	B	C	D
A	2	1	1	3
B	1	1	2	0
C	1	2	0	0
D	3	0	0	0

7. Draw each graph in planar form:

   (a)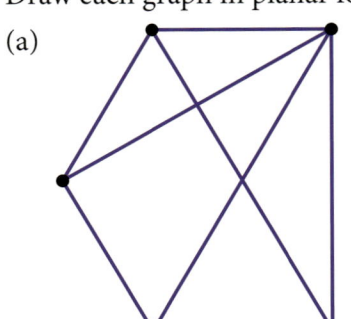
   (b)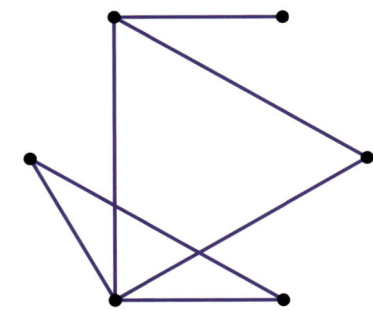

8. Show that each of the graphs is bipartite by listing the two sets of vertices:

   (a)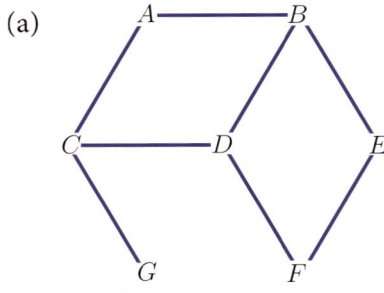
   (b)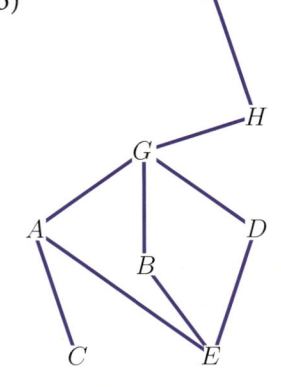

9. Draw an example of each of the following:

   (a) A simple, connected graph with 6 vertices, each of degree 2.
   (b) A simple, non-connected graph with 6 vertices, each of degree 2.
   (c) A simple, connected graph with 6 vertices, each of degree 3.
   (d) A multigraph with 6 vertices with degrees 2, 2, 4, 4, 4, 4.
   (e) A simple, bipartite graph with 7 vertices and 11 edges.

10. (a) Draw the graph κ_5.
    (b) Draw the graph $\kappa_{2,3}$.
    (c) Prove that the number of edges in the graph κ_n is $\binom{n}{2}$.

    [7 marks]

11. The graph κ_n has 36 edges. Find the value of n. [3 marks]

12. (a) Write down the smallest and the largest possible degree of a vertex in a simple connected graph with n vertices.
    (b) Show that in a simple connected graph there must be two vertices with the same degree.
    (c) Draw an example of a connected multigraph with three vertices with degrees 1, 2 and 3. [8 marks]

6C Some important theorems

In this section we will prove some important properties of graphs. You will be expected to learn these proofs for the exam, so they are shown as Worked examples.

Worked example 6.5

Prove that the sum of the degrees of all the vertices in a graph is equal to twice the number of edges.

The degree of a vertex is the number of edges coming out of it; so in determining the degree of a vertex we are actually counting edges

Every edge has two ends, so each edge corresponds to two vertices.
Hence when adding up the degrees of all the vertices, each edge is counted twice.

This result is known as **The Handshaking lemma**, because the edges can be thought of as representing handshakes and vertices as people. It is used in proving many other theorems, such as the one in the next example.

Worked example 6.6

Prove that in any graph, the number of vertices of odd degree is even.

(Below are two proofs of this result; the first one is shorter, but the second one may be more obvious.)

 What is the main function of proof: To establish the truth of the result, to be elegant, or to give better intuitive understanding of the result? Which of the two proofs do you prefer?

What do we know about degrees of vertices? The Handshaking lemma tells us that the sum of all degrees is even. So we can try to write an expression for the sum of all degrees

even + even = even
odd + odd = even but odd + odd + odd = odd

First Proof

Let a be the number of vertices of even degree, and b the number of vertices with odd degree.
The sum of all degrees is the sum of a even numbers and b odd numbers:

$$\underbrace{\sum \text{degrees}}_{\text{even}} = \underbrace{(a \text{ evens})}_{\text{even}} + (b \text{ odds})$$

By the handshaking lemma, LHS is even. The sum of even numbers is always even, so the first bracket is even.
Hence the second bracket must be even. But the sum of odd numbers can only be even if there is an even number of them. Hence b is even, as required.

6 Graph theory 79

continued . . .

> We can think about building up a graph from a single vertex by adding vertices and edges, and think about how the degrees change as we do this

Second Proof

In a graph with a single vertex and no edges, the number of vertices of odd degree is zero, which is even.
We can build up any graph by a sequence of two types of operation:
1. add an edge between two existing vertices
2. add an extra vertex

> Operation 1 only changes the degrees of the two vertices which are being connected. We need to consider different cases, depending on whether those degrees were even or odd before the extra edge was added

With 1: The degrees of the two vertices being connected are increased by 1, and the rest remain unchanged.
If the two degrees were even, they are now odd so the number of odd vertices is increased by 2.
If the two degrees were odd, they are now even so the number of odd vertices is decreased by 2.
If one of the degrees was even and the other one odd, the first one becomes odd and the second becomes even. So the number of odd degrees remains unchanged.

> Operation 2 does not change degrees of existing vertices. The new vertex has no edges yet

With 2: The degree of the new vertex is zero, which is even. The other degrees don't change. So the number of vertices of odd degree remains unchanged.

> Remember that we started with the number of vertices of odd degree equal to zero

Hence as we build up the graph, the number of vertices of odd degree can increase or decrease by 2, or remain unchanged. As it started as an even number, it always remains even.

The rest of the results in this section concern planar graphs. When a graph is drawn so that the edges do not intersect, the plane is divided into a certain number of regions. Counting the 'outside' as one region, the graph shown overleaf divides the plane into 6 regions. In what follows, we denote by f the number of regions, v is the number of vertices and e is the number of edges of the graph. So for the graph overleaf, $v = 5$, $e = 9$, $f = 6$. The result in the next example is called **Euler's relation**.

> **EXAM HINT**
> Euler's relation is given in the Formula booklet.

Worked example 6.7

Prove that for a connected planar graph, $v - e + f = 2$.

(You can check that this result is not true if the graph is not connected. In the proof, we will have to make sure that we are always working with a connected graph.)

As this result is about the number of edges and vertices of a graph, we can try to apply a strategy from the previous example: build up the graph by adding vertices and edges, and see how the numbers e, v and f change

In a graph with a single vertex and no edges, $v = 1$, $e = 0$, $f = 1$, so $v - e + f = 2$.
We can build up any connected graph by a sequence of operations of two types:
(i) add an edge between two existing vertices

To keep the graph connected, whenever we add a vertex we have to join it to something

(ii) add a vertex and an edge joining it to one of the existing vertices.

With (i), v remains unchanged, e increases by 1, and f increases by 1 because the new edge splits one of the regions into two.

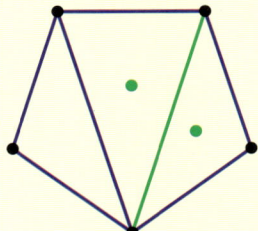

So now we have
$v - (e + 1) + (f + 1) = v - e + f$

continued . . .

When we add a new vertex and an edge, the new edge 'sticks out', so it does not split any of the regions into two

With (ii), v and e increase by 1 but f remains unchanged, because none of the existing regions are split into two.

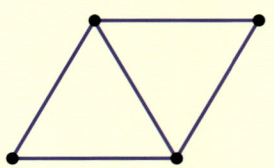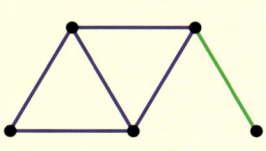

So now we have
$(v+1)-(e+1)+f = v-e+f$

In either case the value $v - e + f$ does not change, so it is always equal to 2.

Euler's relation was first discovered for polyhedra (three dimensional shapes with polygons for faces). In that case, v, e and f stand for the number of vertices, edges and faces. You can imagine a polyhedron being turned into a planar graph by making a hole in one face and stretching it out flat. The face with the hole becomes the 'outside' region.

Euler's formula was originally used to classify platonic solids. It is now an important tool in the study of solid objects with holes, in the branch of mathematics called topology.

EXAM HINT

Both of these results are given in the Formula booklet.

There are two other important results for planar graphs, involving only the number of vertices and the number of edges. The first one (proved in Worked example 6.8) applies to any simple, connected, planar graph. The second one (proved in Worked example 6.9) applies only to certain planar graphs.

Worked example 6.8

(a) Show that for a simple, connected, planar graph with three or more vertices, $e \leq 3v - 6$.

(b) Hence show that the complete graph κ_5 is not planar.

There is no connection between the number of vertices and edges of a graph in general, except that $e \geq n - 1$ if the graph is connected. So there is something special about planar graphs. We know one equation that could be relevant: the Euler's relation

(a) Euler's relation:
$v - e + f = 2$
$\Leftrightarrow e = v + f - 2$

82 Topic 10 – Option: Discrete mathematics

> continued...
> We need to eliminate f. Can we find a connection between the number of regions and the number of vertices or edges? Each region has at least three edges. So the total number of edges is at least $3f$, except each edge belongs to two regions, which means that it is counted twice. So in fact
> $$e \geq \frac{3f}{2}$$

Each region has at least three edges, and each edge belongs to exactly two regions.

So $e \geq \frac{3f}{2}$, i.e. $f \leq \frac{2e}{3}$

Then
$$e = v + f - 2$$
$$\Rightarrow e \leq v + \frac{2e}{3} - 2$$
$$\Leftrightarrow 3e \leq 3v + 2e - 6$$
$$\Leftrightarrow e \leq 3v - 6$$
as required

> Apply the result to κ_5.

(b) κ_5 has $v = 5$ and $e = \binom{5}{2} = 10$

So $3v - 6 = 9 < e$, hence κ_5 is not planar.

We saw in the previous section that the complete bipartite graph $\kappa_{3,3}$ is not planar. However, this graph has $v = 6$ and $e = 9$, so it satisfies the inequality $e \leq 3v - 6$ for planar graphs. To show that $\kappa_{3,3}$ is not planar we need a second result, which applies only to planar graphs with no 'triangles' (cycles with three edges).

Worked example 6.9

(a) Show that if a simple, connected, planar graph with more than three vertices has no triangles then $e \leq 2v - 4$.

(b) Hence show that $\kappa_{3,3}$ is not planar.

(Note that this is a stronger inequality than the one in the previous Worked example, because $2v - 4 < 3v - 6$ for $v \geq 3$. For example, κ_4 has $v = 4$ and $e = 6$ so $e > 2v - 4$, but the graph is still planar. The result does not apply to this graph because it contains closed paths of length 3.)

> This looks very similar to the previous example, except for the condition of no cycles of length 3. This means that each region has at least 4 edges.

(a) Euler's relation:
$$v - e + f = 2$$
$$\Leftrightarrow e = v + f - 2$$
Each region has at least four edges (as the smallest closed path is of length 4), and each edge belongs to exactly two regions.

So $e \geq \frac{4f}{2}$, i.e. $f \leq \frac{e}{2}$

Hence,
$$e \leq v + \frac{e}{2} - 2$$
$$\Leftrightarrow 2e \leq 2v + e - 4$$
$$\Leftrightarrow e \leq 2v - 4$$
as required.

> continued . . .
>
> Apply result from (a) to $\kappa_{3,3}$
> We need to make sure that this graph contains no cycles of length three for the result to apply.
>
> (b) $\kappa_{3,3}$ has $v = 6$ and $e = 3 \times 3 = 9$.
> It has no triangles, because a triangle would have to include two vertices from the same group joined to each other.
> So $2v - 4 = 8 < e$, hence $\kappa_{3,3}$ is not planar.

Exercise 6C

Questions 1 to 3 concern the following four graphs:

(a)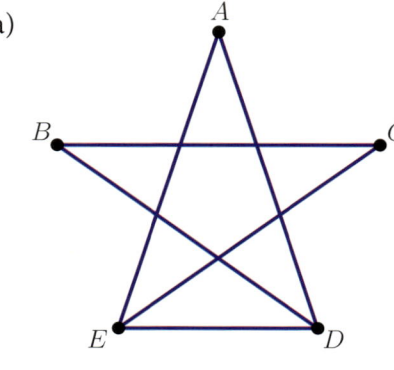

(b)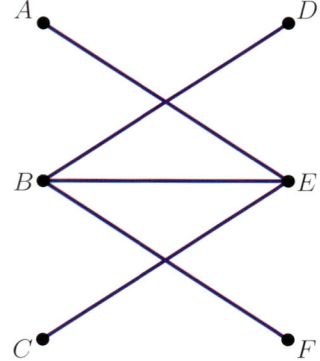

(c)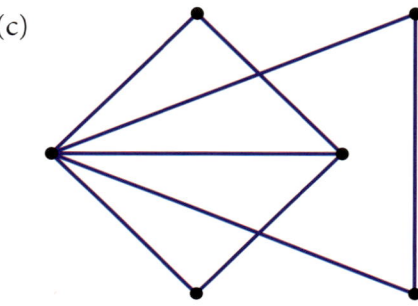

(d)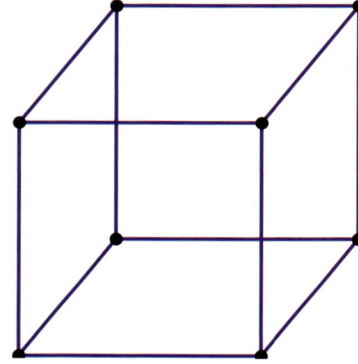

1. Verify that the Handshaking lemma holds for each graph.

2. Write down the number of vertices of odd degree in each graph.

3. Draw each graph in planar form and verify that Euler's relation holds for each graph.

4. A planar graph has 5 vertices and divides the plane into 4 regions.
   (a) How many edges does the graph have?
   (b) Draw an example of such a graph. [4 marks]

5. Draw a simple connected graph in which the vertices have the following degree sequences, or explain why one does not exist.

   (a) 3, 3, 2, 2

   (b) 3, 3, 2, 2, 1

   (c) 2, 2, 2, 1, 1   [9 marks]

6. A graph has 10 vertices and each vertex has degree 5.

   (a) How many edges does the graph have?

   (b) Show that the graph cannot be planar.   [7 marks]

6D Subgraphs and complements

Sometimes we want to concentrate on the vertices which are not joined to each other, rather than those that are. The **complement** of a simple graph G is the graph with the same vertices as G, and an edge joining each pair of vertices which are not adjacent in G. In the diagram shown here, the edges of G are coloured blue and the edges of its complement G' are red.

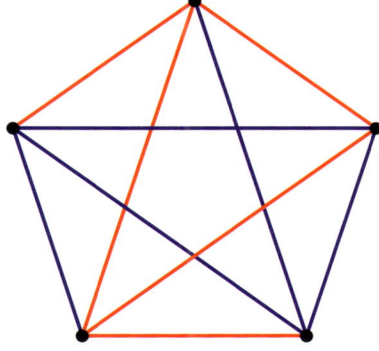

When we take the edges of both G and G' we get a complete graph. Hence if the graphs have v vertices and G has e edges, G' has $\binom{v}{2} - e$ edges.

Sometimes we are only interested in certain edges in a graph. A **subgraph** of G is a graph which contains only some of the edges of G. In the diagram alongside, a subgraph is highlighted in red. Note that every graph with n vertices is a subgraph of the complete graph κ_n.

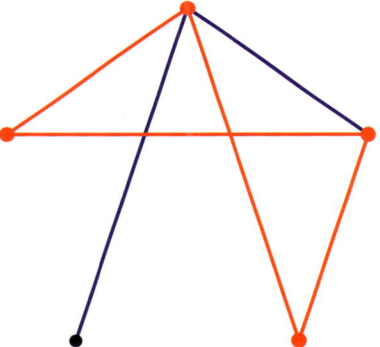

Exercise 6D

1. Draw the complements of the following graphs:

   (a) (i) 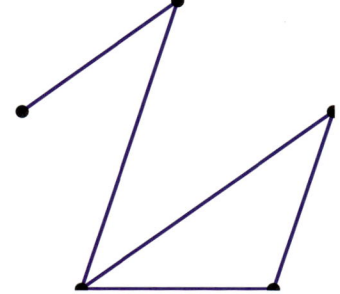   (ii)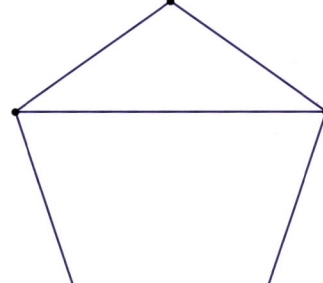

6 Graph theory 85

(b) (i) 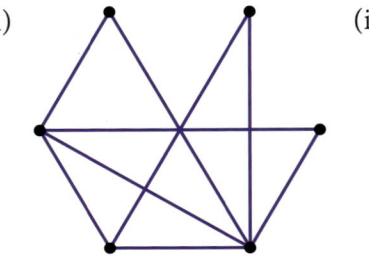   (ii)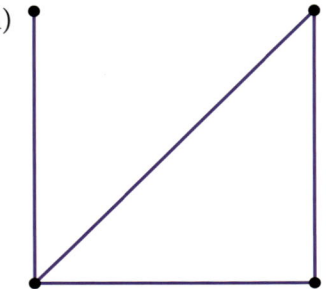

2. Find the adjacency tables for the complements of the following graphs:

(a)
	A	B	C	D
A	0	1	1	0
B	1	0	0	1
C	1	0	0	0
D	0	1	0	0

(b)
	A	B	C	D
A	0	0	1	1
B	0	0	1	0
C	1	1	0	0
D	1	0	0	0

3. For each of the following graphs, draw all subgraphs with exactly 4 edges:

(a) 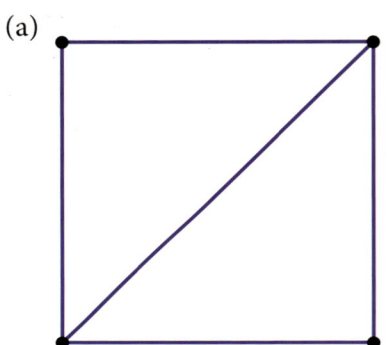   (b)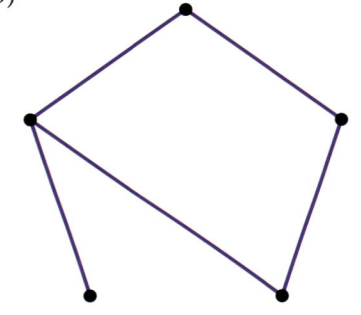

4. Show that each of the following graphs contains K_4 as a subgraph:

(a) 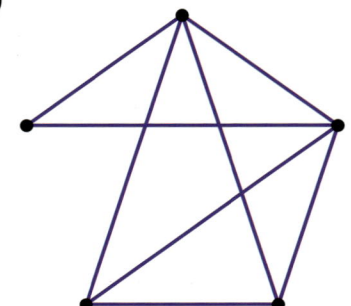   (b)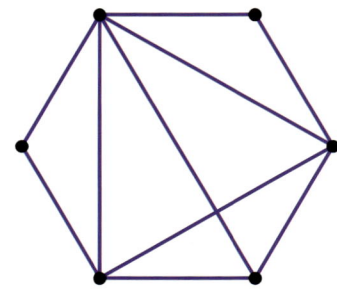

5. Draw a graph G with 5 vertices such that G and its complement are both connected. *[3 marks]*

6. (a) Show that a bipartite graph cannot contain K_3 as a subgraph.

   (b) Hence show that if G is a bipartite graph with more than 4 vertices, then its complement is not bipartite.
   [7 marks]

6E Moving around a graph

In many applications of graph theory we are interested in different ways of getting from one vertex to another. Depending on the problem, we may be required to return to the starting vertex, visit every vertex, or there may be restrictions on whether we are allowed to use each edge more than once. All these different ways of moving around a graph are given names which you must learn.

A **walk** is any sequence of adjacent edges. A **path** is a walk with no repeated vertices, and a **trail** is a walk with no repeated edges.

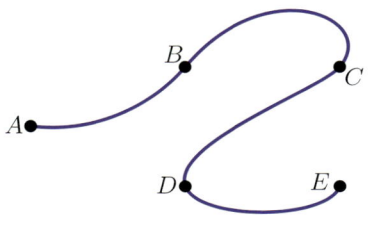
ABCDE: a path

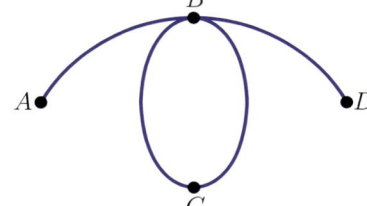
ABCBD: not a path, but a trail

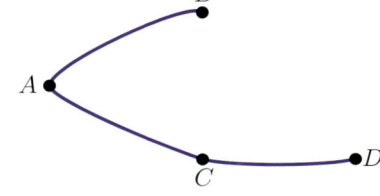
ABACD: not a trail

A **cycle** is a walk that starts and ends at the same vertex and has no other repeated vertices (so it is a closed path). A **circuit** is a walk that starts and ends at the same vertex and has no repeated edges (so it is a closed trail). Note that if there are no repeated vertices then there are also no repeated edges; hence every cycle is also a circuit, but not every circuit is a cycle.

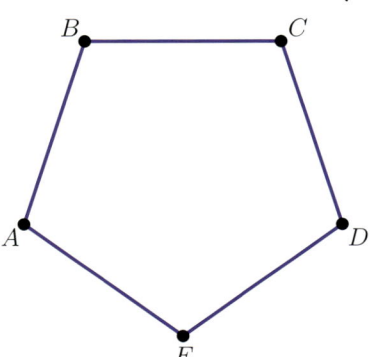
ABCDEA: cycle and circuit

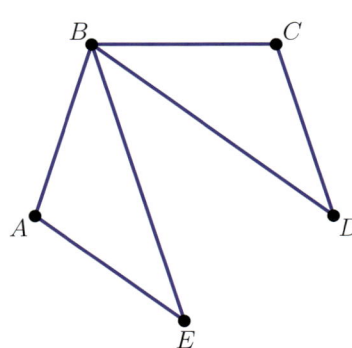
ABCDBEA: circuit but not cycle

Worked example 6.10

For the graph shown in the diagram:

(a) List all paths of length 3 from *A* to *D*.

(b) List all the cycles of length 4 starting and ending at *B*.

(c) Find a trail that uses each edge exactly once.

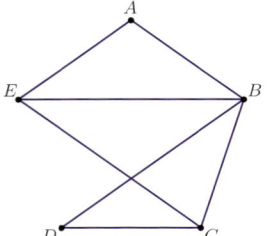

This can only be done by inspection. Think where we can go from *A*
A path of length 3 has four different vertices

(a) ABCD, AEBD, AECD

A cycle of length 4 has four different vertices

(b) BCEAB, BECDB

Some vertices will appear more than once

(c) EABECBDC

In the next section we will see that questions like part (c) can only be solved for some graphs.

Exercise 6E

1. Write down all walks of length 3 from *A* to *D* in the following graphs:

(a) 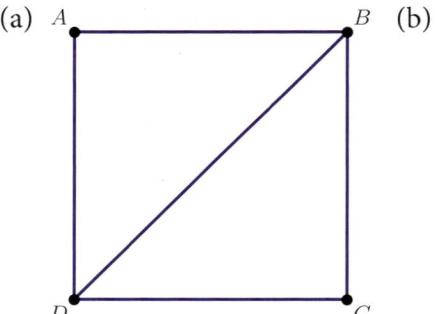 (b)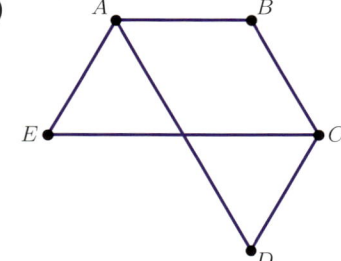

88 Topic 10 – Option: Discrete mathematics

(c)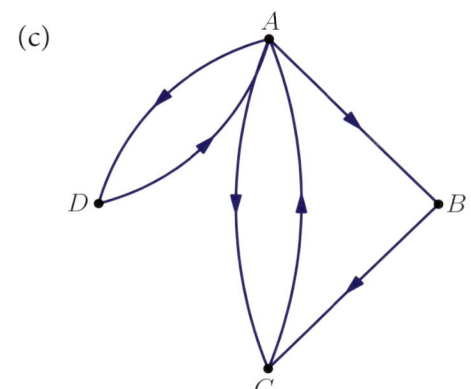

(d)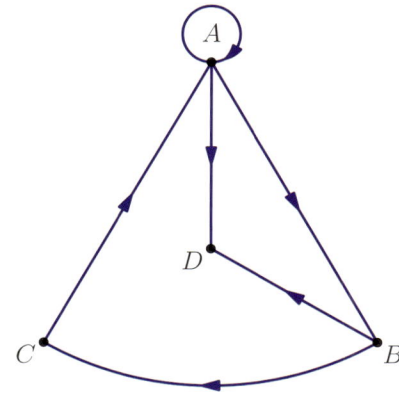

2. Find all cycles of length 4 in the graphs from the previous question.

3. Find the number of different paths of length n between two given vertices in κ_4 if n is:
   (a) 2   (b) 3   (c) 4   *[5 marks]*

4. Find the number of different walks of length n between two given vertices in κ_4 if n is:
   (a) 2   (b) 3   (c) 4   *[5 marks]*

6F Eulerian graphs

The Königsberg bridges problem is considered to be the first published problem in graph theory. Two banks of the river and two islands are represented by vertices of a graph and the seven bridges by its edges. The resulting graph is:

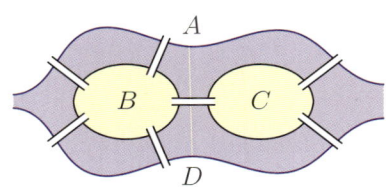

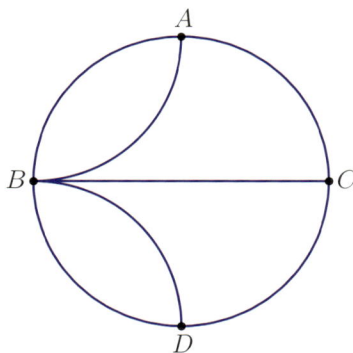

The problem is to find a closed walk that uses each edge exactly once. This corresponds to crossing each bridge exactly once and returning to the starting point. It turns out that this is impossible, and the search for an explanation led Euler to start developing graph theory. The reason lies in the degrees of the vertices of the graph.

> Leonhard Euler (1707–1783) was a Swiss mathematician who made immense contributions to many branches of mathematics. He is responsible for much mathematical notation still in use today: $f(x)$ to represent a function, Σ to represent sums, e as the base of natural logarithms and i as the simplest imaginary number. Is new notation new mathematical knowledge?

A closed walk that uses each edge exactly once is called an **Eulerian circuit**. A graph with an Eulerian circuit is called an **Eulerian graph**.

KEY POINT 6.5

> In an Eulerian graph every vertex has even degree and it is possible to find a closed walk which uses each edge exactly once.

This result can be explained as follows. Every time we visit a vertex we must go in and out of it, which uses up two edges. This also applies to the starting vertex, as we return to it at the end. So the number of edges at each vertex must be even.

Worked example 6.11

Show that the graph in the Königsberg bridges problem is not Eulerian.

Determine the degrees of all vertices

Degrees of vertices: 3, 5, 3, 3

In an Eulerian graph all vertices have even degree

All vertices have odd degree, so the graph is not Eulerian.

Even if we are not required to return to the starting point, it is impossible to cross each bridge exactly once, because of the following result:

KEY POINT 6.6

> A graph with a walk which uses each edge exactly once (without returning to the starting point) is called **semi-Eulerian**, and the walk is called an **Eulerian trail**. In a semi-Eulerian graph there are exactly two vertices with odd degree, and the walk must start at one of them and end at the other.

Remember that the number of vertices with odd degree must be even (Key point 6.4) so we can't have just one vertex with odd degree.

Finding an Eulerian trail is equivalent to drawing the graph without picking up your pen and without going over any edge more than once. This is a good practical way to check that you have found an Eulerian trail.

The explanation is similar to that for an Eulerian graph, with the difference that the starting vertex only needs an 'out' edge and the end vertex only an 'in' edge, so they are the only two vertices that can have odd degree.

Worked example 6.12

Show that the following graph is semi-Eulerian and find an Eulerian trail.

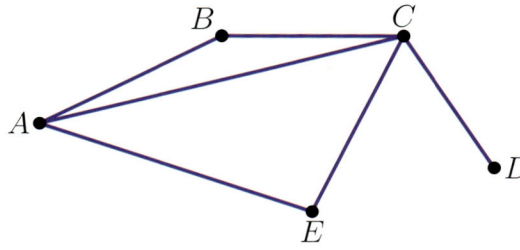

• We need the degrees of all the vertices

Degrees of the vertices:
A = 3, B = 2, C = 4, D = 1, E = 2
There are exactly two vertices of odd degree, so the graph is semi-Eulerian.

• The Eulerian trail starts and ends at the odd vertices, so we can start at A and end at D

Eulerian trail: ABCAECD

> Eulerian and semi-Eulerian graphs will be used in the Route inspection algorithm in Section 7D.

Exercise 6F

1. For each graph shown below say whether it is Eulerian, semi-Eulerian or neither.

   (a) 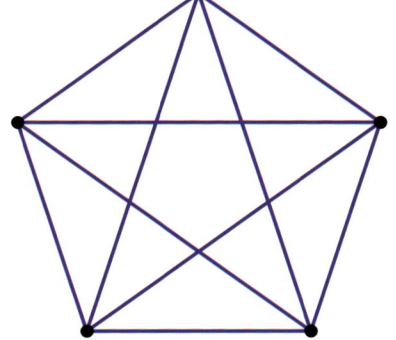   (b)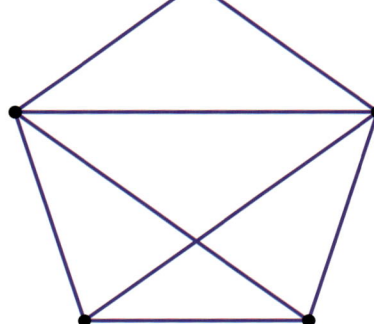

(c) 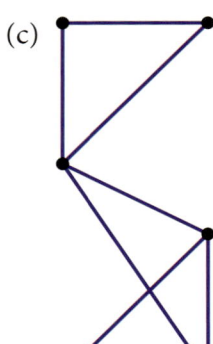   (d)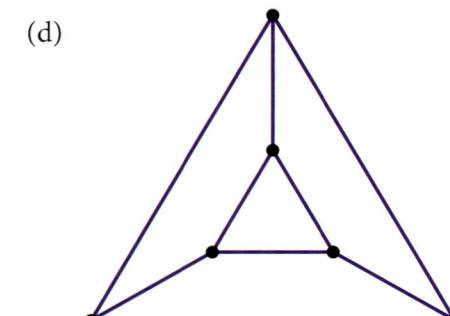

2. Which of the graphs given by the following adjacency tables are Eulerian?

(a)
	A	B	C	D	E
A	0	1	0	1	1
B	1	0	0	0	1
C	0	0	0	0	1
D	1	0	0	0	1
E	1	1	1	1	0

(b)
	A	B	C	D
A	0	0	1	1
B	0	0	1	1
C	1	1	0	0
D	1	1	0	0

(c)
	A	B	C	D	E	F
A	0	1	1	0	0	0
B	1	0	1	1	1	0
C	1	1	0	1	0	1
D	0	1	1	0	0	0
E	0	1	0	0	0	1
F	0	0	1	0	1	0

3. Two graphs, G and H, are shown below:

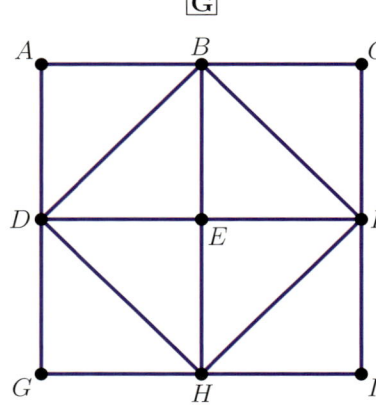 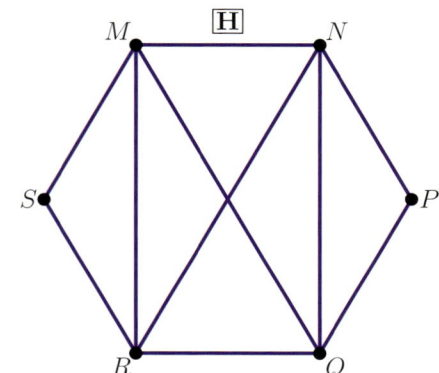

(a) Explain why G is not Eulerian.

(b) Find an Eulerian circuit in H. [5 marks]

4. Explain why the graph shown below is semi-Eulerian, and find an Eulerian trail.

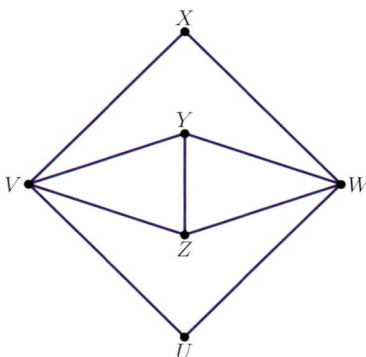

[5 marks]

6G Hamiltonian graphs

A **Hamiltonian path** in a graph visits each vertex exactly once. A **Hamiltonian cycle** visits each vertex exactly once and returns to the starting vertex. Not every graph has a Hamiltonian cycle; if it does it is called a **Hamiltonian graph**.

> **Worked example 6.13**
>
> Show that the following graph is Hamiltonian:
>
>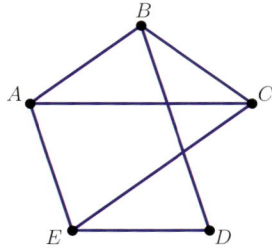
>
> Find a Hamiltonian cycle by inspection
>
>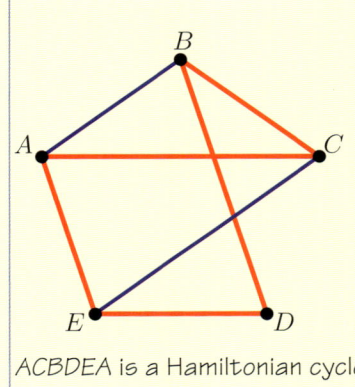
>
> ACBDEA is a Hamiltonian cycle, so the graph is Hamiltonian.

There is no easy way to check that a graph is Hamiltonian, except by finding a Hamiltonian cycle. There is one criterion that is sometimes useful: If in a connected, simple graph with n vertices each vertex has degree at least $\frac{n}{2}$ edges, then the graph is Hamiltonian. This implies that every complete graph is Hamiltonian (as each vertex has degree $n-1$). However, there are many Hamiltonian graphs where vertices have smaller degrees. Two examples are shown here: a cycle and a cube.

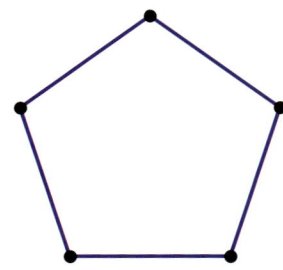
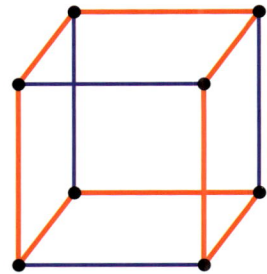

6 Graph theory 93

Problems about Hamiltonian graphs can be difficult as there is no good criterion to decide whether a graph is Hamiltonian or not. We will see this when tackling the Travelling salesman problem in Section 7E.

Exercise 6G

1. Find a Hamiltonian cycle in each of the following graphs:

(a) 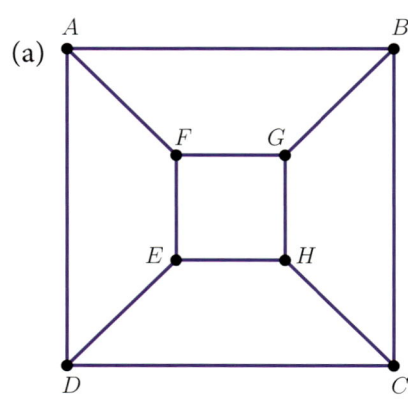 (b)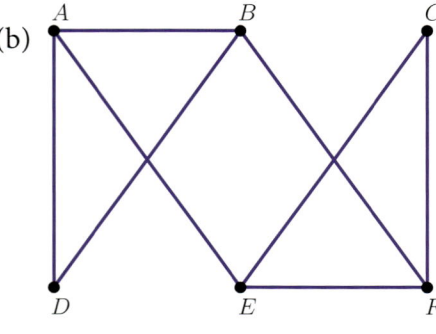

(c) 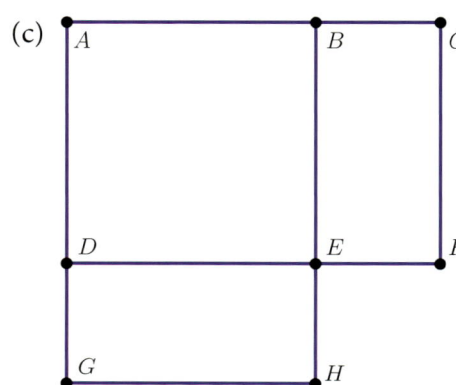 (d)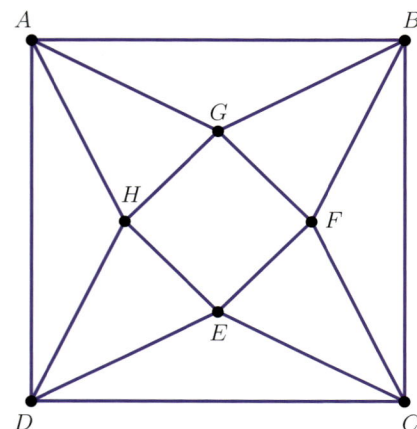

2. Draw each of the following graphs and find a Hamiltonian cycle:
   (a) (i) K_4 (ii) K_5
   (b) (i) $K_{4,4}$ (ii) $K_{3,3}$

3. Find the number of distinct Hamiltonian cycles in $K_{3,3}$. (Two cycles, one of which is the reverse of the other, are considered identical.) *[4 marks]*

Summary

- A **graph** consists of **vertices** joined by **edges**. The number of edges coming out of each vertex is the **degree** of that vertex.
- The sum of degrees of all the vertices is equal to twice the number of edges. The number of vertices of odd degree is even.
- In a **digraph** edges have direction.
- A graph can be represented by its **adjacency table**.
- In a **simple graph** there are no loops or repeated edges.
- In a **connected graph** it is possible to find a path between any two vertices.
- In a **complete graph** every pair of vertices is joined by an edge. The complete graph with n vertices, κ_n, has $\binom{n}{2}$ edges.
- A **tree** is a graph with no cycles. A tree with n vertices has $n-1$ edges.
- A **bipartite graph** has two groups of edges such that only edges from different groups are adjacent.
- A **planar graph** can be drawn without edges crossing.
- The following relations hold for connected planar graphs:

    $v - e + f = 2$ (**Euler's relation**)

    $e \leq 3v - 6$

    $e \leq 2v - 4$ if there are no cycles of length 3 (e.g. for a bipartite graph).

- The **complement** of a simple graph consists of all the edges which are not present in the original graph.
- A **subgraph** contains only some of the edges of the original graph.
- Different types of **walk** around a graph include:

    Path: A walk with no repeated vertices.

    Trail: A walk with no repeated edges.

    Cycle: A closed path.

    Circuit: A closed trail.

- In an **Eulerian graph** each vertex has even degree. It is possible to find an **Eulerian circuit** which uses each edge exactly once and returns to the starting point.
- A **semi-Eulerian graph** has exactly two vertices of odd degree. It is possible to find an **Eulerian trail** between those two vertices which uses each edge exactly once.
- A **Hamiltonian graph** has a **Hamiltonian cycle**, which visits each vertex exactly once and returns to the starting point.

Mixed examination practice 6

1. (a) Draw the complete graph with 4 vertices, κ_4.

(b) Show that the complete graph κ_n has $\frac{1}{2}(n-1)!$ different Hamiltonian cycles.

(Two cycles, one which is the reverse of the other, are considered identical.)

(c) List all the Hamiltonian cycles in your κ_4 graph. *[8 marks]*

2. (a) Decide which of the two graphs shown below is Eulerian, and justify your answer.

(b) Find an Eulerian circuit in the Eulerian graph from part (a). *[5 marks]*

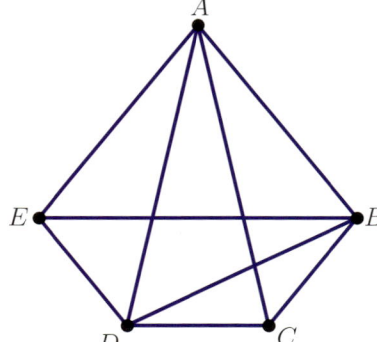 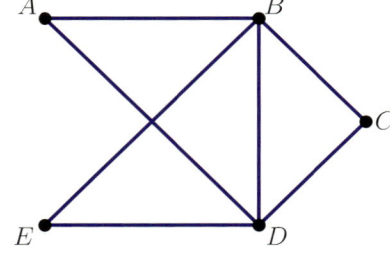

3.

(a) Construct an adjacency table for this graph.

(b) List all the walks of length 3 from B to D. *[7 marks]*

4. (a) Prove that the sum of degrees of all the vertices in a graph is equal to twice the number of edges.

(b) Eleven teams take part in a school football league, so each team has to play ten matches. A teacher wants to produce a schedule such that each team plays exactly five matches in the first term. Show that this is impossible. *[7 marks]*

Topic 10 – Option: Discrete mathematics

5. Graph G is given in the diagram.

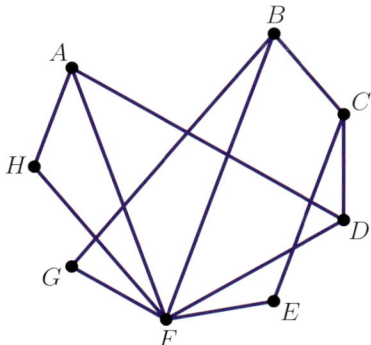

(a) Prove that a planar graph cannot have cycles of length 3.

(b) Hence show that G cannot be drawn in planar form. *[7 marks]*

6. (a) Find the number of edges of a complement, G', of graph G with n vertices and e edges.

(b) Write down the number of edges in a tree with n vertices.

(c) Hence show that G and G' can both be trees only if $n = 4$.

(d) Draw a graph G such that G and G' are both trees. *[8 marks]*

7. A graph G has e edges and n vertices.

(a) Show that the sum of the degrees of the vertices is twice the number of edges.

(b) Deduce that G has an even number of vertices of odd degree.

(c) (i) Graph G is connected, planar and divides the plane into exactly four regions. If $(n-1)$ vertices have degree three and exactly one vertex has degree d, determine the possible values of (n, d).

   (ii) For each possible (n, d), draw a graph which satisfies the conditions described in (c)(i). *[9 marks]*

(© IB Organization 2007)

8. (a) Prove that a bipartite graph cannot contain cycles of odd length.

(b) Show that the complete bipartite graph $\kappa_{3,4}$ is not Hamiltonian.

(c) Is $\kappa_{4,4}$ Eulerian? Justify your answer. *[8 marks]*

9. (a) State Euler's relation for a simple, connected, planar graph.

(b) State and prove the corresponding result for a simple planar graph with two connected components. *[12 marks]*

In this chapter you will learn:

- how to find a tree of minimum weight that connects all the vertices of the graph (Kruskal's algorithm)
- how to find the shortest path between two vertices (Dijkstra's algorithm)
- how to find the shortest route around the graph which uses each edge at least once (Chinese postman problem)
- how to find the shortest route around the graph which visits each vertex at least once (Travelling salesman problem).

7 Algorithms on graphs

In applications where the graphs in question are very large, it can be difficult to find optimal routes. It is therefore important to have algorithms which can be implemented on a computer and are guaranteed to find the best solution. In this chapter we will meet several such algorithms. We will also see an example of a problem for which such an algorithm does not exist and we can only estimate the length of the shortest possible route.

7A Weighted graphs

In a **weighted graph** each edge has a number associated with it. This number is called the **weight**, and can represent the distance, time or cost of travel between the two vertices. Note that this is not the actual length of the edge, and that there is no need to try and draw the graph to scale. Also remember that not all intersections of edges are vertices of the graph.

For example, the graph alongside could represent a road network and the numbers could be times (in minutes) taken to travel between different junctions. So it takes 17 minutes to travel between junctions B and E. To get from B to C, you can go either via A (which takes 19 minutes) or via D (which takes 12 minutes).

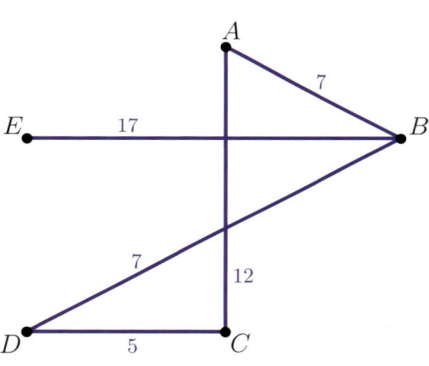

When a graph is large, it may not be possible to draw it and, instead, we can represent it using an adjacency table. For a weighted graph the numbers in the table represent the weights of the edges. The adjacency table shown here represents the above graph. Note that all graphs we consider in this chapter are simple.

The adjacency table showing the weights of the edges is also called the cost adjacency matrix. It is possible to perform algebraic operations on matrices to deduce various properties of a graph.

	A	B	C	D	E
A	-	7	12	-	-
B	7	-	-	7	17
C	12	-	-	5	-
D	-	7	5	-	-
E	-	17	-	-	-

Worked example 7.1

Graph G has the adjacency table:

	A	B	C	D	E	F
A	-	-	9	6	-	6
B	-	-	-	6	4	9
C	9	-	-	6	-	5
D	6	6	6	-	4	-
E	-	4	-	4	-	7
F	6	9	5	-	7	-

(a) Write down the degree of vertex C.

(b) Draw G in planar form.

> The degree of a vertex is the number of non-zero entries in the corresponding row or column

(a) deg (C)=3

> We can start by drawing the graph with vertices in order A,B,C,D,E,F, and then redraw it in planar form

(b)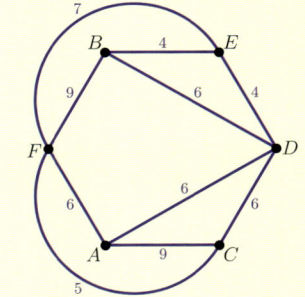

> To draw the graph in planar form, find a Hamiltonian cycle first, and the fit in the rest of the edges. Finally, write the weights on the edges

Hamiltonian cycle: ACDEBFA

Exercise 7A

1. Construct the adjacency table for each weighted graph shown below:

   (a) (i) 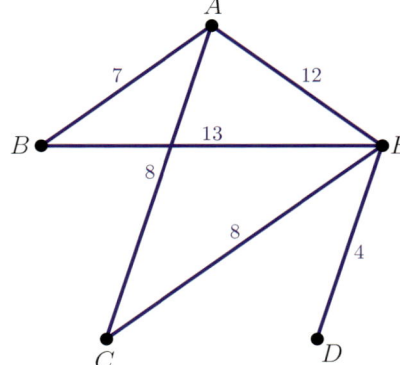   (ii)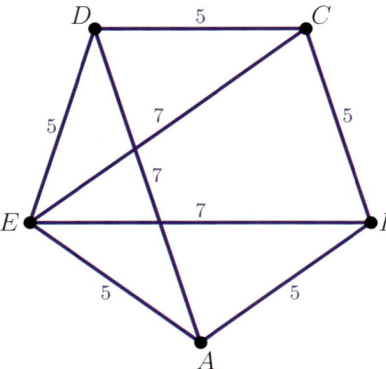

   (b) (i) 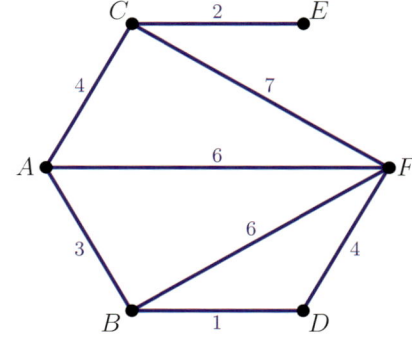   (ii)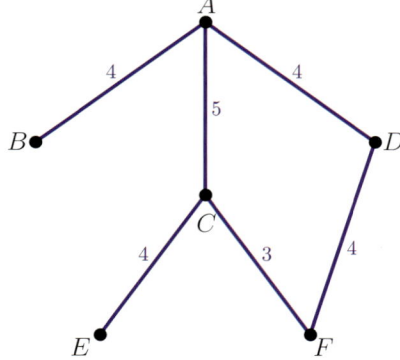

2. Draw a weighted graph with the weights of the edges given in the following tables:

   (a) (i)

	A	B	C	D	E
A	-	6	10	3	-
B	6	-	4	10	12
C	10	4	-	-	9
D	3	10	-	-	-
E	-	12	9	-	-

   (ii)

	A	B	C	D	E
A	-	-	7	4	9
B	-	-	5	-	7
C	7	5	-	4	9
D	4	-	4	-	-
E	9	7	9	-	-

   (b) (i)

	A	B	C	D	E	F
A	-	3	-	-	5	-
B	3	-	5	5	-	-
C	-	5	-	-	-	4
D	-	5	-	-	4	3
E	5	-	-	4	-	-
F	-	-	4	3	-	-

   (ii)

	A	B	C	D	E	F
A	-	-	7	-	-	9
B	-	-	5	8	8	8
C	7	5	-	-	8	-
D	-	8	-	-	7	-
E	-	8	8	7	-	3
F	9	8	-	-	3	-

3. Draw in planar form the graph given by the cost adjacency matrix:

(a)
	A	B	C	D	E
A	-	5	7	-	9
B	5	-	5	10	12
C	7	5	-	4	9
D	-	10	4	-	-
E	9	12	9	-	-

(b)
	A	B	C	D	E
A	-	8	10	10	8
B	8	-	8	-	-
C	10	8	-	8	15
D	10	-	8	-	8
E	8	-	15	8	-

4. The weights of edges in a simple graph G are shown in the following table:

	A	B	C	D	E
A	-	6	-	6	4
B	6	-	4	5	6
C	-	4	-	3	-
D	6	5	3	-	5
E	4	6	-	5	-

(a) Draw the graph and list all Hamiltonian cycles starting at A.

(b) Hence find the Hamiltonian cycle of least weight. *[7 marks]*

5. Draw the weighted graph corresponding to the given table and find the length of an Eulerian path starting at vertex A.

	A	B	C	D	E	F
A	-	12	-	-	-	10
B	12	-	9	12	14	-
C	-	9	-	9	-	-
D	-	12	9	-	-	-
E	-	14	-	-	-	10
F	10	-	-	-	10	-

[7 marks]

6. Consider weighted graph G given by the following table:

	A	B	C	D	E
A	-	4	6	-	-
B	4	-	5	-	-
C	6	5	-	6	5
D	-	-	6	-	5
E	-	-	5	5	-

Without drawing the graph, explain why there is an Eulerian cycle and find its length, explaining your calculation clearly. *[5 marks]*

7 Algorithms on graphs

7. The table for the weighted graph G is:

	A	B	C	D	E	F
A	-	7	-	8	-	-
B	7	-	-	-	5	10
C	-	-	-	8	-	12
D	8	-	8	-	10	9
E	-	5	-	10	-	-
F	-	10	12	9	-	-

(a) Without drawing the graph, explain why G is not Eulerian.

(b) Graph H is obtained from G by deleting one edge. Given that H is Eulerian:

   (i) State which edge should be deleted.

   (ii) Find the length of an Eulerian cycle in H. *[6 marks]*

7B Minimum spanning tree: Kruskal's algorithm

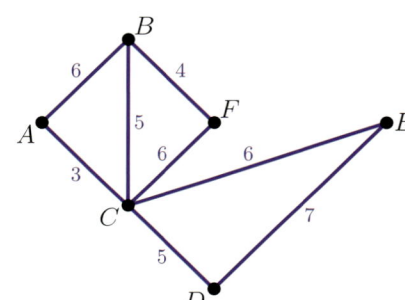

Six villages are to be connected to an internet network by cables. The graph shows distances (in kilometres) between villages where a direct connection is possible. What is the minimum length of the cable required?

This is an example of a **minimum connector problem**. We only need to include enough edges to create a connected subgraph. In particular, there is no need for any cycles: if A is connected to B via C, then the edge AB is not required. This means that we are trying to find a subgraph that is a tree and has minimum possible weight. Such a subgraph is called the **minimum spanning tree**.

There is a simple algorithm for finding the minimum spanning tree, called **Kruskal's algorithm**. It works by adding one edge at a time, starting with the shortest, and checking that we never create cycles. This is an example of a **greedy algorithm**, where at each stage we pick the best possible option (in this case, the shortest possible edge). We will see later that this strategy does not always work for other types of problems.

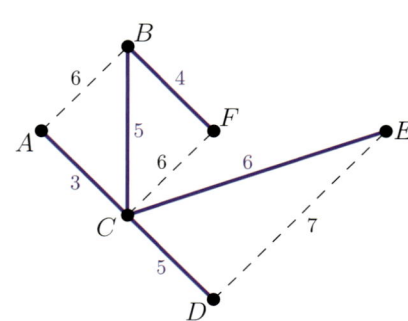

In our example, the shortest edge is AC, so we add it to the graph first. Next we add BF, then BC and CD. There are then three edges of length 6, but AB and CF are not required, as they would create cycles, so we just add CE. All the vertices are now connected, so we have completed our spanning tree.

This algorithm is summarised below:

KEY POINT 7.1

Kruskal's algorithm adds edges to the graph one at a time.
- Start by marking all the vertices.
- At each stage add the shortest remaining edge as long as it does not create a cycle.
- Keep adding edges until all vertices have been connected.

The next example shows how to set out your working so that your method is clear. You need to show the order in which you have considered the edges, note which ones you skipped (because they would create a cycle), and draw your completed tree. It helps to list the edges in order of length first. Remember that a tree with n vertices has $n - 1$ edges, so you know when you have completed the tree. It is also a good idea to draw the tree as you go along.

EXAM HINT

The minimum spanning tree is not necessarily unique; there may be more than one tree with the same weight. You are only required to find one answer unless explicitly told otherwise.

Worked example 7.2

Find the minimum spanning tree for this graph:

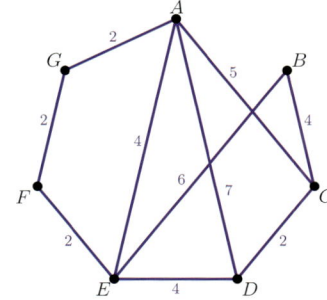

List the edges in the order they were added to the tree, and state the weight of your tree.

We start by listing the edges in order of length first. If two edges have the same length, we can list them in any order

Consider each edge in order and add it to the graph if it does not create a cycle
We skip AE because we already have EF, FG, GA

As there are 7 vertices, we can stop after the 6th edge (ED) has been added

CD 2
EF 2
FG 2
AG 2
BC 4
AE 4 skip
ED 4 stop
AC 5
EB 6
AD 7

continued...

We drew the tree as we added the edges, so we have the complete tree. The weight is the sum of the weights of all the edges

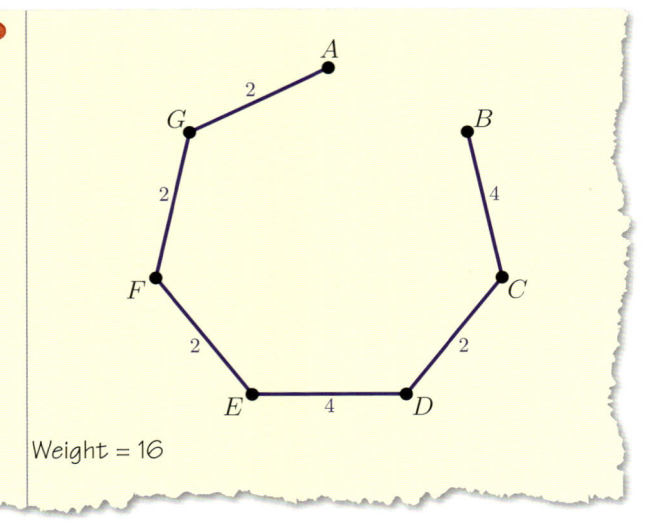

Weight = 16

Kruskal's algorithm is quick and easy to implement on small graphs. However on a large graph it is difficult to check if you are creating a long cycle. Also, for an algorithm to be implemented on a computer, we would need an additional algorithm to check for cycles, and this can be very time-consuming. So for large graphs there is an alternative, called Prim's algorithm.

Exercise 7B

1. Use Kruskal's algorithm to find a minimum spanning tree for the graphs below. Draw each tree and state its weight.

   (a) (i) 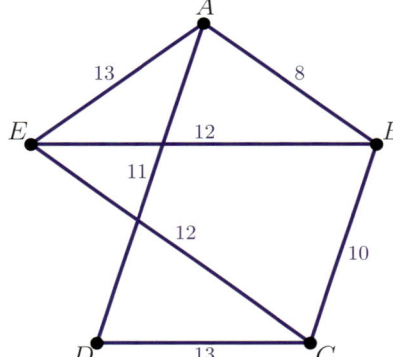   (ii)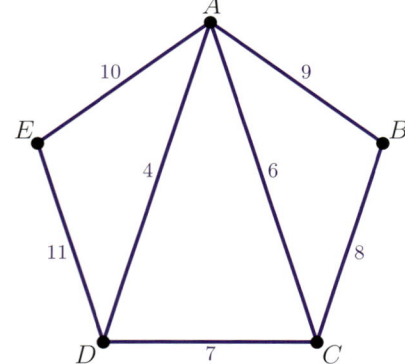

(b) (i) 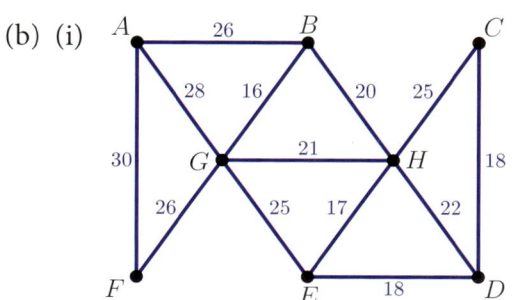   (ii)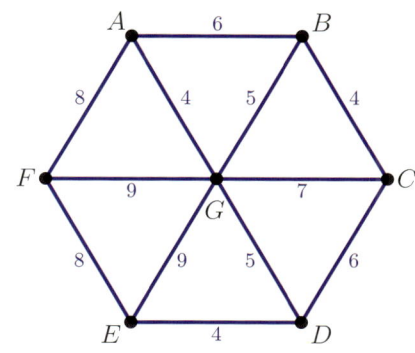

(c) (i) 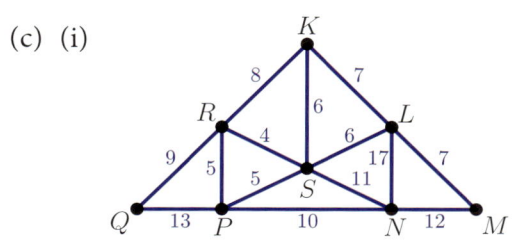   (ii)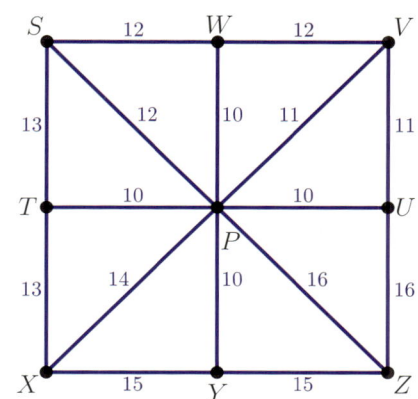

2. Use Kruskal's algorithm to find the minimum spanning tree for each of the graphs represented by the following tables. Draw each tree and state its weight.

(a) (i)

	A	B	C	D	E
A	-	10	8	7	10
B	10	-	5	4	9
C	8	5	-	7	10
D	7	4	7	-	8
E	10	9	10	8	-

(ii)

	A	B	C	D	E
A	-	12	16	11	16
B	12	-	13	14	19
C	16	13	-	15	18
D	11	14	15	-	18
E	16	19	18	18	-

(b) (i)

	A	B	C	D	E	F	G
A	-	-	30	-	-	50	45
B	-	-	70	35	40	-	-
C	30	70	-	50	-	-	20
D	-	35	50	-	10	-	15
E	-	40	-	10	-	15	-
F	50	-	-	-	15	-	10
G	45	-	20	15	-	10	-

(ii)

	A	B	C	D	E	F	G
A	-	25	35	40	-	-	-
B	25	-	50	35	40	-	-
C	35	50	-	45	45	-	40
D	40	35	45	-	20	35	30
E	-	40	45	20	-	15	25
F	-	-	-	35	15	-	-
G	-	-	40	30	25	-	-

(c) (i)

	A	B	C	D	E	F
A	-	4	-	6	-	10
B	4	-	5	-	5	-
C	-	5	-	6	-	4
D	6	-	6	-	7	-
E	-	5	-	7	-	2
F	10	-	4	-	2	-

(ii)

	A	B	C	D	E	F
A	-	5	7	-	8	8
B	5	-	6	-	5	-
C	7	6	-	4	4	3
D	-	-	4	-	5	2
E	8	5	4	5	-	-
F	8	-	3	2	-	-

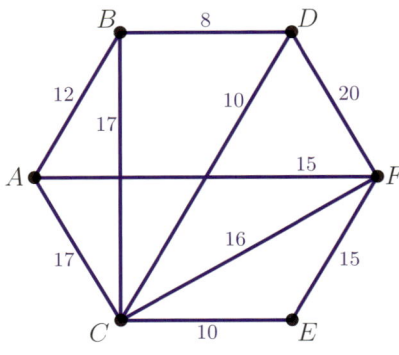

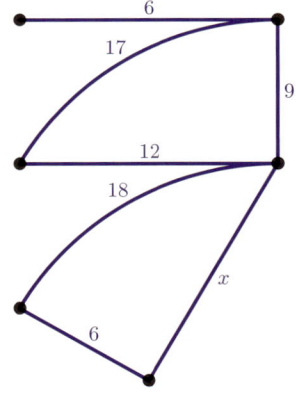

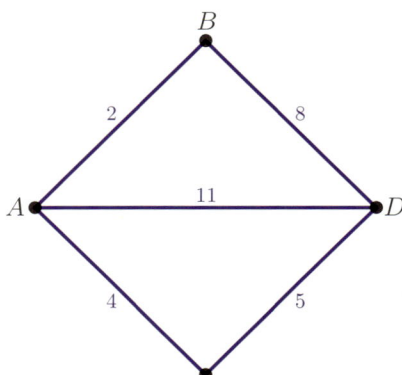

3. The diagram shows graph K.
   (a) Draw the minimum spanning tree for K.
   (b) It is required to find a spanning tree of least weight which includes the edge CF. Explain how you can adapt Kruskal's algorithm to do this. You do not need to find the tree. *[6 marks]*

4. (a) Explain briefly what is meant by the minimum spanning tree of a graph.
   (b) Find the minimum spanning tree of the graph given by the table alongside. Draw your tree and state its weight. *[7 marks]*

5. (a) State the number of edges in a tree with n vertices.
   (b) In a graph with 12 vertices all edges have different weights and the shortest edge has weight 8. Sharon finds that the minimum spanning tree has weight 139. Explain why this can't be right. *[6 marks]*

6. A simple connected graph has 5 vertices and 7 edges of lengths 10, 11, 13, 15, 18, 20 and 22. Find the:
   (a) minimum possible weight of the minimum spanning tree
   (b) maximum possible weight of the minimum spanning tree. *[5 marks]*

7. The minimum spanning tree of the graph shown in the diagram has weight 51. Find the range of possible values of x. *[5 marks]*

7C Finding the shortest path: Dijkstra's algorithm

We often need to use graph theory to find the shortest path between two vertices. An example might be when the graph represents a road network and we want to find the shortest or the quickest route between two places. There can be many possible routes, so calculating the length of each one is not practical. In this section we will meet an algorithm which can be implemented on the computer.

The difficulty is that the shortest path does not necessarily start with the shortest edge. Consider the graph alongside. The shortest edge from A is AB, but the shortest path from A to D is via C. So we need to look at different ways of getting through the network, but avoid having to look at all possible paths.

Dijkstra's algorithm considers all the vertices in the graph, but only keeps track of the shortest path from the start to the current vertex. When the algorithm is completed, we can recover the shortest path from the start to any vertex. In order to do this, we need to keep some information for each vertex as we go along. This is usually done by drawing a box next to each vertex as follows:

order of labelling	distance from start	previous vertex
temporary labels		

A **temporary label** shows the shortest distance from start found so far. This information is updated whenever we find a shorter path.

The labels in the top row are called **permanent labels**. They are only written in once we know that we have found the shortest possible path to this vertex.

Order of labelling is the order in which the vertices are given permanent labels. The starting vertex will always be labelled 1, but the end vertex will not necessarily be last. We can only be certain that we have found the shortest possible path once the end vertex has a permanent label.

Distance from start is the shortest distance from the starting vertex to the current vertex.

In the last box we write the *previous vertex* in the final shortest path. This allows us to work back from end to start vertex to recover the shortest path.

The algorithm is much clearer when illustrated on an example. We show in red the information added at each stage.

Worked example 7.3

(a) Find the shortest path from S to T in this graph:

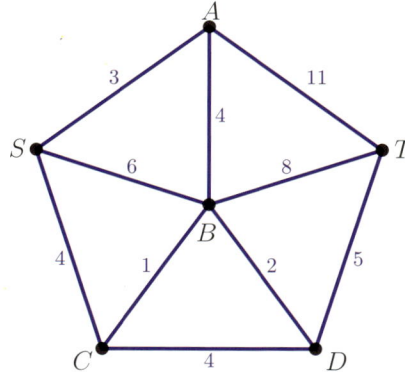

(b) Write down the length of the shortest path from S to D.

(c) If we are not allowed to use the edge BD, what is now the shortest path from S to T?

continued . . .

Start by labelling *S* and the vertices adjacent to it.
Vertex *A* has the least distance from *S*, so it gets a permanent label, which we write in the top row

We now look at vertices which are adjacent to *A*. *T* is labelled with $3 + 11 = 14$.
For *B*, $3 + 4 = 7$, but *B* already has label 6, so this is not updated.
The vertex with the smallest temporary label is *C*, so this is made permanent

Vertices adjacent to *C* are *B* and *D*.
B: $4 + 1 = 5 < 6$, so this is updated.
D: $4 + 4 = 8$
Vertex *B* now gets a permanent label, noting that the previous vertex in the path of length 5 was *C*

Vertices adjacent to *B* are *D* and *T*.
D: $5 + 2 = 7 < 8$, so it is updated
T: $5 + 8 = 13 < 14$, so it is updated
Vertex *D* now gets a permanent label, noting that it was reached from *B*

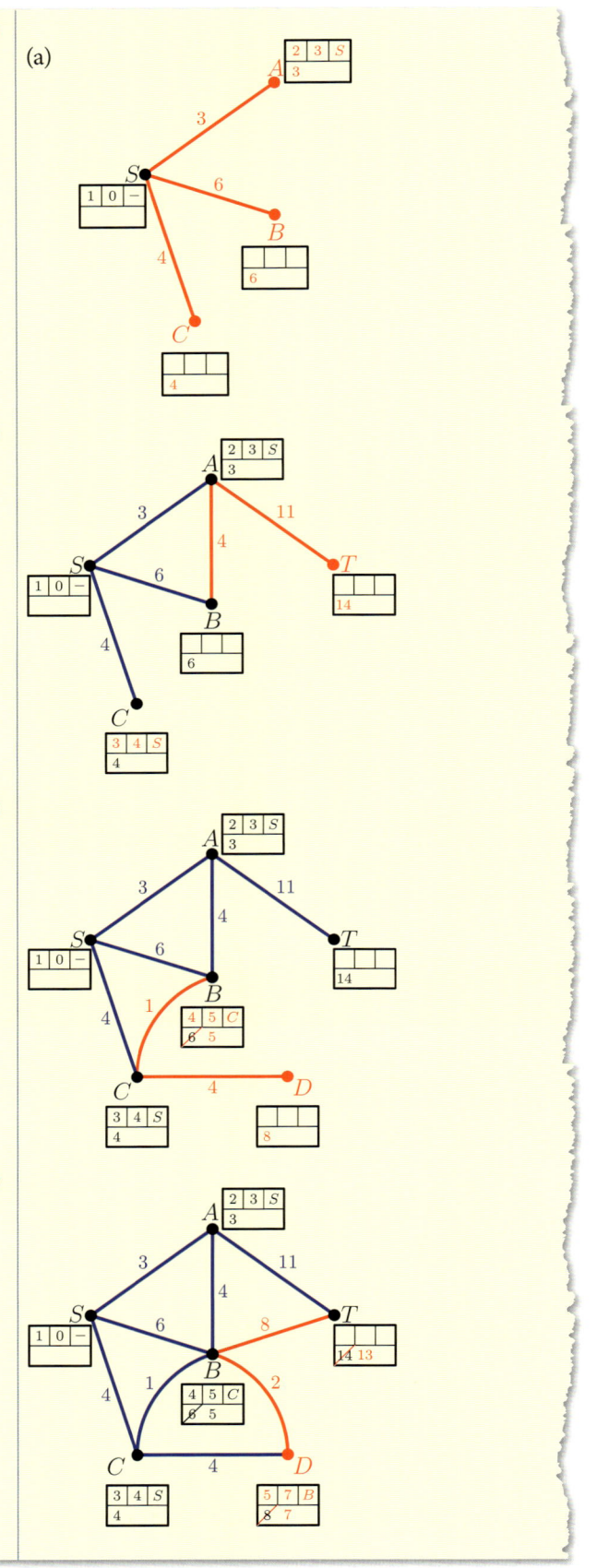

continued...

T: 7 + 5 = 12 < 13, so T is updated again
It is the last remaining vertex, so it gets a permanent label
All vertices have permanent labels, so we can stop

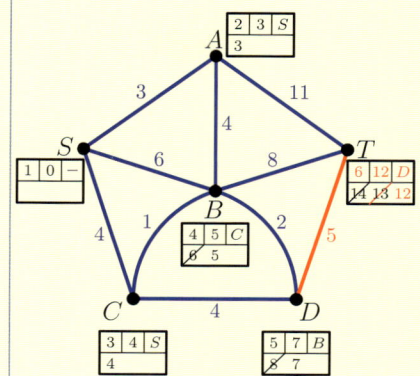

The length of the shortest path is the middle number in the T's box

The length of the shortest path is 12.

We can work back from T to find the actual path

Working back from T:
T-D-B-C-S
So the shortest path is S-C-B-D-T.

We can use the completed diagram to go back from D to S

(b) Working back from D:
D-B-C-S
So the shortest path from S to D is S-C-B-D, of length 7.

We look back to when we added BD: If this can't be done, then D is not changed from 8 to 7, so T would stay at 13. But notice that 13 can be got in two different ways.

(c) without BD:
S-C-B-T and S-C-D-T both have length 13.

> **EXAM HINT**
>
> Your solution must contain a diagram with a completed box for each vertex, like the final diagram in part (a). Don't forget to list the shortest path and state its length.

> **EXAM HINT**
>
> If a graph is given in a cost adjacency matrix you can follow Dijkstra's algorithm as you draw the graph. Begin with the start vertex and all the edges starting from it. Then add temporary labels before moving on to more edges and vertices.

Exercise 7C

1. For each of the following networks:
   - fill in the boxes to carry out Dijkstra's algorithm
   - find the shortest path (or paths) from S to F
   - write down the lengths of the shortest paths from S to D, E and F.

   For larger versions of the diagrams that can be photocopied and filled in, see the end of this chapter (pages 131–133).

(a) (i) 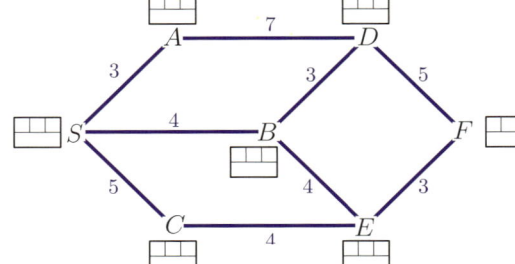 (ii)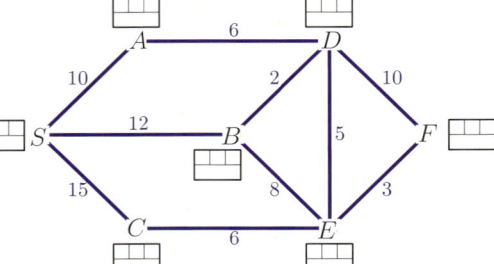

(b) (i) 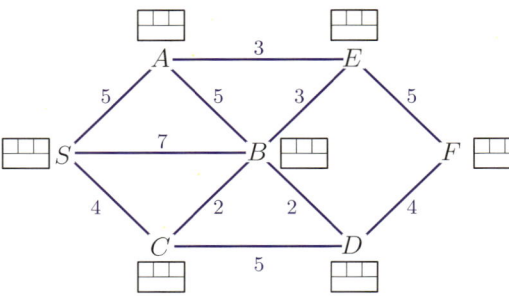 (ii)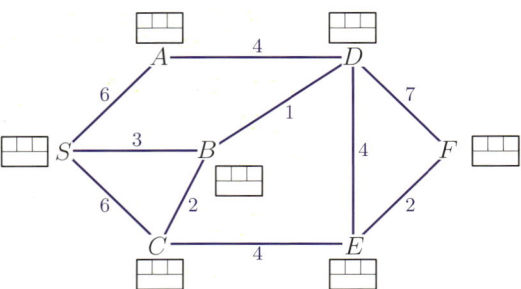

(c) (i) 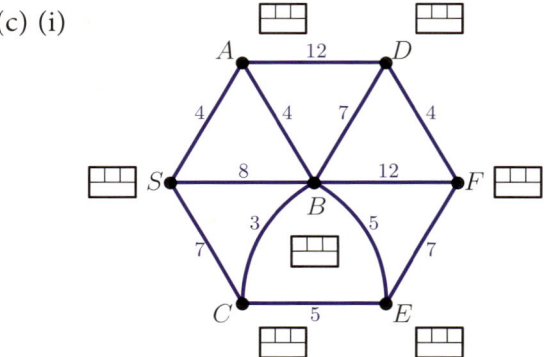 (ii)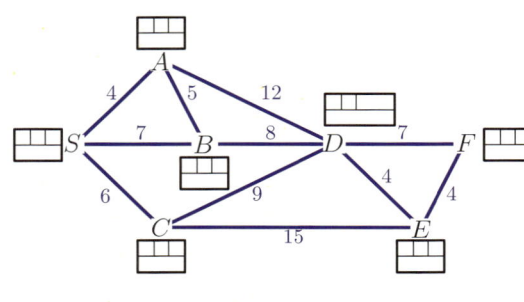

2. Use Dijkstra's algorithm to find the shortest path from S to T:

   (a) (i) 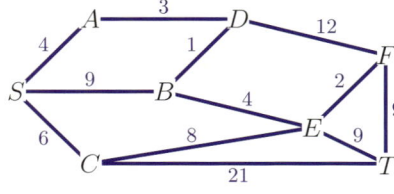 (ii)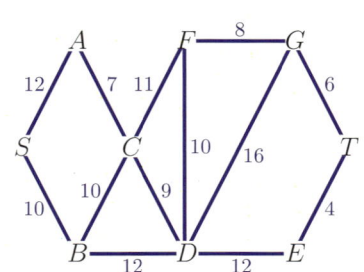

(b) (i) 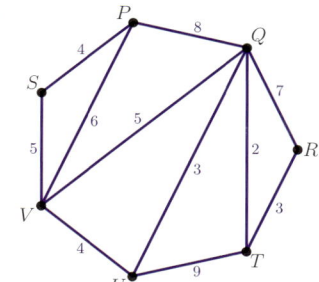   (ii)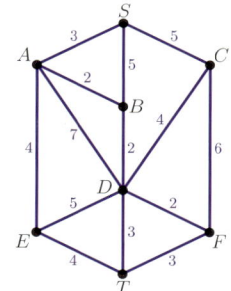

3. Use Dijkstra's algorithm to find shortest path from S to F in the weighted graphs given by the following tables:

(a) (i)

	S	A	B	C	D	E	F	G	H
S	-	6	8	8	-	-	-	-	-
A	6	-	4	-	7	-	-	-	-
B	8	4	-	6	8	5	-	-	-
C	8	-	6	-	7	-	12	-	-
D	-	7	8	7	-	6	11	-	8
E	-	-	5	-	6	-	12	9	5
F	-	-	-	12	11	12	-	6	3
G	-	-	-	-	-	9	6	-	5
H	-	-	-	-	8	5	3	5	-

(ii)

	S	A	B	C	D	E	F	G	H
S	-	6	4	5	-	-	-	-	-
A	6	-	-	-	6	2	-	-	-
B	4	-	-	-	5	5	-	-	-
C	5	-	-	-	-	6	6	4	-
D	-	6	5	-	-	-	5	-	2
E	-	2	5	6	-	-	4	3	3
F	-	-	-	6	5	4	-	5	2
G	-	-	-	4	-	3	5	-	1
H	-	-	-	-	2	3	2	1	-

(b) (i)

	S	A	B	C	D	G	H	I	J	E
A	7									
B	4									
C	9	8	3							
D		15	12	7						
G		18	18		8					
H				22	21	30				
I					24	16				
J					56	31	40	50		
E						42	26	39		
F								33	23	

EXAM HINT

Note an unusual format of the table, which has appeared in exam questions in the past.

7 Algorithms on graphs 111

(ii)

	S	P	Q	A	B	C	D	E	F	G
P	42									
Q	31	17								
A		41	32							
B		38	25							
C			28		7					
D				24	22	29				
E					31	23	29	16		
F							46	41	22	
G								42		21
H									31	19	12

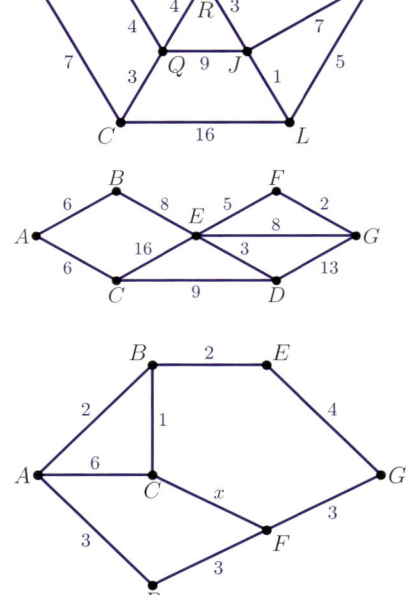

4. The graph represents the cost of train journeys between different towns.

   (a) Use Dijkstra's algorithm to find the cheapest route from S to M. State your route and its cost.

   (b) Write down the cost of the cheapest route from S to J.

   [8 marks]

5. The diagram shows a network of roads and their lengths.

   (a) Find the length of the shortest path from A to G.

   (b) The road BE is closed for repairs. Find the new shortest path from A to G, making your method clear.

   [8 marks]

6. The diagram shows a weighted graph. The unknown length x is a positive integer. If the unique shortest path from A to G is $ABCFG$, show that there is only one possible value of x.

   [6 marks]

7D Travelling along all the edges: Chinese postman problem

The **Chinese postman problem**, also called the **Route inspection** problem, is to find a route of minimum length which uses each edge at least once and returns to the starting vertex. Think about a postman delivering letters: He needs to travel along every street at least once.

If all the vertices have even degree, there is an Eulerian circuit which uses each edge exactly once. If there is more than one such circuit they all have the same length, which is equal to the sum of the weights of all the edges.

> This problem was originally posed and studied by the Chinese mathematician Mei-Ku Kuan in 1962.

> We met Eulerian graphs in Section 6F.

If there are some vertices of odd degree the graph is not Eulerian, so some edges need to be repeated. We know that there can only be an even number of vertices of odd degree. For your exam, you only need to know how to solve the Chinese postman problem for graphs with two or four vertices of odd degree. If there are two vertices of odd degree you can use the following algorithm:

KEY POINT 7.2

Chinese postman algorithm

- Identify the vertices of odd degree.
- Find the shortest path between those two vertices, either by inspection or using Dijkstra's algorithm.
- The edges in this shortest path need to be used twice, and all the other edges are used only once.
- The length of the route is the total weight of all the edges plus the length of the above shortest path.

Worked example 7.4

(a) Find the length of the shortest Chinese postman route for this graph.
(b) State which edges need to be used twice.
(c) Find one such route starting and finishing at A.

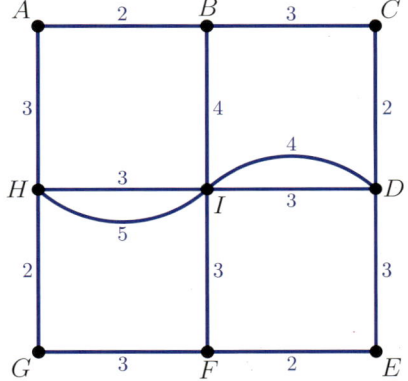

Check the degrees of all the vertices

(a) There are two odd vertices: B and F

Find the shortest path from B to F. In this case, we can do this by inspection

B to F: B-I-F (length=7)

The length is the weight of all the edges plus 7

Total length = 42 + 7 = 49

(b) The edges BI and IF are used twice.

Find one possible route by inspection, remembering that BI and IF can be used twice. The easiest way to achieve this, if possible, is to include BIFIB at some point

(c) A possible route: ABIFIBCDIDEFGHIHA

7 Algorithms on graphs   113

If there are four vertices of odd degree we need to look at the lengths of the paths between all possible pairs and pick the best combination. For example, if the four odd vertices are called A, B, C and D then they can be paired up in three possible ways:

AB and CD

AC and BD

AD and BC

To calculate the length of the repeated edges for the first pairing we need to add the length of the shortest path from A to B and the length of the shortest path from C to D. When we have done this for all three pairings we then choose the one that gives the shortest total length of repeated edges.

> **EXAM HINT**
> You need to write down the lengths of routes for all possible combinations, even if it seems obvious which one is the shortest.

KEY POINT 7.3

To solve the Chinese postman problem for a graph with four vertices of odd degree:

- consider all three possible ways of pairing up the four vertices
- find the shortest path for each pair of vertices and add up those lengths for each combination
- pick the combination with the lowest total; those edges need to be repeated.

Worked example 7.5

Find the length of the optimal Chinese postman route for the graph shown in the diagram and state which edges need to be used twice.

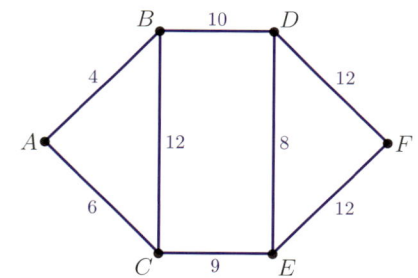

Identify the odd vertices	Odd vertices: B, C, D, E
Write down all three pairings and find shortest paths. Remember that the shortest paths do not need to be direct	BC and DE: 10 + 8 = 18 (using BAC) BD and CE: 10 + 9 = 19 BE and CD: 18 + 17 = 35 (using BDE and CED)
Select the lowest total; those edges need to be repeated	Repeat edges BA, AC and DE. The length of the route is: (all edges) + 18 = 73 + 18 = 91

Topic 10 – Option: Discrete mathematics

Exercise 7D

1. For each graph G below:

(i)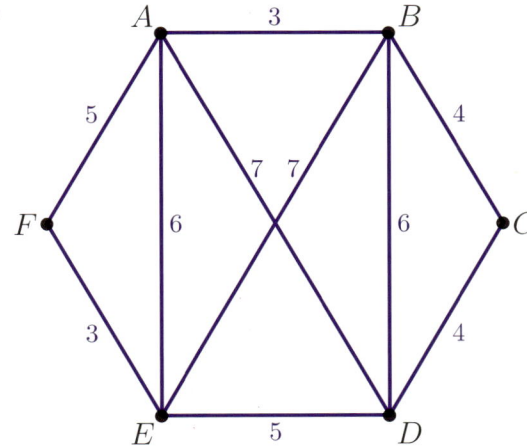

(ii)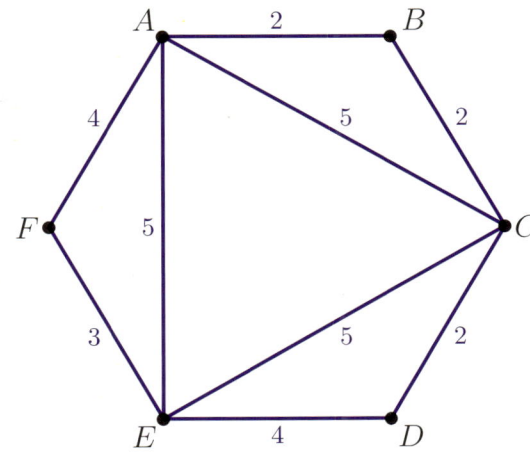

  (a) Show that G is Eulerian.
  (b) Write down the length of a Chinese postman route.
  (c) Find a Chinese postman route starting and finishing at C.

2. For each graph:

(i)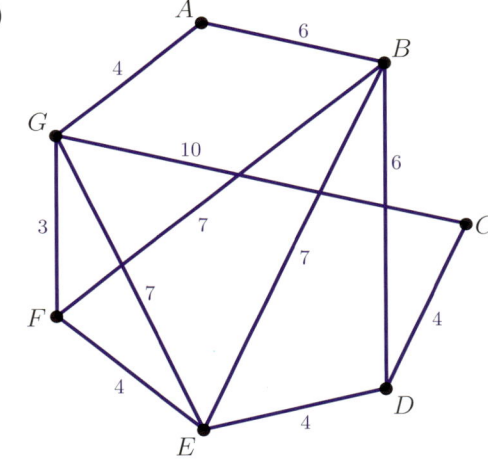

(ii)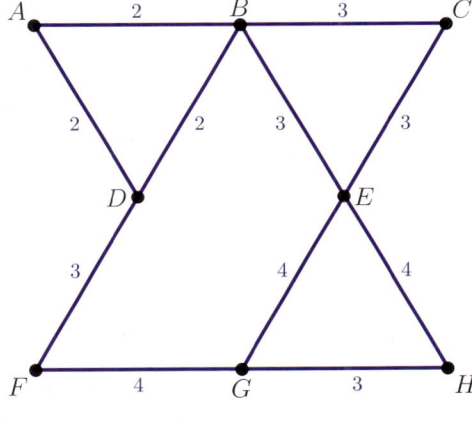

  (a) Explain why it is impossible to walk along each edge of the graph exactly once, starting and finishing at A.
  (b) Use the Chinese postman algorithm to find the route of minimum length, starting and finishing at A, and using every edge of the graph at least once. State the weight of your route.

7 Algorithms on graphs 115

3. For each of the graphs below:

(i) 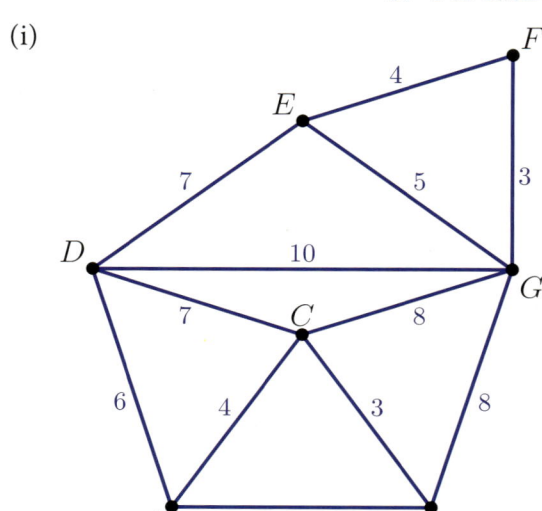 (ii)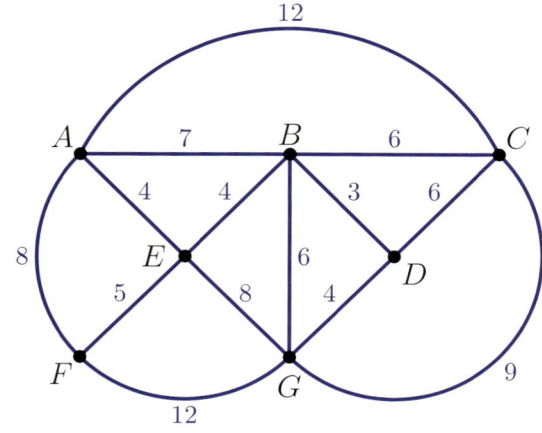

(a) List the vertices of odd degree.

(b) Find the length of the optimal Chinese postman route and state which edges need to be repeated.

4.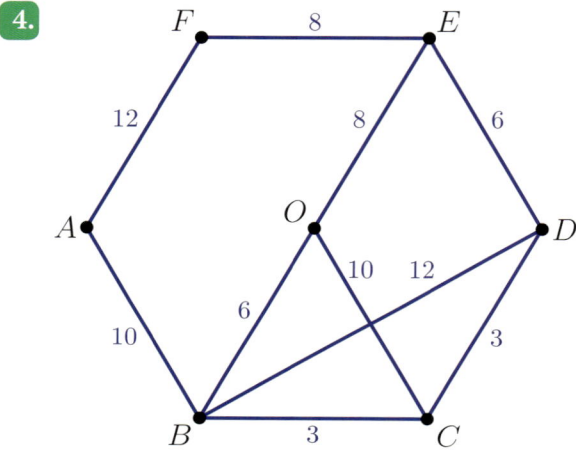

(a) Write down the two vertices of odd degree.

(b) State the length of the shortest path between the two vertices of odd degree.

(c) Hence find the length of the shortest route which starts and finishes at C and uses every edge of the graph at least once. [6 marks]

5. The graph represents the network of roads in a small town, with the weights of the edges representing the lengths of the roads. A salesman wants to visit all the houses in the town, so he must walk along each road once. He wants to start and finish at his shop, which is located at junction C.

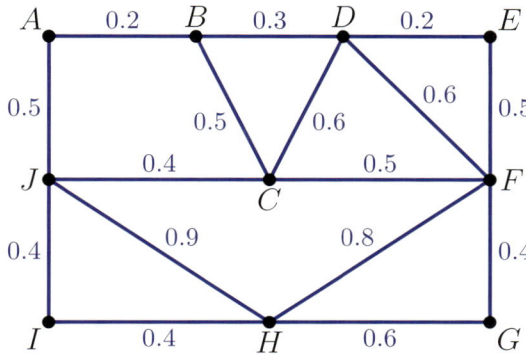

Use the Chinese postman algorithm to find the shortest possible route for the salesman. *[8 marks]*

6. (a) The diagram shows the town of Königsberg with its two islands and seven bridges. The bridge between the North bank (NB) and the second island (I_2) is closed. In the corresponding graph, the weights of the edges represent the time, in minutes, to walk between different places.

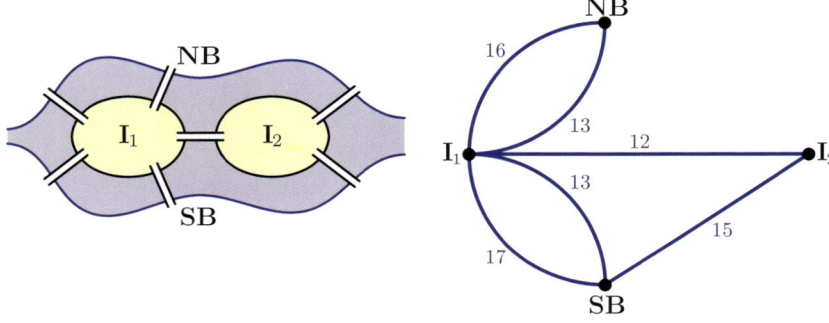

A tour around the town starts at the North bank, crosses every bridge at least once (except for the closed one), and returns to the North bank. Find the shortest possible time taken by such a tour. You must make your method clear.

(b) The bridge between NB and I_2 reopens, and it takes 16 minutes to walk between the two places. Find the shortest possible time for a route which crosses every bridge at least once, starting and finishing at the North bank. *[9 marks]*

7. (a) For the graph shown in the diagram, find the shortest route, which starts and finishes at A and uses each edge of the graph at least once. Make your method clear and state the length of your route.

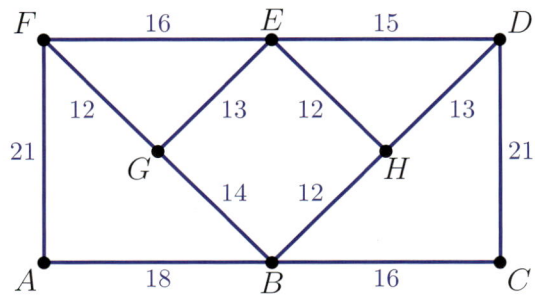

7 Algorithms on graphs 117

(b) The edge *GH* of weight 16 is added to the graph. Find the length of the new shortest route which uses each edge at least once, starting and finishing at *A*. *[9 marks]*

8. Weighted graph K has the weights of the edges shown in the following table.

	A	B	C	D	E	F
A		21	18			
B	21		8	14	42	
C	18	8		21	4	16
D		14	21		6	4
E		42	4	6		11
F			16	4	11	

(a) Explain why K is not Eulerian.

(b) Find the shortest path between vertices *C* and *F* in K.

(c) Find the shortest route, starting and finishing at *D*, which uses each edge of K at least once. Make your method clear and state the length of your route.

(d) It is required to find the shortest route which uses each edge of K at least once, but does not need to return to the starting vertex.

  (i) Find the least possible length of such a route.

  (ii) What start and finish vertices should be used to achieve this shortest route? *[10 marks]*

7E Visiting all the vertices: Travelling salesman problem

The **travelling salesman problem** is to find the shortest route around a graph which visits each vertex at least once and returns to the starting point. Think about a salesman who wants to visit every town in a region. There are several versions of this problem, depending on whether the graph is complete and whether we are allowed to repeat vertices. If the graph is not complete it may not have a Hamiltonian cycle, so visiting each vertex exactly once may be impossible.

◁ *Hamiltonian cycles were introduced in Section 6G.* ◁

The version we will solve is to find a Hamiltonian cycle of least weight in a complete graph. In other words, we want to find the shortest route around a complete graph which visits each vertex exactly once and returns to the starting point.

One way to solve this problem is to list all Hamiltonian cycles and find their weights. (We know that a complete graph is always Hamiltonian.) This is guaranteed to find the shortest cycle, but is inefficient, or even not feasible, for large graphs.

118 Topic 10 – Option: Discrete mathematics

This is because a complete graph with n vertices has $\frac{1}{2}(n-1)!$ Hamiltonian cycles, and this number becomes very large, very quickly.

This problem is more difficult than it seems. In fact, there is no known algorithm (other than listing all possible cycles) which guarantees finding the shortest Hamiltonian cycle. The best we can do is find upper and lower bounds for the problem. These are two numbers such that we can guarantee that the shortest possible Hamiltonian cycle has length somewhere between them.

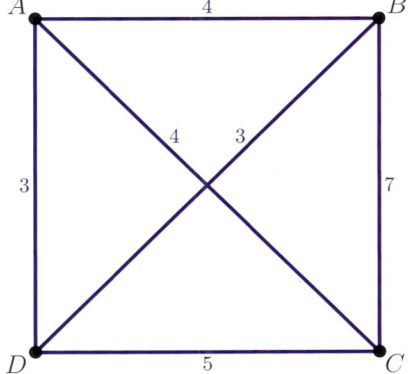

For example, in the graph shown here, one Hamiltonian cycle is $ABCDA$ with length 19. We therefore know that there is a Hamiltonian cycle of length 19, so the shortest one cannot be longer than this. In other words, the shortest possible Hamiltonian cycle has length $L \leq 19$. We say that 19 is an **upper bound** for the travelling salesman problem. This is not the best possible upper bound. For example, the cycle $ABDCA$ has length 16 so we know that in fact $L \leq 16$. It turns out that 16 is the shortest possible length (so the best possible upper bound), but we cannot know this without checking all possible cycles.

On the other hand, we can be certain that there is no Hamiltonian cycle shorter than 12. This is because we know that every Hamiltonian cycle in a K_4 graph consists of 4 edges, and the shortest edge in our graph has weight 3. Therefore $L \geq 12$; we say that 12 is a **lower bound** for the travelling salesman problem. So in conclusion, we can say that the length of the shortest possible Hamiltonian cycle, L, satisfies $12 \leq L \leq 16$.

Upper and lower bounds are only useful if they are quite close to each other. Knowing that, for example, $3 \leq L \leq 97$ is not very useful. However if, in a large graph, we can say that $21 \leq L \leq 24$, then we have quite a lot of information about the graph. In many practical problems this level of accuracy is sufficient.

The method used above for finding upper and lower bounds is unlikely to give us a sufficiently narrow range for the value of L. We will now look at some methods which are more complicated, but result in much better upper and lower bounds.

KEY POINT 7.4

Nearest neighbour algorithm for finding an upper bound:
- pick a starting vertex
- go to the closest vertex not yet visited
- repeat until all the vertices have been used
- add one more edge to return to the starting vertex.

This clearly gives a Hamiltonian cycle, so it provides an upper bound; the shortest possible Hamiltonian cycle will be less than this value. In the graph below, choosing A as the starting vertex gives the cycle *ADBCA* of length 17.

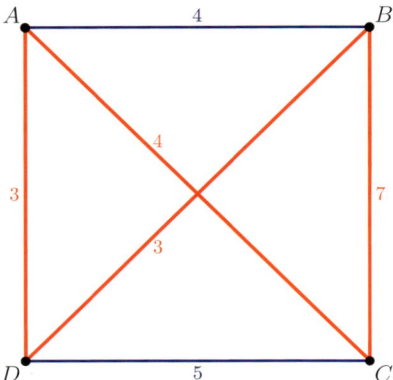

> **KEY POINT 7.5**
>
> An improved upper bound can be found by starting from a different vertex.
>
> We want the upper bound to be as small as possible.

In this example, whichever vertex we pick we get the same upper bound of 17. We know that the shortest possible Hamiltonian cycle has length 16 (*ABDCA*), so this illustrates that the nearest neighbour algorithm will not always find the best possible solution.

We now look at finding a lower bound.

> **KEY POINT 7.6**
>
> A lower bound for the travelling salesman problem can be found by using the following algorithm:
>
> - remove one vertex (and all the associated edges) from the graph
> - find the length of the minimum spanning tree for the remaining graph
> - add the two shortest edges connecting the removed vertex.
>
> We want the lower bound to be as large as possible.

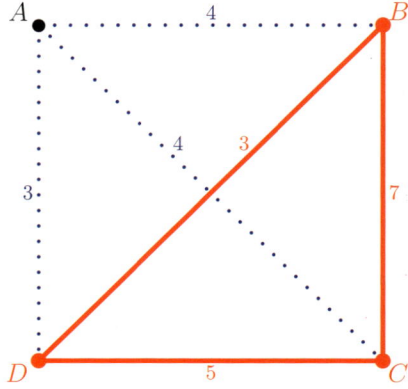

For example, removing vertex A from our graph leaves the subgraph shown in red. Its minimum spanning tree consists of edges *BD* and *CD* and has weight 8. The two shortest edges from A are *AD* and either *AB* or *AC*, with the total length 7. Hence the lower bound for the travelling salesman problem is $8 + 7 = 15$. Combining this with the upper bound we found earlier, we can conclude that $15 \leq L \leq 17$. We saw earlier that the actual minimal Hamiltonian cycle has length 16.

It may not be immediately clear why this method gives a lower bound, especially as the edges selected above do not even form a cycle. We have selected the correct number of edges (if there are n vertices, any Hamiltonian cycle will have n edges), including the two shortest edges from A and two shortest edges connecting the remaining vertices. So it seems likely that any Hamiltonian cycle cannot be shorter than this. If the edges selected in this way happen to form a cycle, then we have found the solution to the travelling salesman problem.

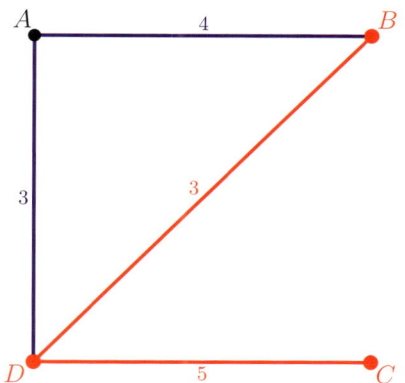

If we remove a different vertex from the graph we get a different lower bound. Removing vertices B, C and D from the above graph gives lower bounds of 14, 13 and 14, respectively. Remember that we want to make the lower bound as large as possible, because that brings it closer to the actual solution. So in this case the best lower bound we can find is 15.

Worked example 7.6

For the graph shown in the diagram:

(a) Use the nearest neighbour algorithms starting at A and going to D first, to find an upper bound for the travelling salesman problem.

(b) By removing vertex A find a lower bound for the travelling salesman problem.

(c) Write down an inequality satisfied by the length, L, of the shortest Hamiltonian cycle in the graph.

(d) By removing vertex C find an improved lower bound.

(e) Explain why we have actually found the solution of the travelling salesman problem for this graph.

Start from A and always go to the closest vertex not yet visited

(a) AD (2)
DB (2)
BC (3)
CE (4)

We have visited all the vertices, so return to A

EA (4)
upper bound = 15

Find a minimum spanning tree for the graph with A removed, then add the two shortest edges from A

(b) remove A:

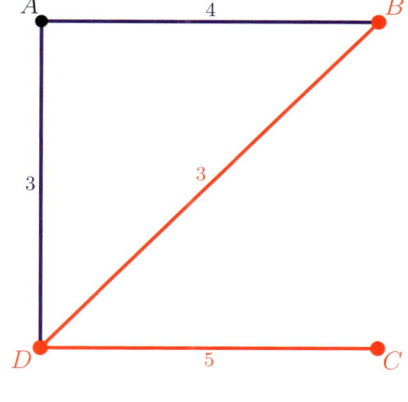

BD (2)
BC (3)
CE (4)
Add edges AD and AB:
lower bound = $(2 + 3 + 4) + (2 + 2) = 13$

7 Algorithms on graphs 121

> continued...
> *L is somewhere between the upper and the lower bound*

(c) $13 \leq L \leq 15$

> *Find a minimum spanning tree for the graph without vertex C*

(d) remove C:

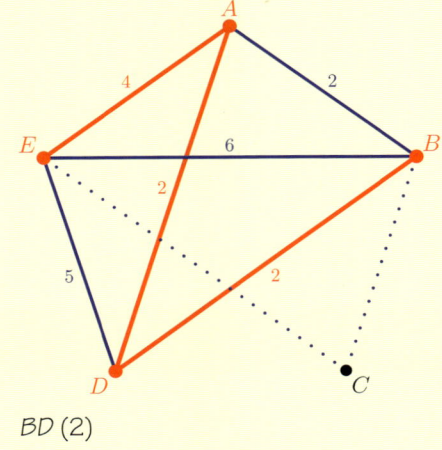

BD (2)
AD (2)
AE (4)

> *Add the two shortest edges from C*

Add edges CE and CB:
lower bound $= (2 + 2 + 4) + (3 + 4) = 15$

> *The upper and lower bounds we have found are the same*

(e) Upper and lower bounds are the same:
$15 \leq L \leq 15$
so $L = 15$ is the solution.

Note that in finding an upper bound in part (a), we created a cycle. This cycle is not necessarily the best one, because it could be that $L < 15$. The improved lower bound in part (d) also creates a cycle. This *is* the best possible cycle because $L \geq 15$, so we cannot find one shorter than 15.

KEY POINT 7.7

We know that we have found the exact solution to the travelling salesman problem in either of these two cases:

(1) The lower bound and the upper bound are equal.

(2) We have found a cycle with the same length as the lower bound.

Exercise 7E

Questions 1 to 2 refer to the travelling salesman problem on the following graphs:

(a) (i) 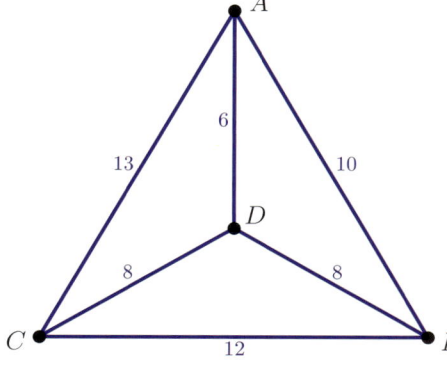   (ii)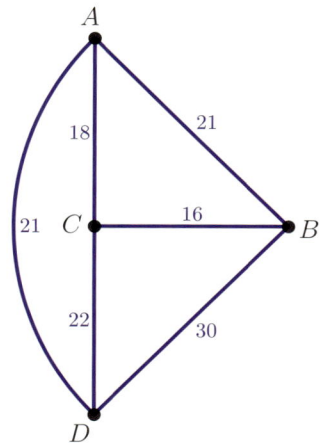

(b) (i) 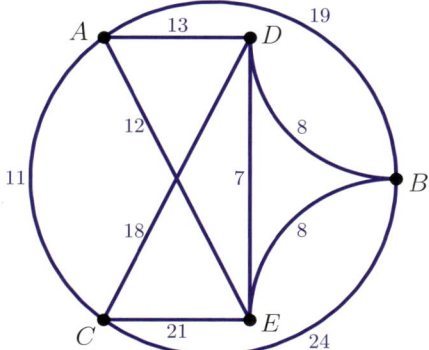   (ii)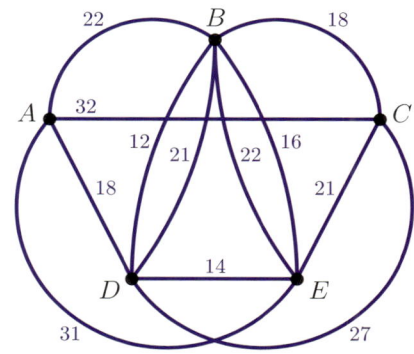

(c) (i)

	A	B	C	D	E
A		32	28	26	19
B	32		14	21	26
C	28	14		18	18
D	26	21	18		22
E	19	26	18	22	

(ii)

	A	B	C	D	E
A		22	21	17	22
B	22		22	23	31
C	21	22		18	31
D	17	23	18		26
E	22	31	31	26	

1. Use the nearest neighbour algorithm starting at A to find an upper bound.
2. By deleting vertex A, find a lower bound for each graph.
3. The weights of edges of graph G are given in the table:

	A	B	C	D
A		16	12	8
B	16		18	8
C	12	18		9
D	8	8	9	

(a) List all Hamiltonian cycles starting and finishing at A.
(b) Hence solve the travelling salesman problem for G.

[5 marks]

4. The weights of the edges of a simple graph G are given in this table:

	A	B	C	D	E
A		4	3	7	6
B	4		3	9	7
C	3	3		8	5
D	7	9	8		9
E	6	7	5	9	

(a) Explain why the upper bound for the travelling salesman problem for G is at most 29.

(b) Use the nearest neighbour algorithm, starting with each vertex in turn, to find an improved upper bound.

(c) By deleting vertex D from the graph find a lower bound for the travelling salesman problem for G. *[11 marks]*

5. Consider the graph given by this table:

	A	B	C	D	E	F
A		5	10	11	8	7
B	5		6	7	8	7
C	10	6		7	10	12
D	11	7	7		9	10
E	8	8	10	9		6
F	7	7	12	10	6	

(a) Use the nearest neighbour algorithm starting from A to find an upper bound for the travelling salesman problem on G.

(b) By deleting vertex B and using Kruskal's algorithm to find the minimum spanning tree for the resulting graph, find a lower bound for the travelling salesman problem.

(c) Explain how you know that you have found a solution to the travelling salesman problem, and write down the weight of the optimal route. *[9 marks]*

Summary

- In a **weighted graph** edges have associated numbers, called **weights**.
- A **minimum spanning tree** of a weighted graph is a subgraph of smallest possible weight which is also a tree.
- **Kruskal's algorithm** for finding a minimum spanning tree involves adding edges in order of weight and skipping edges which would form a cycle.
- To perform **Dijkstra's algorithm** for finding the shortest path between two vertices:
  - Start by labelling each vertex connected to the start vertex with a **temporary label** which is its distance from the start vertex.
  - At each stage find the vertex with the smallest temporary label, make it a **permanent label**, and then give temporary labels to all vertices connected to it.

- If a vertex already has a temporary label, it is updated only if the new one would be smaller.
- Once the end vertex has a permanent label, we can work backwards to find the shortest path.
- The labels for each vertex are recorded in a box, with permanent labels in the top row.

order of labelling	distance from start	previous vertex
temporary labels		

- The **Chinese postman problem** is to find the shortest route around a graph which uses each edge at least once and returns to the starting vertex.
  - If the graph is Eulerian, the solution is any Eulerian path.
  - If the graph is not Eulerian, we use the **Route inspection algorithm**
    - find the shortest path between pairs of vertices of odd degree
    - the edges in this path need to be used twice, all the other edges are used once
    - the weight of the route is the sum of all the edges in the graph plus the weight of the shortest path.

- The **travelling salesman problem** is to find the Hamiltonian cycle of least weight in a complete graph (i.e. the shortest route which visits every vertex and returns to the starting point).
  - The exact solution can only be found by checking all Hamiltonian cycles, which is inefficient.
  - An **upper bound** can be found by using the nearest neighbour algorithm.
  - An improved upper bound can be found by starting from a different vertex.
  - A **lower bound** can be found by removing one vertex, finding the weight of the minimum spanning tree for the remaining graph, and adding the weights of the two shortest edges from the removed vertex.
  - The required least weight of a Hamiltonian cycle is somewhere between the lower bound and the upper bound, $LB \leq L \leq UB$.
  - In order to get a more accurate estimate for L we aim to make the lower bound as large as possible and the upper bound as small as possible.

Mixed examination practice 7

1. (a) Explain what is meant by a minimum spanning tree.
   (b) Use Kruskal's algorithm to find the minimum spanning tree for this graph.

   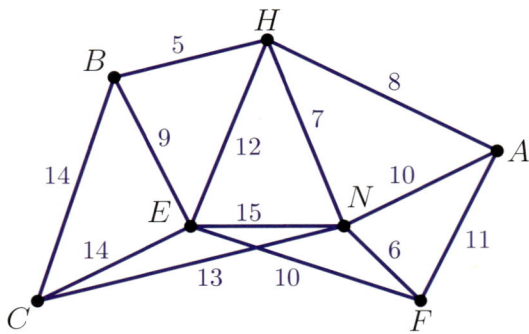

   List edges in the order you added them to the tree, draw your tree and state its weight.   *[7 marks]*

2. (a) Outline briefly Kruskal's algorithm for finding the minimum spanning tree.
   (b) Use Kruskal's algorithm to find the minimum spanning tree for the graph represented by the following table. Draw the tree and state its weight.

	A	B	C	D	E	F	G	H	I	J
A		14							15.5	15
B	14		8.5						12	
C		8.5		22.5			10	16.5	13	
D			22.5		21		25			
E				21		8	16			
F					8		20.5			
G				25	16	20.5		19		
H			16.5				19		18	
I	15.5	12	13					18		11.5
J	15								11.5	

   [9 marks]

3. The weights of the edges of a graph with vertices A, B, C, D and E are given in the following table.

	A	B	C	D	E
A		10	15	11	16
B	10		12	19	13
C	15	12		18	14
D	11	19	18		17
E	16	13	14	17	

   (a) Use any method to find an upper bound for the travelling salesman problem for this graph.

(b) (i) Use Kruskal's algorithm to find and draw a minimum spanning tree for the subgraph obtained by removing the vertex E from the graph.

(ii) State the total weight of this minimum spanning tree and hence find a lower bound for the travelling salesman problem for this graph.

[11 marks]

(© IB Organization 2006)

4. We want to solve the travelling salesman problem for the graph K shown here.

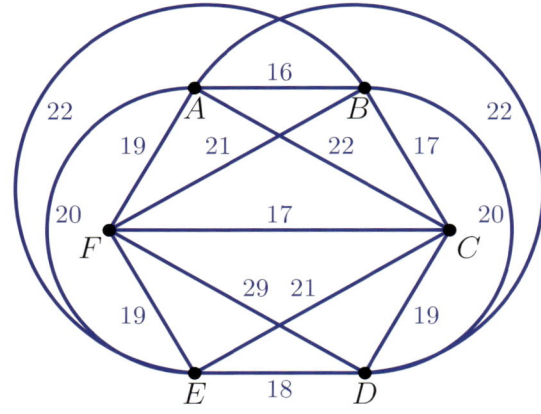

(a) Use the nearest neighbour algorithm starting at vertex B to find an upper bound for the travelling salesman problem.

(b) By removing vertex B find a lower bound.

(c) Write down an inequality satisfied by L, the length of the shortest Hamiltonian cycle in K.

[10 marks]

5. A graph has edges with weights given in this table:

	A	B	C	D	E	F	G	H	I	J
A	-	34	22	-	-	-	-	-	-	-
B	34	-	-	20	11	-	-	-	-	-
C	22	-	-	-	24	34	21	-	-	-
D	-	20	-	-	-	-	16	-	-	-
E	-	11	24	-	-	-	26	-	-	-
F	-	-	34	-	-	-	-	-	10	-
G	-	-	-	16	26	-	-	26	-	12
H	-	-	21	-	-	-	26	-	25	-
I	-	-	-	-	-	10	-	25	-	18
J	-	-	-	-	-	-	12	-	18	-

(a) Use Dijkstra's algorithm to find the shortest path from A to J. Write down the length of your path.

(b) It is required that the path includes edge FI. Find the length of the new shortest path.

(c) The path does not need to include FI any more, but the edge GJ is removed from the graph. Find the new shortest path and its length.

[12 marks]

6. Consider the travelling salesman problem for this graph:

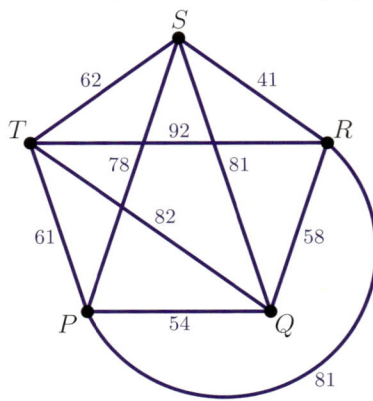

By deleting each vertex in turn, find a lower bound for the travelling salesman problem.

[10 marks]

7. The diagram shows a plan of a house, with doors connecting adjacent rooms.

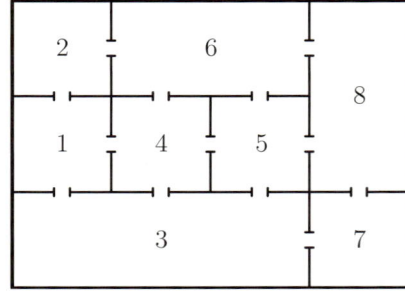

(a) Represent the plan on a graph, with vertices representing rooms and edges representing doors.

(b) Explain why it is not possible to walk through each door once and return to the starting room.

The table shows distances between the centres of adjacent rooms.

	2	3	4	5	6	7	8
1	4	6	5				
2				5			
3			3	2		4	
4				4	7		
5					2		4
6							5
7							3

(c) Use Dijkstra's algorithm to find the shortest route between rooms 1 and 8.

(d) Hence find the shortest tour of the house which passes through each door at least once and returns to the starting point.

[13 marks]

8. For the graph shown in the diagram:

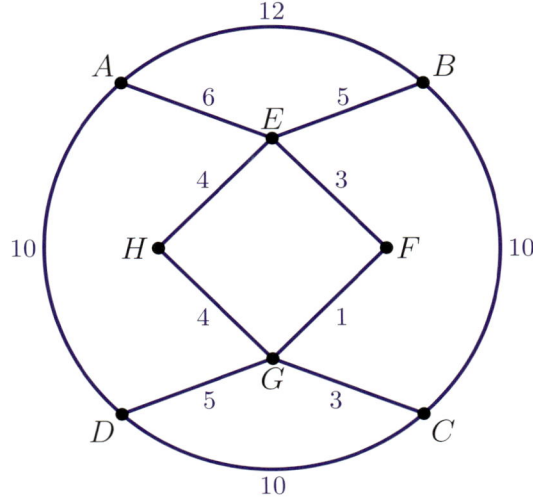

(a) List the vertices of odd degree.

(b) Solve the Chinese postman problem for this graph. Show your method clearly, list the edges which need to be used twice, and state the length of the optimal route. *[9 marks]*

9. The graph below represents a network of paths connecting seven fountains in a park:

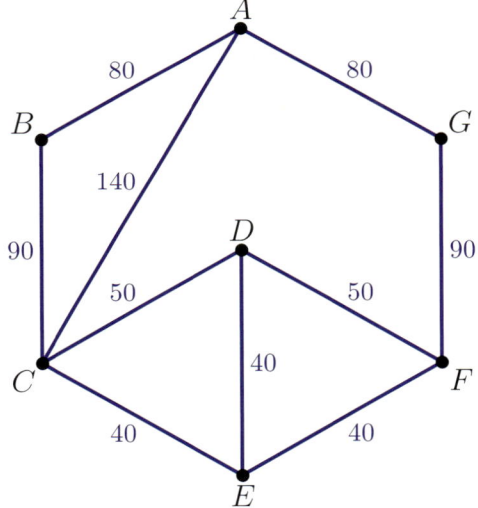

(a) Explain why it is not possible to start from fountain A, walk along each path exactly once and return to A.

(b) Find the length of the shortest route which uses each path at least once and returns to A.

(c) A new path is to be built so that it becomes possible to walk along each path exactly once and return to the starting point. Between which two fountains should this new path be built? *[11 marks]*

10. The table shows the lengths (in km) of main roads between eight villages.

	A	B	C	D	E	F	G	H
A		7	9		9			
B	7		10	12		12	8	
C	9	10			11			
D		12			10	8	8	5
E	9		11	10			12	7
F		12		8	12		11	6
G		8		8		11		8
H				5	7	6	8	

(a) A road inspector needs to drive along each road to inspect it.

  (i) Explain why he cannot return to the starting village without using some roads more than once.

  (ii) Can he use each road exactly once if he does not have to return to the starting village? Justify your answer.

(b) A snowplough needs to clear all the roads. To do this, it must travel along each road twice (not necessarily in opposite directions).

  (i) Explain why the snowplough can start from village A, travel along each road exactly twice, and return back to A.

  (ii) Find the distance the snowplough needs to cover. *[9 marks]*

11. Graph G has the following cost adjacency table:

	A	B	C	D	E
A	-	6	10	9	7
B	6	-	9	8	8
C	10	9	-	6	10
D	9	8	6	-	5
E	7	8	10	5	-

(a) By deleting each vertex in turn, find a lower bound for the travelling salesman problem for G.

(b) Explain why this lower bound is in fact the solution to the travelling salesman problem.

Appendix A

Fill-in diagrams for Exercise 7C

1. Photocopy and, for each of the following networks:
   - fill in the boxes to carry out Dijkstra's algorithm
   - find the shortest path (or paths) from S to F
   - write down the lengths of the shortest paths from S to D, E and F.

(a) (i)

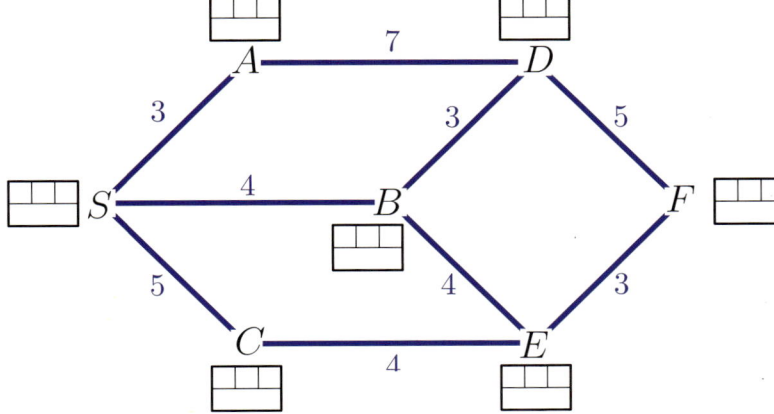

(ii)

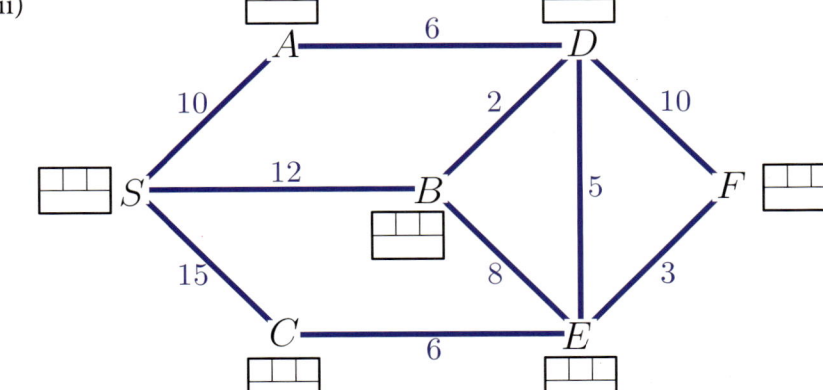

(b) (i)

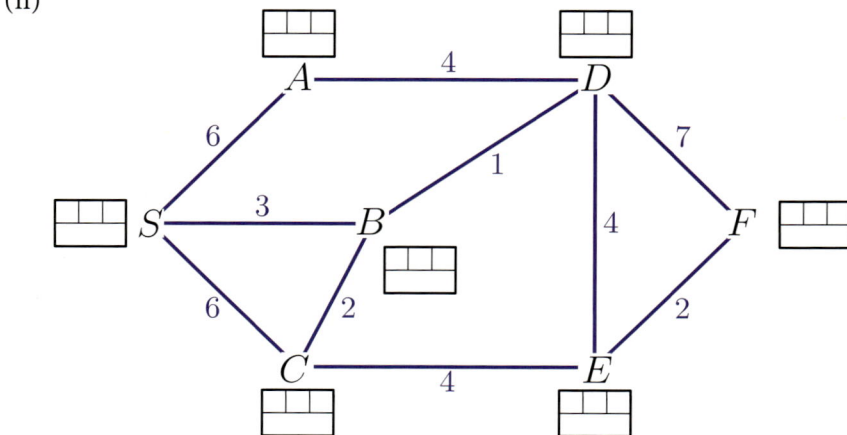

(ii)

(c) (i)

(ii)

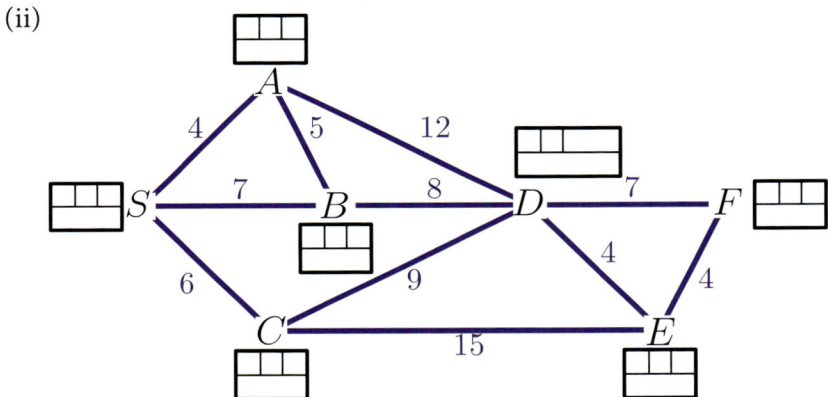

In this chapter you will learn:

- about different ways to define a sequence
- how to find the formula for the *n*th term for some sequences defined by recurrence relations
- how to use recurrence relations to model various situations.

8 Recurrence relations

Sequences often satisfy rules, which link each term to one or more previous terms; for example, $u_1 = 2$, $u_{n+1} = 2u_n$. By looking at the numbers in the sequence we can sometimes spot a pattern; in this case the sequence is $2, 4, 8, \ldots$ so $u_n = 2^n$. But sometimes the pattern in the numbers is not so easy to spot. In this chapter we will learn a systematic way to find a formula for some special types of sequences.

8A Defining sequences recursively

You should have seen from the core course that there are two main ways we can define a sequence:

- Deductive rules that link the value of the term to its position in the sequence, for example $u_n = n^2$.

- Recursive definitions link new terms to previous terms in the sequence, for example $u_{n+1} = 2u_n$.

This type of rule is also called a **recurrence relation**, and does not fully define a sequence. For example, the recurrence relation $u_{n+1} = 2u_n$ could generate the sequences:

$1, 2, 4, 8, \ldots$ or $3, 6, 12, 24, \ldots$ or $0.7, 1.4, 2.8, 5.6, \ldots$

To define the sequence fully, we need a starting value. For example, if we also know that $u_1 = 0.7$ then the recurrence relation generates the third sequence.

Recurrence relations are classified by how many previous terms are needed to find the new term. In a **first order recurrence** the value of each term depends only on one previous term; $u_{n+1} = 2u_n$ is an example of a first order recurrence. If a new term depends on two previous terms, this is called a **second order recurrence** and an example of this is the Fibonacci sequence, $u_{n+2} = u_{n+1} + u_n$. In this case we need two starting values to fully define the sequence. Higher order recurrences are defined in the same way, but in this course we will only consider first and second order recurrence relations.

Topic 10 – Option: Discrete mathematics

Worked example 8.1

Find the first five terms of the sequence, defined by the recurrence relation:

$$u_{n+2} = 3u_{n+1} - 2u_n \text{ with } u_1 = 1, u_2 = 2$$

Apply the recurrence relation from third term onwards

$u_1 = 1$
$u_2 = 2$
$u_3 = 3u_2 - 2u_1 = 4$
$u_4 = 3u_3 - 2u_2 = 8$
$u_5 = 3u_4 - 2u_3 = 16$

These first five terms suggest that there is a pattern in the sequence which looks like $u_n = 2^{n-1}$. There is, of course, no guarantee that this pattern continues unless we can prove it. Results about recurrence relations are often best proved using induction.

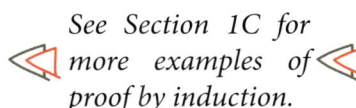
See Section 1C for more examples of proof by induction.

Worked example 8.2

A sequence is defined by the recurrence relation $u_{n+2} = 3u_{n+1} - 2u_n$ with $u_1 = 1, u_2 = 2$. Prove by induction that $u_n = 2^{n-1}$.

As each term depends on two previous terms, we need two base cases

When $n = 1: u_1 = 1 = 2^{1-1}$
When $n = 2: u_2 = 2 = 2^{2-1}$
So the statement is true for $n = 1$ and $n = 2$.

As each term depends on more than one previous term we need to use strong induction

Suppose the statement is true for all $n < k$. Then for $n = k$:
$u_k = 3u_{k-1} - 2u_{k-2}$

The expression $u_n = 2^{n-1}$ is valid for $n = k - 1$ and $n = k - 2$

$= 3(2^{k-2}) - 2(2^{k-3})$
$= 3(2^{k-2}) - 2^{k-2}$
$= 2(2^{k-2})$
$= 2^{k-1}$
So the statement is true for $n = k$

Always write a conclusion

The statement $u_n = 2^{n-1}$ is true for $n = 1$ and $n = 2$, and if it is true for all $n < k$ then we can prove that it is also true for $n = k$. Hence it is true for all n by strong induction.

Exercise 8A

1. Find the first five terms of the sequences defined by the following recurrence relations:

   (a) $u_{n+1} = 4u_n + 1$, $u_1 = 1$

   (b) $u_n = 4 - u_{n-1}$, $u_1 = 3$

   (c) $u_{n+2} = u_{n+1}u_n$, $u_1 = 1, u_2 = 2$

   (d) $u_n = nu_{n-1}$, $u_1 = 2$

2. Given that $u_1 = 3, u_2 = 5$ and $u_{n+2} = 3u_{n+1} - 2u_n$ prove by induction that $u_n = 2^n + 1$.

3. A sequence is defined by the recurrence relation $a_{n+1} = 2a_n - a_{n-1}$ with $a_1 = 5$ and $a_2 = 7$. Prove by induction that $a_n = 2n + 3$.

4. The terms of a sequence satisfy the recurrence relation $u_{n+1} = u_n + 2n - 1$ with $u_1 = 1$. Show that $u_n = n^2$ for all $n \geq 1$.

8B First order linear recurrence relations

In a first order recurrence each term in the sequence depends only on the previous term; so we can write $u_{n+1} = f(u_n)$. The sequence is fully determined if we know the first term.

Although we can find any term in the sequence by applying the recurrence sufficiently many times, a solution for u_n in terms of n can only be found in some special cases. For example, even for a simple-looking recurrence like $u_{n+1} = 4u_n(1 - u_n)$ with $u_1 = 0.6$ there is no known expression for u_n in terms of n. If you plot the first twenty terms using your calculator, you will find that they do not appear to follow any recognisable pattern.

This recurrence relation is an example of a *logistic map*, which can be used to model population growth.

In this course we will study only **linear recurrence relations**, where the function $f(u_n)$ involves only multiples of u_n and no higher powers, roots, or any other functions. We will only learn a general method for solving recurrences with **constant coefficients** and so we will not consider recurrence relations such as $u_{n+1} = (n+1)u_n$, where the coefficient of u_n depends on n.

Sequences defined by the logistic map exhibit a range of behaviours (depending on the starting value). These range from periodic, where a few values repeat again and again, to chaotic, where the pattern never repeats. In a chaotic sequence, a small change in the starting value can have a large effect on subsequent terms. To analyse these sequences we need a range of mathematical techniques, from quadratic equations to differentiation.

The general form of a first order recurrence relation with constant coefficients is $u_{n+1} = au_n + g(n)$ (so although the coefficient of u_n does not depend on n, another part of the equation does); an example is $u_{n+1} = u_n + n$. We will mainly look at cases where $g(n)$ is a constant, although the method can be extended to deal with many other functions $g(n)$.

So the most general first order recurrence relation we will learn how to solve in this section is $u_{n+1} = au_n + b$. We have already met two special cases of this recurrence: When $a = 1$, $u_{n+1} = u_n + b$

produces an arithmetic sequence, so $u_n = u_1 + (n-1)b$; if $b = 0$ we get a geometric sequence, $u_n = u_1 a^{n-1}$.

To find the solution for other values of a and b, let us start with a particular example:
$$u_{n+1} = 3u_n + 1 \text{ with } u_1 = 2$$

If there was no '+1' in the equation, the sequence would be geometric and the solution would be of the form $c \times 3^n$ were c is a constant whose value depends on the first term. When we check this, it does not satisfy our equation so we need to try something different. The simplest way we can modify the solution is by adding a constant, and this works if we select the right constant:

If $u_n = c \times 3^n + d$ then:
$$c \times 3^{n+1} + d = 3(c \times 3^n + d) + 1$$
$$\Rightarrow c \times 3^{n+1} + d = c \times 3^{n+1} + 3d + 1$$
$$\Rightarrow \quad d = 3d + 1$$
$$\Rightarrow \quad d = -\frac{1}{2}$$

We can check that $u_n = c \times 3^n - \frac{1}{2}$ satisfies the recurrence relation for all values of c. We call this the *general solution* of the recurrence relation. To find the formula for our particular sequence we need to choose the value of c which makes the first term $u_1 = 2$:

$$c \times 3^1 - \frac{1}{2} = 2 \Rightarrow c = \frac{5}{6}$$

So the formula for our sequence is $u_n = \left(\frac{5}{6}\right)3^n - \frac{1}{2}$.

You can check that this works by substituting into the recurrence relation.

We can use this method to solve any first order linear recurrence relation of the form $u_{n+1} = au_n + b$.

KEY POINT 8.1

To solve the recurrence relation $u_{n+1} = au_n + b$:
- set $u_n = c \times a^n + d$
- substitute into the recurrence relation to find d
- substitute in the value of the first term to find c.

This method works whenever $a \neq 1$. When $a = 1$ we already know how to find the solution, as it is an arithmetic sequence given by $u_n = u_1 + (n-1)b = bn + (u_1 - b)$.

> This is an example of an application of Occam's razor, a philosophical principle that states that the simplest solution is often the correct one. What role can this sort of principle play in mathematics?

> This has some analogies with using integration to find the equation of a curve. Integration gives an arbitrary constant '+c' which can be found by using the coordinates of one point on the curve.

> In Section 8D we will use more complicated recurrence relations to model situations involving counting, but you will not need to know how to solve them.

> We can extend this method to deal with linear recurrence relations of the form $u_{n+1} = au_n + g(n)$ for various functions g.

8 Recurrence relations 137

Worked example 8.3

Find the formula for the nth term of the sequence defined by the recurrence relation
$u_{n+1} = \frac{1}{2} u_n - 3$ with $u_1 = 6$.

Follow the method above: Write down the general form of the solution

Let $u_n = c\left(\frac{1}{2}\right)^n + d$

Substitute into the recurrence to find d

Then:

$$c\left(\frac{1}{2}\right)^{n+1} + d = \frac{1}{2}\left(c\left(\frac{1}{2}\right)^n + d\right) - 3$$

$$\Rightarrow c\left(\frac{1}{2}\right)^{n+1} + d = c\left(\frac{1}{2}\right)^{n+1} + \frac{d}{2} - 3$$

$$\Rightarrow \qquad d = \frac{d}{2} - 3$$

$$\Rightarrow \qquad d = -6$$

$$\therefore u_n = c\left(\frac{1}{2}\right)^n - 6$$

Use the first term to find c

$u_1 = 6$

$$\Rightarrow 6 = c\left(\frac{1}{2}\right) - 6$$

$$\Rightarrow \qquad c = 24$$

$$\therefore u_n = 24\left(\frac{1}{2}\right)^n - 6$$

Exercise 8B

1. Find the formula for u_n in terms of n for the sequences below:
   (a) (i) $u_{n+1} = 2u_n - 1, u_1 = 3$ (ii) $u_{n+1} = 2u_n + 3, u_1 = 1$
   (b) (i) $u_{n+1} = -3u_n + 2, u_1 = 1$ (ii) $u_{n+1} = -3u_n + 5, u_1 = -2$
   (c) (i) $u_{n+1} = \frac{1}{3} u_n + 1, u_1 = 3$ (ii) $u_{n+1} = \frac{1}{3} u_n - 2, u_1 = 8$

2. Apply the method from this section to a geometric sequence defined by $u_{n+1} = r u_n$ and first term u_1.

3. Try applying the method to an arithmetic sequence $u_{n+1} = u_n + d$, where $d \neq 0$. Where does it fail?

4. A sequence is given by the recurrence relation $u_{n+1} = 5u_n + 8$ with $u_1 = 8$.
   (a) Write down the first three terms of the sequence.
   (b) Find an expression for u_n in terms of n. [9 marks]

5. (a) Find the general solution of the recurrence relation $u_{n+1} = 2u_n - 1$.

(b) Find the sequence with first term $u_1 = 1$ satisfying the above recurrence relation. *[8 marks]*

8C Second order recurrence relations

We will now look at second order recurrence relations, where u_{n+2} depends on two previous terms: $u_{n+2} = f(u_{n+1}, u_n)$. This means that we need to know the first two terms to fully define the sequence. As before, a solution is only easy to find for linear recurrences with constant coefficients, $u_{n+2} = au_{n+1} + bu_n + g(n)$. Moreover, we will only look at the case when $g(n) = 0$; such recurrence relations are called **homogeneous**.

To develop a method for solving these recurrence relations, let us look at a particular example:

$$u_{n+2} = 5u_{n+1} - 6u_n \text{ with } u_1 = 1 \text{ and } u_2 = -1$$

Motivated by the method for the first order recurrence we can try to see if there is a solution of the form $u_n = c \times k^n$ for some constant k. Substituting this into the recurrence gives:

$$c \times k^{n+2} = 5c \times k^{n+1} - 6c \times k^n$$
$$\Rightarrow k^{n+2} = 5 \times k^{n+1} - 6 \times k^n$$
$$\Rightarrow k^2 = 5k - 6$$
$$\Rightarrow k^2 - 5k + 6 = 0$$
$$\Rightarrow k = 2 \text{ or } 3$$

It looks like there are two possible solutions: $u_n = c_1 \times 2^n$ and $u_n = c_2 \times 3^n$. You can check that neither solution by itself works, as it is not possible to find c_1 or c_2 to make the first two terms 1 and -1. However, substituting into the recurrence shows that the sum of the two possible solutions, $u_n = c_1 \times 2^n + c_2 \times 3^n$ satisfies the recurrence as well. It is now possible to use the values of u_1 and u_2 to find the constants:

$$u_1 = 1 \Rightarrow 2c_1 + 3c_2 = 1$$
$$u_2 = -1 \Rightarrow 4c_1 + 9c_2 = -1$$

Solving these two equations gives $c_1 = 2, c_2 = -1$, so the *n*th term of the sequence is given by $u_n = 2 \times 2^n - 3^n$.

We can apply the same method to any recurrence relation of the form $u_{n+2} = au_{n+1} + bu_n$. Trying a solution of the form $u_n = c \times k^n$

will result in a quadratic equation $k^2 = ak + b$. This is called the **auxiliary equation**. The full method is summarised below.

KEY POINT 8.2

To solve a second order recurrence relation:
$$u_{n+2} = au_{n+1} + bu_n$$

- Find the solutions, k_1 and k_2, of the auxiliary equation:
$$k^2 = ak + b$$
- The general solution is $u_n = c_1 k_1^n + c_2 k_2^n$.
- Use the values of u_1 and u_2 to find the values of c_1 and c_2.

In the above example the auxiliary equation had two distinct real roots. We will see later how to deal with the case of repeated roots or complex roots. First let us apply the method to find the formula for the nth term of the Fibonacci sequence.

Worked example 8.4

Solve the recurrence relation $u_{n+2} = u_{n+1} + u_n$ with $u_1 = u_2 = 1$.

Write down the auxiliary equation and solve it

$u_n = c \times k^n$ where

$$k^2 = k + 1$$
$$\Rightarrow k^2 - k - 1 = 0$$
$$\Rightarrow k = \frac{1 \pm \sqrt{5}}{2}$$

$$u_n = c_1 \left(\frac{1+\sqrt{5}}{2}\right)^n + c_2 \left(\frac{1-\sqrt{5}}{2}\right)^n$$

Use u_1 and u_2

$$u_1 = 1: c_1 \frac{1+\sqrt{5}}{2} + c_2 \frac{1-\sqrt{5}}{2} = 1 \qquad [1]$$

$$u_2 = 1: c_1 \left(\frac{1+\sqrt{5}}{2}\right)^2 + c_2 \left(\frac{1-\sqrt{5}}{2}\right)^2 = 1$$

$$\Leftrightarrow c_1 \frac{3+\sqrt{5}}{2} + c_2 \frac{3-\sqrt{5}}{2} = 1 \qquad [2]$$

If we subtract the two equations we can eliminate $\sqrt{5}$

$[2] - [1] \Rightarrow c_1 + c_2 = 0 \Rightarrow c_2 = -c_1$

$[1] \Rightarrow c_1 \frac{1+\sqrt{5}}{2} - c_1 \frac{1-\sqrt{5}}{2} = 1$

$\Leftrightarrow c_1 \sqrt{5} = 1$

$\therefore c_1 = \frac{1}{\sqrt{5}}, c_2 = -\frac{1}{\sqrt{5}}$

So $u_n = \frac{1}{\sqrt{5}} \left(\left(\frac{1+\sqrt{5}}{2}\right)^n - \left(\frac{1-\sqrt{5}}{2}\right)^n \right)$

This method also works when the roots of the auxiliary equation are complex. The constants c_1 and c_2 will be such that the imaginary parts cancel and all u_n are real.

Worked example 8.5

Solve the recurrence relation $u_{n+2} + 4u_n = 0$ with $u_1 = 0, u_2 = 1$.

Write down the auxiliary equation and solve it

$$k^2 + 4 = 0$$
$$\Rightarrow k = \pm 2i$$
$$u_n = c_1(2i)^n + c_2(-2i)^n$$

Use the values of u_1 and u_2

$u_1 = 0 \Rightarrow 2c_1 - 2c_2 i = 0$ [1]
$u_2 = 1 \Rightarrow -4c_1 - 4c_2 = 1$ [2]

$[1] \Rightarrow c_1 = c_2$
$[2] \Rightarrow -8c_1 = 1 \Rightarrow c_1 = c_2 = -\dfrac{1}{8}$

$$\therefore u_n = -\dfrac{1}{8}\left((2i)^n + (-2i)^n\right)$$

Raising a complex number to a power is easier if it is written in polar form

$$= -\dfrac{1}{8}\left(\left(2\operatorname{cis}\dfrac{\pi}{2}\right)^n + \left(2\operatorname{cis}\dfrac{-\pi}{2}\right)^n\right)$$

$$= -\dfrac{2^n}{8}\left(\operatorname{cis}\dfrac{n\pi}{2} + \operatorname{cis}\dfrac{-n\pi}{2}\right)$$

$\operatorname{cis}\theta + \operatorname{cis}(-\theta) = 2\cos\theta$

$$= -\dfrac{2^n}{8} \times 2\cos\dfrac{n\pi}{2}$$

$$= -2^{n-2}\cos\dfrac{n\pi}{2}$$

If the last answer seems complicated, you can write out the first few terms to see that the sequence is correct. The final answer confirms that all terms of the sequences are real numbers. However, you won't always have to simplify fully, in most cases $u_n = -\dfrac{1}{8}\left((2i)^n + (-2i)^n\right)$ would be an acceptable answer.

We now look at what happens when the auxiliary equation has a repeated root.

Consider the recurrence relation $u_{n+2} = 6u_{n+1} - 9u_n$ with $u_1 = 6, u_2 = 9$. The auxiliary equation is $k^2 - 6k + 9 = 0$ and has only one root, $k = 3$. If we try to set $u_n = c \times 3^n$, then $u_1 = 6$ implies $c = 2$, but then $u_2 \neq 9$. So we need to modify the solution slightly. If we try the next simplest form, $u_n = (c + dn) \times 3^n$, we can use the values of u_1 and u_2 to find constants c and d:

$$u_1 = 6 \Rightarrow (c+d) \times 3 = 6$$
$$u_2 = 9 \Rightarrow (c+2d) \times 9 = 9$$

Solving this gives $c = 3, d = -1$. You can check that $u_n = (3-n)3^n$ satisfies the recurrence relation. This form of the solution will work whenever the auxiliary equation has a repeated root.

KEY POINT 8.3

To solve a second order linear homogeneous recurrence relation when the auxiliary equation has a repeated root k, set $u_n = (c+dn)k^n$.

Worked example 8.6

Solve the recurrence relation $u_{n+2} = 2u_{n+1} - u_n$ given that $u_1 = 1, u_2 = 2$.

Write down the auxiliary equation and solve it

$$k^2 - 2k + 1 = 0 \Rightarrow k = 1$$

Let $u_n = (c + dn) \times 1^n$

Use the values of u_1 and u_2

Then
$$u_1 = 1 \Rightarrow c + d = 1$$
$$u_2 = 2 \Rightarrow c + 2d = 2$$
$$\therefore c = 0, d = 1$$

So $u_n = n$

Exercise 8C

1. Solve the following second order recurrence relations:
   (a) $u_{n+2} = 5u_{n+1} - 6u_n$; $u_1 = 5, u_2 = 13$
   (b) $u_{n+2} = 4u_n$, $u_1 = 4, u_2 = 0$
   (c) $u_{n+2} = 3u_{n+1} - 2u_n$, $u_1 = 9, u_2 = 13$

2. Find the formula for the nth terms of the sequence given by the recurrence relation:
   (a) $u_{n+2} - 4u_{n+1} + 4u_n = 0$, $u_1 = 4, u_2 = 12$
   (b) $u_{n+2} = 2u_{n+1} - u_n$, $u_1 = 5, u_2 = 7$

3. Solve the following recurrence relations, leaving your answer in the complex form.
   (a) $u_{n+2} = 2(u_{n+1} - u_n)$, $u_1 = -6$, $u_2 = 0$
   (b) $u_{n+2} = 4u_{n+1} - 13u_n$, $u_1 = -10$, $u_2 = -40$

4. Solve the following recurrence relations and write the solutions explicitly in real form.
   (a) $u_{n+2} = u_{n+1} - u_n$, $u_1 = 1, u_2 = -1$
   (b) $u_{n+2} = 2(u_{n+1} - u_n)$, $u_1 = -6, u_2 = -12$

5. A sequence is defined by the recurrence relation $u_{n+2} = 4u_{n+1} - 2u_n$ for $n \geq 1$, and $u_1 = 1$, $u_2 = 3$. By solving the recurrence relation find an expression for u_n in terms of n.

   [11 marks]

6. Two sequences, a_n and b_n, satisfy the recurrence relations
   $$a_{n+1} = 3a_n + b_n \qquad b_{n+1} = 5a_n - b_n$$
   with $a_1 = 6$, $b_1 = -6$.
   (a) Find the value of a_2.
   (b) Show that $a_{n+2} = 2a_{n+1} + 8a_n$.
   (c) Solve the second order recurrence relation for a_n.
   (d) Hence find an expression b_n in terms of n.   *[18 marks]*

8D Modelling using recurrence relations

In this section we will look at some examples of the application of recurrence relations. First order recurrence relations can be used to model situations that involve repeated percentage increases, for example savings accounts or debt repayment schemes.

Worked example 8.7

A savings account pays 0.3% monthly interest added to the account at the end of each month. At the start of each month $100 is paid into the account. Let u_n be the amount of money in the account at the end of month n (after the interest has been paid). Find an expression for u_n in terms of n and hence calculate the amount of money in the account after two years.

| We can find a recurrence relating u_{n+1} to u_n. In month $n + 1$, add 100 and then increase by 0.3% | $u_{n+1} = 1.003(u_n + 100)$ |

continued . . .

> *This is a linear recurrence relation, so we know what form of solution to try*

Set $u_n = c \times 1.003^n + d$:
$c \times 1.003^{n+1} + d = 1.003c \times 1.003^n$
$\qquad\qquad\qquad + 1.003d + 100.3$
$\Rightarrow -0.003d = 100.3$
$\Rightarrow d = -33433\frac{1}{3}$

> *Find the first term and use it to find c*

At the end of first month
$u_1 = 100 \times 1.003 = 100.3$
$c \times 1.003^1 - 33433\frac{1}{3} = 100.3$
$\Rightarrow c = 33433\frac{1}{3}$
$\therefore u_n = 33433\frac{1}{3}(1.003^n - 1)$

> *'After 2 years' is the end of month 24*

After 2 years:
$u_{24} = 2492$
There will be $2492 in the account.

We can also use recurrence relations to solve some counting problems. In fact the Fibonacci sequence was first written down to model the size of a rabbit population. We look at this in the next example.

Worked example 8.8

A farmer starts with a pair of rabbits. Assume rabbits do not breed in their first year, but from the second year onwards each pair produces one pair per year, a male and a female.

(a) Find a second order recurrence relation for the number of pairs of rabbits, u_n in year n.

(b) Hence find how many pairs of rabbits the farmer will have after ten years (assuming all survive).

> *In year n, there are all the rabbits from the previous year plus all the new ones born that year*

(a) The number of pairs in year n is:
all the rabbits from the previous year (u_{n-1})
PLUS
new rabbits (u_{n-2}, because they only born to pairs which are two or more years old)
$\therefore u_n = u_{n-1} + u_{n-2}$

continued . . .

> We need the starting values

(b) Year 1: $u_1 = 1$
Year 2: $u_2 = 1$

> We recognise this as the Fibonacci sequence for which we already know the formula

Fibonacci sequence:
$$u_n = \frac{1}{\sqrt{5}}\left(\left(\frac{1+\sqrt{5}}{2}\right)^n - \left(\frac{1-\sqrt{5}}{2}\right)^n\right)$$

Hence $u_{10} = 55$

There are many other recurrence relations that model population growth, taking into account various factors such as death rate and competition for resources. Models that involve two interacting species give particularly interesting results. Find out about the Lotka-Volterra equations for the predator-prey model.

Exercise 8D

1. £1000 is invested in a bank account, which pays compound interest at the rate of 4% per annum. By first writing a recurrence relating the amount of money in year $n + 1$ to the amount of money in year n, find how much the investment will be worth at the end of the 15th year (after the interest is added). [8 marks]

2. A savings account pays 5% interest per year. At the start of each year $2000 is paid into the account and the interest is added at the end of the year. Let u_n be the amount of money in the account in year n, after the money for that year is paid in but before the interest is added. By solving a recurrence relation find an expression for u_n in terms of n. [10 marks]

3. A loan of €16 000 is to be paid off in monthly instalments of €350. The interest charged on the loan is 1% per month, and is added *before* the payment for that month is made. Let u_n be the amount owed at the start of month n (so $u_1 = 16\,000$).
   (a) Explain why $u_{n+1} = 1.01 u_n - 350$.
   (b) Solve the above recurrence relation.
   (c) Hence find how many months it will take for the debt to be paid off. [11 marks]

4. Chung climbs up the stairs either one or two steps at a time. Let u_n be the number of ways in which she can reach the nth step.
   (a) Explain why $u_n = u_{n-1} + u_{n-2}$.
   (b) Write down the values of u_1 and u_2.
   (c) Hence find the number of different ways Chung can climb a flight of 12 stairs. *[10 marks]*

5. Omar decides to vary the amount of time he spends on his mathematics homework so that each day he spends the average of the amount of time that he spent on the previous two days. Let t_n be amount of time, in minutes, Omar spent on his homework on day n.
   (a) Write down a recurrence relation for t_{n+2} in terms of t_{n+1} and t_n.
   (b) Given that Omar spent 15 minutes on his homework on day 1 and 27 minutes on day 2, find an expression for the time he spends on his homework on day n.
   (c) Describe the long-term behaviour of the sequence t_n. *[11 marks]*

6. n lines are drawn in the plane so that no two are parallel and no three pass through the same point. Let P_n be the number of intersection points.
   (a) Explain why $P_{n+1} = P_n + n$.
   (b) Write down the value of P_2.
   (c) Prove by induction that $P_n = \dfrac{n^2 - n}{2}$ for all $n \geq 2$. *[10 marks]*

7. Let u_n be the number of sequences consisting of 0s and 1s, which do not contain two consecutive 0s.
   (a) By considering the possibilities for the last digit of a string of length n, explain why $u_n = u_{n-1} + u_{n-2}$.
   (b) Write down the values of u_1 and u_2.
   (c) Hence find the number of 16-digit strings consisting of 0s and 1s which do not contain two consecutive 0s. *[10 marks]*

8. In the game of *Towers of Hanoi* there are n rings of different sizes and three pins. The rings start on the first pin, arranged in order of size so that the largest one is at the bottom. The object of the game is to end up with all rings on a different pin, still in decreasing order of size. At no point can a larger ring be placed on top of a smaller ring.
   Let H_n be the minimum number of moves needed to complete the game with n rings.
   (a) Find the values of H_1 and H_2.

The strategy for the game is as follows:
- Move all rings, other than the largest one, to the second pin.
- Move the largest ring to the third pin.
- Move all the other rings from the second to the third pin.

(b) Explain why, if this strategy is followed, $H_n = 2H_{n-1} + 1$.

(c) Find an expression for H_n in terms of n, and hence find the minimum number of moves needed to complete the game with 10 rings. *[13 marks]*

9. A bank charges 5% annual interest on a loan. At the end of each year, the interest is added and then a fixed amount, R, is paid off.

(a) If the amount borrowed is $1000, show that the amount owed at the start of year n is $(1000 - 20R)(1.05)^{n-1} + 20R$.

(b) Find the minimum value of R, correct to the nearest dollar, so that the loan is completely repaid after 10 years.

(c) For this value of R, what is the total amount repaid (to the nearest dollar)?

(d) What is the minimum annual repayment required so that the loan is eventually paid off? *[12 marks]*

Summary

In this chapter we looked at methods for solving linear **recurrence relations**.

- A first order linear recurrence $u_{n+1} = au_n + b$ has solution of the form $u_n = ca^n + d$.

- To solve a second order linear homogeneous recurrence $u_{n+2} = au_{n+1} + bu_n$ we first need to solve the auxiliary equation $k^2 = ak + b$.
    - If the equation has two distinct roots k_1, k_2 then the solution is $u_n = c_1 k_1^n + c_2 k_2^n$.
    - If the equation has a repeated root then the solution is $u_n = (c + dn)k^n$.

- The constants can be found by substituting into the recurrence relation and using starting values of u_n.

- You need to be able to write down recurrence relations to model counting problems and financial situations.

Mixed examination practice 8

1. Find an expression for u_n in terms of n for the sequence defined by
   $u_1 = 0, u_{n+1} = 5u_n + 1$ for $n \geq 1$. [8 marks]

2. The value of a car decreases by 8% each year.
   (a) Write down an equation for the value of the car after n years, u_n, in terms of its value in the previous year.
   (b) Given that the value of the car after one year was $8500 find how long it will take for it to fall below $4000. [9 marks]

3. Solve the recurrence relation $u_{n+2} = 5u_{n+1} - 6u_n$ given that $u_1 = 1$ and $u_2 = 3$. [10 marks]

4. Solve the recurrence relation $u_{n+2} + 4u_{n+1} + 4u_n = 0$ with $u_1 = -4$ and $u_2 = 4$. [10 marks]

5. Given that $u_1 = 6, u_2 = -36$ and $u_{n+2} + 9u_n = 0$ for $n \geq 1$, find an expression for u_n in terms of n. [10 marks]

6. Solve the recurrence relation $a_{n+1} = \frac{1}{2}(a_{n-1} + a_n)$ given that $a_1 = 1, a_2 = 4$. [10 marks]

7. A magic crystal produces several new crystals every day. The crystals that were produced the previous day produce only one new crystal, but the older ones produce 9 new crystals each.
   (a) If c_n is the number of crystals on day n:
       (i) Write down the numbers of crystals on days $n - 1$ and $n - 2$.
       (ii) Write down the number of crystals which are exactly one day old on day n.
       (iii) Find an expression for the total number of new crystals created on day n.
       (iv) Hence explain why $u_n = 2u_{n-1} + 8u_{n-2}$.
   (b) Harry was given two newly-formed magic crystals on the first day of term.
       (i) How many crystals does he have on the second day?
       (ii) Find an expression for the number of crystals Harry has on the nth day of term. [16 marks]

8. A sequence has the first term $a_1 = \frac{b}{3}$ and satisfies the recurrence relation $a_{n+1} = 3a_n - b$.

   Find an expression for a_n in terms of n and b. [6 marks]

9. n straight lines are drawn in the plane so that no two are parallel and no three pass through the same point. They divide the plane into u_n regions.
   (a) Explain why $u_{n+1} = u_n + n + 1$.
   (b) Prove by induction that $u_n = \frac{1}{2}n^2 + \frac{1}{2}n + 1$. [8 marks]

Topic 10 – Option: Discrete mathematics

9 Summary and mixed examination practice

Introductory problem revisited

> Suppose you have a large supply of 20 cent and 30 cent stamps. In how many different ways can you make up $5 postage?

Let x and y be the number of 20 cent and 30 cent stamps, respectively. We want to solve the equation $20x + 30y = 500$ with x and y non-negative integers. This is a linear Diophantine equation, so we use the method from chapter 4.
As $\gcd(20, 30) = 10$, we write $10 = 20(-1) + 30(1)$.
Hence one solution of the equation is $x = -50, y = 50$.
The general solution is $x = -50 + 3k, y = 50 - 2k$.
We need $x, y \geq 0$ and, remembering that x, y are integers, this gives $k \geq 17$ and $k \leq 25$. There are 9 pairs (x, y) satisfying these conditions, so there are 9 different ways to make up the required postage.

Although number theory and graph theory have a surprising number of real world applications, their mathematical significance is due to the beauty of the proofs which are associated with these areas. In this option we focussed on three new types of proof which allowed us to justify the methods we use: *proof by contradiction*, the *pigeonhole principle* and *strong induction*.

The main thrust of the number theory section was working towards solving *Diophantine equations*. To do this, the *Euclidean algorithm* was needed which arose based upon the study of *greatest common divisors*.

Modular arithmetic, the study of remainders when a number is divided, provides another useful tool to look at divisibility. Easier modular arithmetic problems can be solved using linear congruences. One application of Diophantine equations is in the solution of hard problems in modular arithmetic, particularly the *Chinese remainder theorem*. Also, *Fermat's little theorem* provides a very powerful tool for determining the remainder when we are working with powers of numbers.

Graphs are a way of representing information about connections between objects. Once a graph has been drawn several questions can be asked about it, such as:

- Can a walk around the graph go through every vertex exactly once (*Hamiltonian path*)?
- Can a walk around the graph go along every edge exactly once (*Eulerian trail*)?

There are also optimisation problems which can be solved such as:

- Finding the minimum spanning tree (solved using *Kruskal's algorithm*)
- Finding the shortest path between two vertices (solved using *Dijkstra's algorithm*)

- Finding the shortest route around a graph using each edge at least once (the *Chinese postman problem*, solved using the *Route inspection algorithm*)
- Finding the shortest route which visits every vertex and returns to the starting point (the *travelling salesman problem*). This problem cannot in general be efficiently solved, but we can find upper and lower bounds.

Finally, *recurrence relations* are a way of defining sequences based upon previous terms in the sequence. They can be solved by applying standard trial functions and fixing the constants. Sequences defined using recurrence relations arise both within mathematics and in applied fields such as finance and biology.

Mixed examination practice 9

1. (a) Show that $2^{42} - 1$ is divisible by 43.
   (b) Show that if $d \mid n$ then $(2^d - 1) \mid (2^n - 1)$.
   (c) Hence show that $2^{42} - 1$ is divisible by 63. [8 marks]

2. A simple, connected graph has 5 vertices, each with the same degree, $d > 0$.
   (a) What are the possible values of d? Justify your answer.
   (b) For each possible value of d:
      (i) Draw an example of such a graph.
      (ii) State whether or not your graph is Eulerian, and if it is find an Eulerian circuit.
   (c) For the graph with the largest possible value of d find a Hamiltonian cycle. [12 marks]

3. (a) A number N has digits $(a_k a_{k-1} \ldots a_1 a_0)$, so that:
   $N = a_k 10^k + a_{k-1} 10^{k-1} + \ldots + 10a_1 + a_0$. Prove that if N is divisible by 3 then $a_k + a_{k-1} + \ldots + a_1 + a_0$ is also divisible by 3.
   (b) State a similar result if N is divisible by 11.
   (c) Find all possible values of digits a and b so that the number $(1991ab)$ is divisible by 33.
   (d) Show that a number is divisible by 5 if and only if the sum of its base 6 digits is divisible by 5.
   (e) Hence show that $(223412)_6$ is not divisible by 5. [21 marks]

4. (a) Use the Eulidean algorithm to find $\gcd(610, 366)$.
   (b) Solve the linear congruence $366x \equiv 732 \pmod{610}$. [13 marks]

5. (a) Define the complement of a graph.
   (b) If H is a simple graph with 20 edges and its complement has 16 edges, how many vertices does H have? [6 marks]

6. (a) Define the following terms:
      (i) bipartite graph
      (ii) degree of a vertex.

The diagram shows two graphs, K and L.

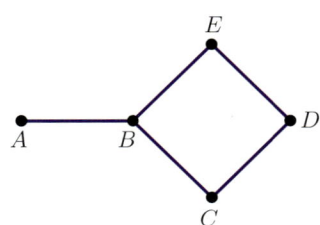
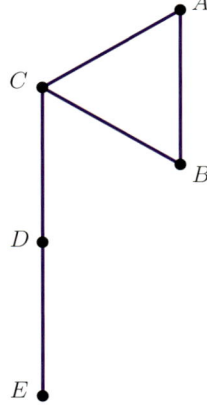

(b) Determine whether or not K is bipartite.

(c) Find an Eulerian trail in L. [6 marks]

7. (a) Use Fermat's little theorem to prove that $x \equiv a^{p-2}b \pmod{p}$ is a solution of the linear congruence $ax \equiv b \pmod{p}$, where p is a prime which does not divide a.

(b) Hence, or otherwise, solve $2x \equiv 11 \pmod{17}$.

(c) Solve the system of linear congruences:
$$2x \equiv 11 \pmod{17}, \ 5x \equiv 1 \pmod{11}$$ [10 marks]

8. (a) Show that if a base 12 number is divisible by 9 then the number formed by its last two digits is divisible by 9.

(b) (i) Find the remainder when 3^{50} is divided by 13.

(ii) Find the last digit in the base 13 expansion of 3^{50}.

(c) (i) Show that if a base 13 number is divisible by 12 then the sum of its digits is divisible by 12.

(ii) Hence show that $(3114CC)_{13}$ is not divisible by 12. [16 marks]

9. (a) Show that the number of distinct Hamiltonian cycles in a complete graph with n vertices is $\frac{1}{2}(n-1)!$

(b) List all the Hamiltonian cycles for the graph shown in the diagram.

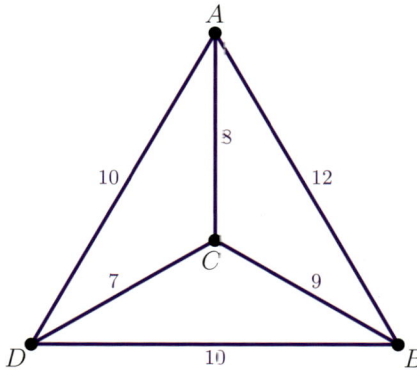

(c) Hence solve the travelling salesman problem for this graph. [9 marks]

10. Graph K is shown in the diagram.

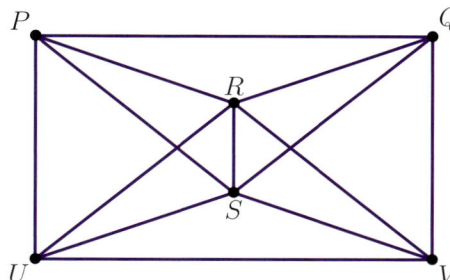

(a) Show that K is not planar, but that every subgraph of K is planar.

(b) Which edge should be removed from K so that the resulting graph is Eulerian?

(c) Find a spanning tree for K.

(d) Show that K has a Hamiltonian cycle.

11. (a) Find two integers m and n such that $90m + 48n = \gcd(90, 48)$.

(b) (i) Find the general solution of the Diophantine equation
$$90x + 48y = 624.$$

(ii) Show that there are no solutions with both x and y positive.

(c) Solve the linear congruence $48x \equiv 54 \pmod{90}$. List all the non-congruent solutions $\pmod{90}$.

12.

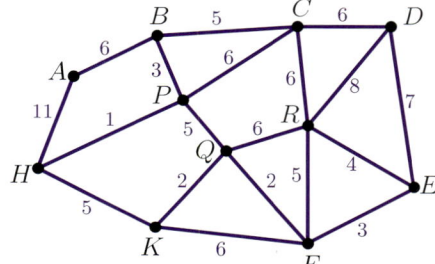

The weighted graph G is shown above. Graph G' is produced by deleting vertex A from G.

(a) Use Kruskal's algorithm to find the minimum spanning tree of graph G' and state its weight.

(b) Hence find the weight of a lower bound for the Hamiltonian cycle in G beginning at vertex A.

(c) Prove for a complete graph with n vertices (with $n \geq 3$), that no more than $\dfrac{(n-1)!}{2}$ Hamiltonian cycles have to be examined to find the Hamiltonian cycle of least weight.

(d) How many cycles in G would have to be examined to find the one with the least weight?

[12 marks]

(© IB Organization 2007)

13. For the graph shown below:

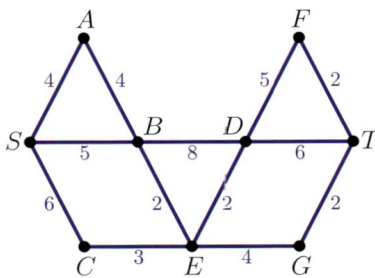

   (a) Explain why it is not possible to find a route, starting and finishing at A, which uses each edge exactly once.
   (b) Use Dijkstra's algorithm to find the length of the shortest path from S to T.
   (c) Hence find the length of the shortest route which starts at A, goes over each edge at least once, and returns to A. Give an example of such a route.
   (d) Show that the number of vertices of odd degree in a graph must be even.
   [17 marks]

14. (a) Draw the complete graph with 5 vertices, κ_5.
    (b) Explain why a bipartite graph cannot contain cycles of odd length.
    (c) Hence show that κ_5 is not bipartite.
    (d) Use the result of part (b) to prove that the complete bipartite graph $\kappa_{4,3}$ is not Hamiltonian.
    (e) For what values of m, n is the graph $\kappa_{m,n}$ Hamiltonian? Justify your answer.
    [12 marks]

15. For the graph shown in the diagram:

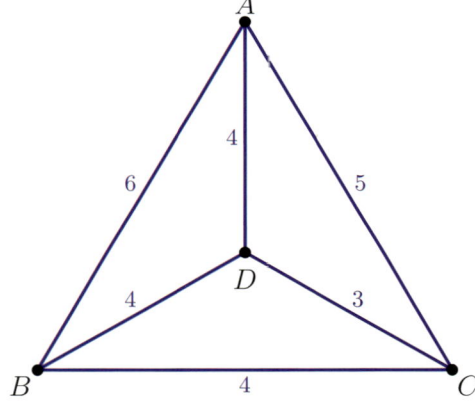

    (a) Explain why this graph is not Eulerian.
    (b) Find the minimum length of a route which uses each edge exactly once and returns to the starting point.
    [6 marks]

16. (a) Use the Euclidean algorithm to find gcd(66, 42).
    (b) Explain why the equation $66x + 42y = 9$ has no integer solutions.
    (c) For which values of m does the equation $66x + 42y = m$ have integer solutions?
    (d) Solve the equation for $m = 18$.
    [12 marks]

17. (a) Prove that for two positive integers a and b, $\text{lcm}(a,b) \times \gcd(a,b) = ab$.
    (b) Use Euclid's algorithm to show that $7n+2$ and $4n+1$ are always coprime.
    (c) Use the result of part (b) to find $\text{lcm}(702, 401)$. *[12 marks]*

18. (a) Prove that in a planar graph, $e \leq 3v - 6$.
    (b) G is a simple graph with $n \geq 3$ vertices and e edges such that both G and its complement, G', are connected and planar.
        (i) Write down the number of edges in G'.
        (ii) Show that $n \leq 10$. *[10 marks]*

19. Consider this graph:

    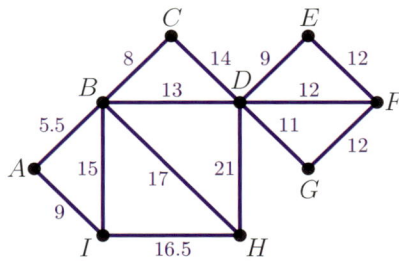

    (a) Find a minimum spanning tree for this graph. Draw your tree and state its weight.
    (b) How many spanning trees are there of the same length as the tree you found in part (a)? *[8 marks]*

20. (a) Solve the simultaneous congruences $3x \equiv 6 \pmod{5}$, $4x \equiv 6 \pmod 2$.
    (b) Consider the simultaneous congruences $3x \equiv 6 \pmod 5$, $4x \equiv 6 \pmod 2$, $x \equiv 7 \pmod{11}$. How many non-congruent solutions $(\text{mod } 550)$ are there? Explain your reasoning. *[7 marks]*

21. A sequence is given by the recurrence relation $u_{n+2} = u_{n+1} + 6u_n$ with $u_1 = -1, u_2 = 17$.
    (a) Write down the first five terms of the sequence.
    (b) Solve the recurrence relation. *[10 marks]*

22. (a) The weighted graph H is shown below.

    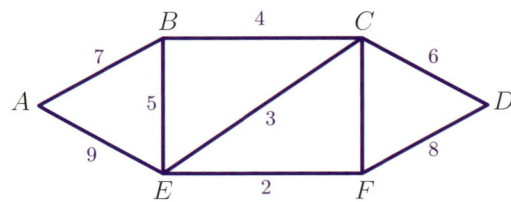

    Use Kruskal's Algorithm, indicating the order in which the edges are added, to find and draw the minimum spanning tree for H.

(b) (i) A tree has v vertices. State the number of edges in the tree, justifying your answer.

(ii) We will call a graph with v vertices a 'forest' if it consists of c components each of which is a tree.

Here is an example of a forest with 4 components.

How many edges will a forest with v vertices and c components have?

(c) A graph has an odd number of vertices. Prove that the degree of at least one of the vertices must be even. *[17 marks]*

(© IB Organization 2008)

23. (a) Prove that a tree with n vertices has $n-1$ edges.

(b) The table shows distances (in metres) between five workstations in an office.

	A	B	C	D	E
A		3	6	3	8
B	3		3	5	5
C	6	3		4	6
D	3	5	4		3
E	8	5	6	3	

(i) Find the minimum spanning tree for the graph represented by this table.

(ii) State the minimum length of cable required to connect all the workstations.

(c) (i) Explain how you can tell that the graph is Eulerian.

(ii) Find an Eulerian cycle and state its length. *[18 marks]*

24. Consider the weighted graph with the weights of the edges shown in the following table:

	A	B	C	D	E	F
A	-	36	41	44	50	52
B	36	-	38	42	48	40
C	41	38	-	35	41	52
D	44	42	35	-	44	50
E	50	48	41	44	-	48
F	52	40	52	50	48	-

(a) Use Kruskal's algorithm to find the minimum spanning tree.

(b) For the travelling salesman problem on this graph:

(i) Remove vertex A to find a lower bound.

(ii) Remove vertex B to find another lower bound.

(iii) State which of the two lower bounds is better.

(c) By considering the cycle *ABCDEFA* find an upper bound, and hence write an inequality satisfied by the solution of the travelling salesman problem.

[15 marks]

25. Julie borrowed £1050 which is to be paid back with the annual interest rate of 5%. At the end of each year, Julie pays back £100 before the interest is added. Let u_n be the amount Julie owes at the start of year n.

    (a) Explain why $u_{n+1} = 1.05u_n - 105$.
    (b) Find an expression for u_n in terms of n.
    (c) Find how long it will take for Julie to pay off the debt. *[12 marks]*

Answers

ANSWER HINT

For this Option, when you are asked to prove or show, there will not be any answers supplied; in some cases hints have been provided.

Chapter 1

Exercise 1A

1. Assume that n^2 is even but n is odd, and consider $n \times n$.
2. Assume that there are such numbers and factorise the expression.
3. Assume that $\log_2 5 = \dfrac{p}{q}$ and rearrange this expression to get even = odd.
4. Suppose that L is the largest even integer and consider $L + 2$.
5. If this was not true, all of them would be under 18; what can you say about the average?
6. Assume that $a + b = c$ where a and c are rational and b is irrational, and consider $c - a$.
7. Assume that $\hat{C} \neq 90°$, and consider two possible cases: $\hat{C} < 90°$ and $\hat{C} > 90°$. In each case draw a perpendicular line from C and apply Pythagoras to the resulting triangle.
8. (a) -0.682
   (b) Write $x = \dfrac{p}{q}$ and show that p and q must both be even.

Exercise 1B

1. 11
2. Think about possible remainders when a number is divided by 7.
3. Let the 'pigeonholes' be (1 and 8), (2 and 7), (3 and 6) and (4 and 5).
4. What happens when you add 10 numbers which have the same last digit?
5. (b) How many different numbers of friends are possible?
6. Cut along a great circle passing through two of the points.
7. Consider an equilateral triangle of side 1 cm.
8. Divide the square into 25 equal squares and find the radius of the circle which covers one of the squares.
9. Pick one vertex and look at the five lines from it. Three of them must be the same colour. Then consider the three endpoints of those lines and the three lines connecting them.

Exercise 1C

4. Express F_{n+1} in terms of F_n and look at the last digit.
6. You can go from $n - 4$ to n. How many base cases are needed?
7. In the inductive step, use proof by contradiction and double angle identity.
9. Think about how the number of regions increases when another line is added.

Chapter 2

Exercise 2A

1. (a) (i) 3, 4   (ii) 4, 11
   (b) (i) 3   (ii) 3
   (c) (i) 3, 4   (ii) 4
   (d) (i) 4, 11   (ii) 4, 11
2. (a) (i) $(a, b) = (0,0), (9,0), (5,4), (1,8)$
       (ii) $(3,2), (8,6)$
   (b) (i) $(0,8), (4,4), (8,0)$
       (ii) $(2,8), (6,4)$
3. $(a,b) = (0,7), (4,0), (7,3)$
5. Write $q = kp$
6. Factorise the expression
9. 525, 555, 585
10. (a) n a multiple of 9   (b) n even

Exercise 2B

1. (a) (i) 4, 612   (ii) 7, 210
   (b) (i) 45, 900   (ii) 45, 1080
   (c) (i) 1, 4536   (ii) 1, 4165
   (d) (i) 28, 56   (ii) 35, 105
   (e) (i) 8, 576   (ii) 9, 54
   (f) (i) $3pq, 18p^2 q^3$
       (ii) $75 pq^2$
3. Write $p = md$, $q = nd$ and show that $d \leq 1$
4. Write $a + b = md$, $a - b = nd$ and show that if $d > 2$ then $d | a, b$

Exercise 2C

1. (a) 1
   (b) 1
   (c) 21
   (d) 80
   (e) 2
2. (a) $m = 3, n = -1$
   (b) $m = -25, n = 8$

(c) $m = -1, n = 1$
(d) $m = 1, n = 0$
(e) $m = 67, n = -29$

3. (b) $x = 11, y = -21$

4. $p = 2, q = -3$

Exercise 2D

1. (a) (i) $2^3 \times 3 \times 5$ (ii) $2^3 \times 5^2$
   (b) (i) $2^2 \times 43$ (ii) $2 \times 3 \times 23$
   (c) (i) 5×31 (ii) 5×47

2. (a) $2 \times 3 \times 3 \times 47$
   (b) (i) 94 (ii) 26 508

Mixed examination practice 2

1. (2,2), (5,2), (8,2), (1,6), (4,6), (7,6)

2. (b) $m = -27, n = 137$ is one possibility

4. (a) $(a-b)(a+b)(a^2+b^2)$

Chapter 3

Exercise 3A

1. (a) (i) 0, 1, 2, 3, 4, 5
       (ii) 0, 1, 2, 3
   (b) (i) 0, 1, 2, 3, 4, 5, 6, 7, 8, 9, A, B
       (ii) 0, 1, 2, 3, 4, 5, 6, 7, 8, 9, A, B, C, D, E

2. (a) (i) 19 (ii) 50
   (b) (i) 313 (ii) 182
   (c) (i) 646 (ii) 1425
   (d) (i) 74 (ii) 199
   (e) (i) 3494 (ii) 436
   (f) (i) 1613 (ii) 287

3. 124

4. 999

Exercise 3B

1. (a) (i) 111 110 (ii) 20 220
   (b) (i) 351 (ii) 1321
   (c) (i) 687 (ii) 2A1
   (d) (i) 4AF (ii) BBC

2. (a) (i) 221
       (ii) 1 000 111 100
   (b) (i) 1 000 111 100
       (ii) 11 020 120
   (c) (i) 3226 (ii) 31E
   (d) (i) 5E6 (ii) 170B

3. 888 888

Exercise 3C

1. (a) (i) 443 (ii) 410
   (b) (i) 1693 (ii) BA0

2. (a) (i) 1065 (ii) 2505
   (b) (i) B2C (ii) 3678

3. (a) 7
   (b) 2, 3, 4, 6, 12
   (c) ends in 00

4. (a) 0, 7
   (b) sum of digits divisible by 13
   (c) $(k,m) = (0,0), (0,D), (7,6)$

Mixed examination practice 3

1. (a) 94 (b) 59F

2. (a) 1 010 101 100 101 111
   (b) 100

3. (a) 120 064

4. (a) 314
   (b) 211 211
   (c) 7056

5. (b) The sum of the digits is divisible by 5
   (c) $(a,b) = (3,0), (0,3), (5,3)$

6. (a) 6170

Chapter 4

Exercise 4A

1. 6 and 9 are both divisible by 3, but 137 is not

2. (a) $x = 2, y = 1$

3. (b) $k = 0$

4. Equation $15 + 9x + 9y = 2007$ has no solution

Exercise 4B

1. a,c,d,f

2. (a) (i) $x = 1, y = -2$
       (ii) $x = 2, y = -3$
   (b) (i) $x = 5, y = -7$
       (ii) $x = 2, y = -3$

3. (a) (i) $x = 2, y = -6$
       (ii) $x = 1, y = -1$
   (b) (i) $x = 3, y = -6$
       (ii) $x = -3, y = 9$

4. (a) 3
   (b) $3 \nmid 28$

5. (a) 6
   (b) Multiples of 6
   (c) $x = 3, y = -5$ (other answers are possible)

6. (a) $\gcd(\lambda, 5) = 1$
   (b) $x = 3, y = -7$ (other answers are possible)

Exercise 4C

1. (a) (i) $x = 1 + 4k, y = -2 - 9k$
       (ii) $x = 2 + 7k, y = -3 - 11k$
   (b) (i) $x = 3 + 12k, y = -7 - 17k$
       (ii) $x = 2 + 7k, y = -3 - 11k$
   (c) (i) $x = 2 + 10k, y = -6 - 33k$
       (ii) $x = 1 + 4k, y = -1 - 9k$
   (d) (i) $x = 3 + 4k, y = -6 - 9k$
       (ii) $x = -3 + 7k, y = 9 - 20k$

2. (a) 6
   (b) $x = 2 - 13k, y = 4 - 27k$

3. (b) $m = 9, n = 13$
   (c) $x = 9 - 38k, y = 13 - 55k$

4. $(26 + 5k, -13 - 3k)$

Exercise 4D

1. (a) $x = -126, y = 84$ (there are others)
   (b) $x = 2, y = 4$

2. (a) 2
   (b) $x = 6 - 37k, y = 5 - 31k$
   (c) x and y are positive for all $k \leq 0$

3. (a) $x = 3 + 13k, y = -5 - 22k$
   (b) $(-10, 17), (3, -5), (16, -27)$

4. (a) Multiples of 3
   (b) Yes, all integer weights
   (c) All weights ≥ 117 and 59 others (investigate!)

Mixed examination practice 4

1. (b) $m = 11, n = -24$
   (c) $x = 220 + 27k, y = -480 + 59k$

2. 51; no solutions as 51 does not divide 41

3. (a) 3
   (c) $x = 25 + 37k, y = -10 - 15k$

4. (a) $\gcd(\lambda, 3) = 1$
   (b) $x = 2 + 3k, y = -1 - 4k$

5. (a) $m = 4, n = -1$ (there are others)
   (b) $x = 4 + 3k, y = -1 - 5k$
   (c) $x = 1, y = 4$ and $x = 4, y = -1$

Chapter 5

Exercise 5A

1. (a) (i) 10   (ii) 6
   (b) (i) 7   (ii) 2
   (c) (i) 4   (ii) 4

2. (a) 1
   (b) 3
   (c) 1
   (d) 0

3. (a) 1, 4, 7
   (b) 3, 8, 13

4. (a) 9
   (b) 6

5. (a) Divisible by 3
   (b) $6k + 1$

Exercise 5B

1. (a) (i) 5   (ii) 4
   (b) (i) 0   (ii) 0
   (c) (i) 2   (ii) 2

2. (a) (i) 3   (ii) 4
   (b) (i) 3   (ii) 4
   (c) (i) 4   (ii) 3
   (d) (i) 6   (ii) 4

3. 2

4. 3

5. 5

Exercise 5C

1. (a) (i) $x \equiv 6 \pmod{11}$
       (ii) $x \equiv 6 \pmod{15}$
   (b) (i) $x \equiv 10 \pmod{11}$
       (ii) $x \equiv 8 \pmod{9}$
   (c) (i) $x \equiv 0 \pmod{3}$
       (ii) $x \equiv 0 \pmod{3}$
   (d) (i) $x \equiv 4 \pmod{9}$
       (ii) $x \equiv 2 \pmod{9}$
   (e) (i) $x \equiv 0 \pmod{3}$
       (ii) $x \equiv 4 \pmod{8}$

2. $x \equiv 4 \pmod{13}$

3. $x \equiv 4 \pmod{7}$

4. (a) $6x = 9k + 4$ is impossible because 3 divides $6x$ and 9 but not 4.
   (b) $x \equiv 2 \pmod{3}$
   (c) $-7, -4, -1, 2, 5, 8$

5. (a) $x \equiv 3, 8, \text{ or } 13 \pmod{15}$
   (b) 7

6. $a = 2$

Exercise 5D

1. (a) (i) $x \equiv 18 \pmod{35}$
       (ii) $x \equiv 24 \pmod{55}$
   (b) (i) $x \equiv 32 \pmod{70}$
       (ii) $x \equiv 21 \pmod{60}$

2. (a) (i) $x \equiv 215 \pmod{209}$
       (ii) $x \equiv 201 \pmod{286}$
   (b) (i) $x \equiv 542 \pmod{630}$
       (ii) $x \equiv 225 \pmod{408}$

3. $x \equiv 5 \pmod{21}$

4. $x \equiv 20 \pmod{105}$

5. (a) 3   (b) $x \equiv 3 \pmod{35}$

6. $x \equiv 4 \pmod{15}$

7. $x \equiv 207 \pmod{527}$

8. (a) Show that $x = 6a + 2 = 9a + 4$ is impossible
   (b) (i) $m = 5 + 3a, n = 3 + 2a$
       (ii) $x \equiv 4 \pmod{18}$

Exercise 5E

1. (a) (i) 9   (ii) 14
   (b) (i) 4   (ii) 5
   (c) (i) 1   (ii) 1
   (d) (i) 2   (ii) 1

2. 4

3. (b) $x \equiv 5 \pmod{13}$
   (c) $x^{12} \equiv 1$ or $0 \pmod{13}$ by FLT

Mixed examination practice 5

1. 9
2. 6
3. $x \equiv 9 \pmod{11}$
4. 1
6. (a) 4   (b) $x \equiv 3 \pmod 8$
7. Apply Fermat's little theorem to find $x^{12} \pmod 7$
8. (a) 24
   (c) 31
9. $x \equiv 28 \pmod{65}$
10. $x \equiv 82 \pmod{170}$
12. (b) 1
    (c) 183
13. (b) $x \equiv 16 \pmod{341}$
14. $k = 2, 15, 28, 41, 54$

Chapter 6

Exercise 6B

1.
	G1	G2	G3	G4	G5	G6
v	4	5	7	7	3	5
e	5	5	8	6	6	6

2.
	A	B	C	D	E	F	G
G1	1	3	3	3			
G2	3	3	1	2	1		
G3	1	4	2	3	2	3	1
G4	1	3	1	1	3	1	2
G5	5	2	5				
G6	2	3	2	3	2		

3.
	G1	G2	G3	G4	G5	G6
Connected	✓		✓	✓	✓	✓
Simple			✓	✓		✓
Complete					✓	
Tree				✓		
Bipartite		✓		✓		✓

4.
G1	A	B	C	D
A	0	1	0	0
B	1	0	1	1
C	0	1	0	2
D	0	1	2	0

G2	A	B	C	D	E
A	1	1	0	0	0
B	1	1	0	0	0
C	0	0	0	1	0
D	0	0	1	0	1
E	0	0	0	1	0

G3	A	B	C	D	E	F	G
A	0	1	0	0	0	0	0
B	1	0	1	0	0	1	1
C	0	1	0	1	0	0	0
D	0	0	1	0	1	1	0
E	0	0	0	1	0	1	0
F	0	1	0	1	1	0	0
G	0	1	0	0	0	0	0

G4	A	B	C	D	E	F	G
A	0	1	0	0	0	0	0
B	1	0	1	0	1	0	0
C	0	1	0	0	0	0	0
D	0	0	0	0	1	0	0
E	0	1	0	1	0	0	1
F	0	0	0	0	0	0	1
G	0	0	0	0	1	1	0

G5	A	B	C
A	1	1	2
B	1	0	1
C	2	1	1

G6	A	B	C	D	E
A	0	1	0	1	0
B	1	0	1	0	1
C	0	1	0	1	0
D	1	0	1	0	1
E	0	1	0	1	0

5. (a) (i)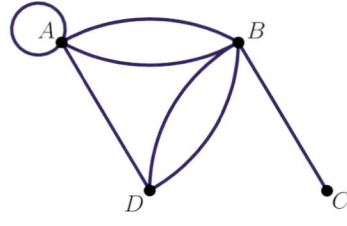

(ii)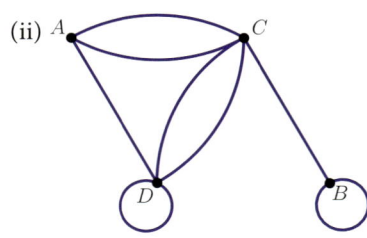

(b) (i)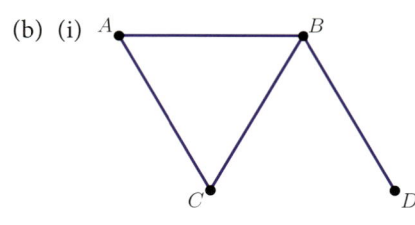

(ii)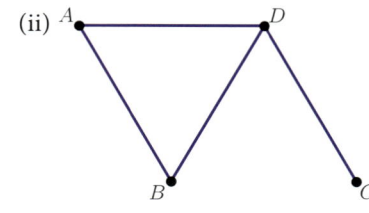

(c) (i)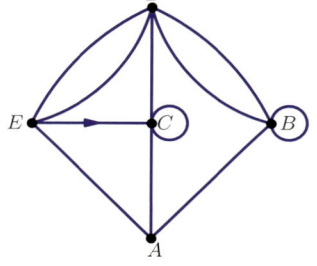

(ii)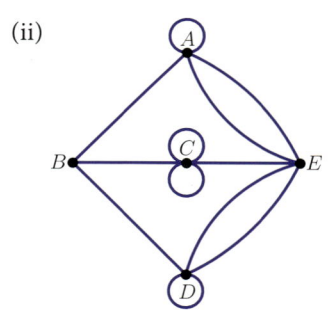

6. (a) (i) A-2, B-3, C-2, D-2, E-2
(ii) A-3, B-2, C-2, D-3
(b) (i) A-4, B-7, C-3, D-7, E-7
(ii) A-9, B-5, C-3, D-3

7. There are many possible answers, for example:

(a)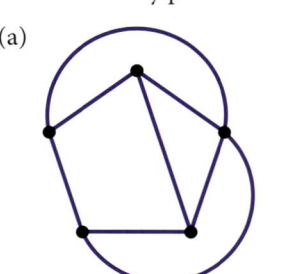

(b)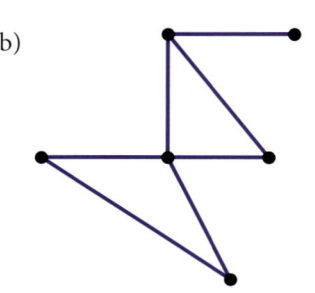

8. (a) A, D, E, G and B, C, F
(b) A, B, D, H and C, E, F, G

9. (a)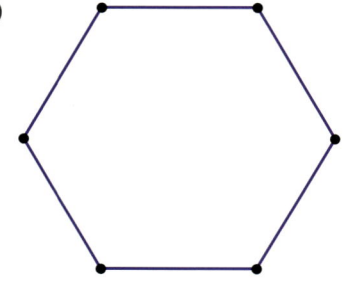

(b)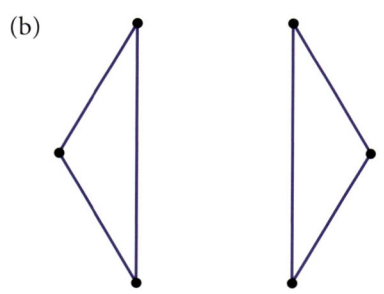

(c)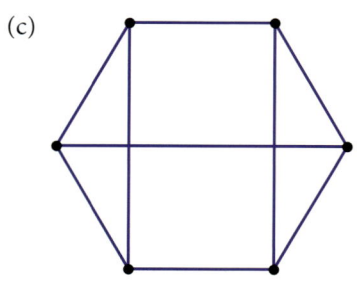

(d)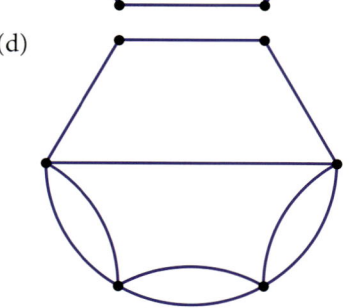

(e)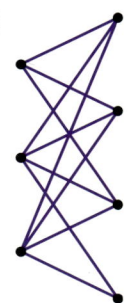

(There are other possible answers)

10. (a)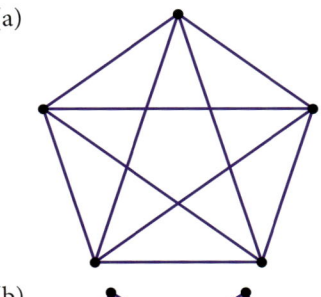

(b)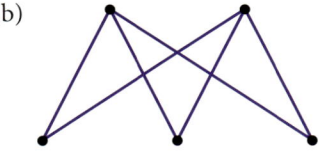

11. $n = 9$

12. (a) $1, n-1$

(c)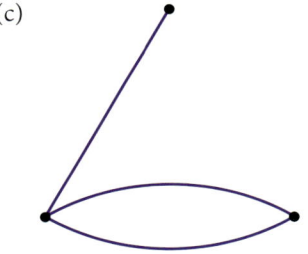

Exercise 6C

2. (a) 2
   (b) 6
   (c) 2
   (d) 8

3. (a)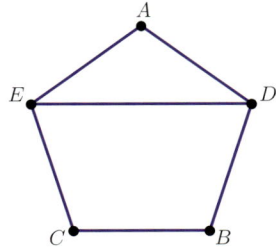

(b)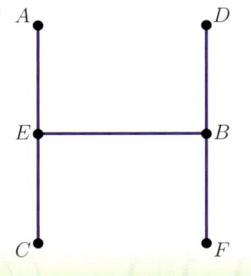

(c)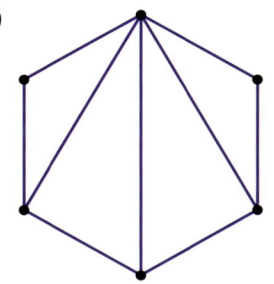

(d)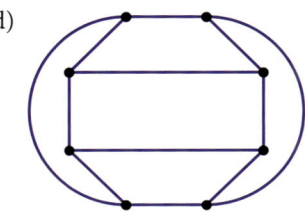

4. (a) 7
   (b)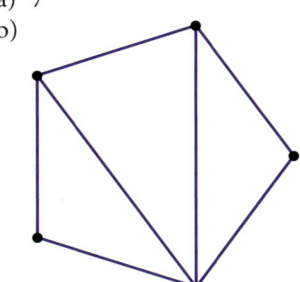

5. (a)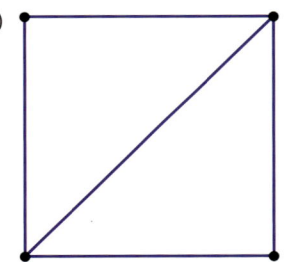

(b) Doesn't exist (odd number of odd vertices)

(c)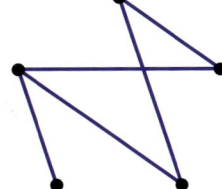

6. (a) 25
   (b) $e > 3v - 6$

Exercise 6D

1. (a) (i)

(ii)

(b) (i)

(ii)

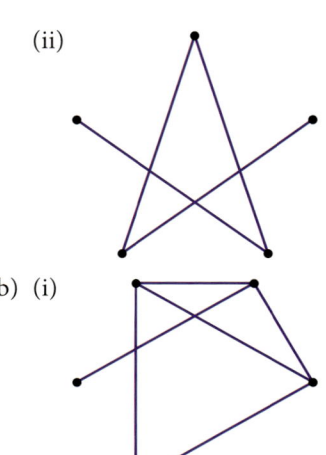

2. (a)

	A	B	C	D
A	0	0	0	1
B	0	0	1	0
C	0	1	0	1
D	1	0	1	0

(b)

	A	B	C	D
A	0	1	0	0
B	1	0	0	1
C	0	0	0	1
D	0	1	1	0

3. (a)

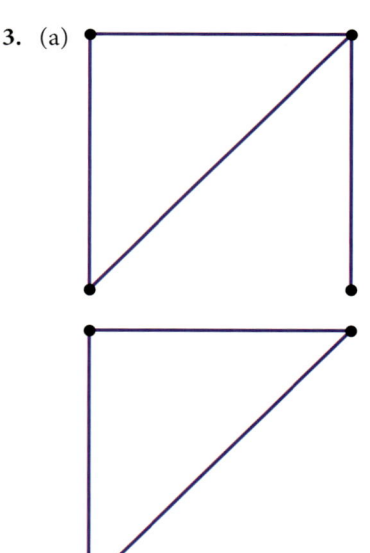

(c)

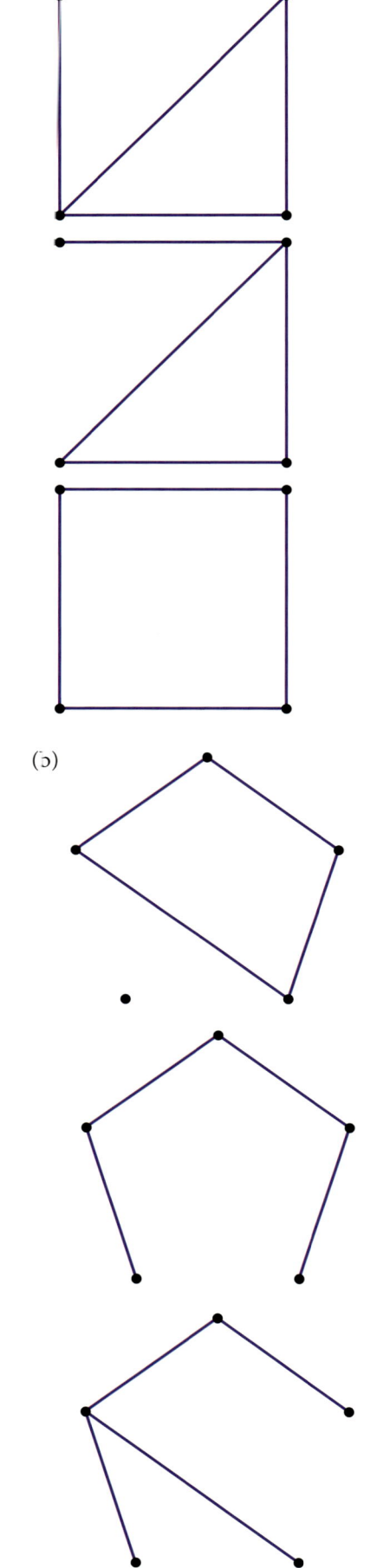

164   Answers

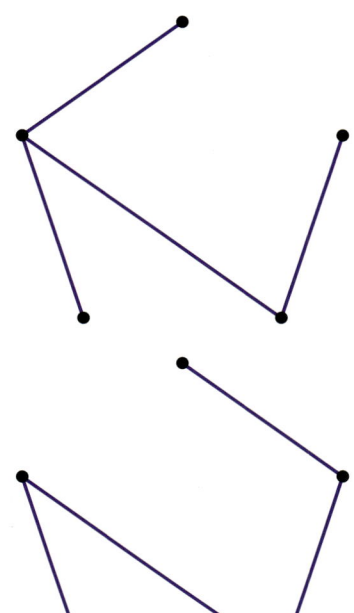

4. (a)

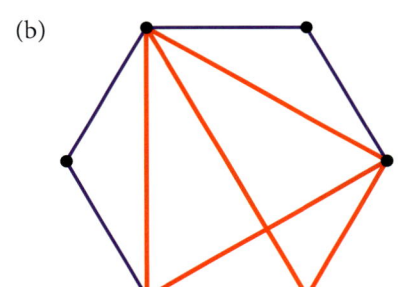

(b)

5. There are many possible answers

6. (b) At least one group of vertices must have at least 3 vertices, so in the complement there will be cycles of length 3.

Exercise 6E

1. (a) *ABCD, ADBC, ADCD, ADAD*
   (b) *AECD, ADAD, ADCD, ABCD, ABAD, AEAD*
   (c) *ADAD, ACAD*
   (d) *AABD, AAAD*

2. (a) *ABCDA*
   (b) *ABCDA, ABCEA, ADCEA*
   (c) None
   (d) None

3. (a) 2
   (b) 2
   (c) 0

4. (a) 2
   (b) 4
   (c) 20

Exercise 6F

1. (a) Eulerian
   (b) Semi-Eulerian
   (c) Semi-Eulerian
   (d) Neither

2. (b) and (c)

3. (a) Four vertices have odd degree
   (b) *SMNPQNRQMRS*

4. There are two vertices of odd degree; *YWXVYZWUVZ*

Exercise 6G

1. (a) *AFGHEDCBA*   (b) *ADBFCEA*
   (c) *ABCFEHGDA*   (d) *ABCDEFGHA*

2. (a) (i) *ABCDA*

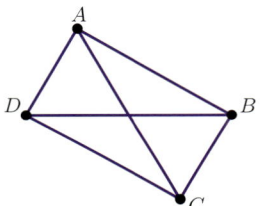

   (ii) *ABCDEA*

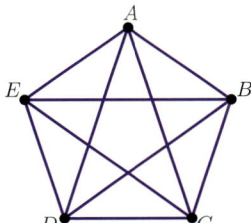

   (b) (i) *AEBFCGDHA*

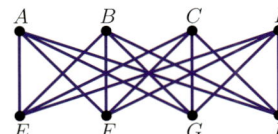

   (ii) *ADBECFA*

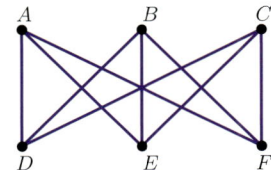

3. 6

Mixed examination practice 6

1. (a)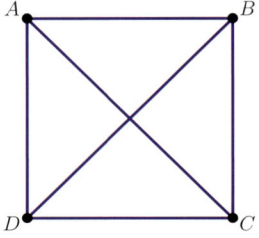

   (c) ABCDA, ABDCA, ACBDA

2. (a) G2; degrees are all even: 2, 4, 2, 4, 2
   (b) ABCDEBDA

3. (a)

	A	B	C	D	E
A	0	0	0	1	1
B	0	0	1	1	1
C	0	1	0	1	0
D	1	1	1	0	0
E	1	1	0	0	0

   (b) BCBC, BCBD, BEBD, BEAD

6. (a) $\binom{n}{2} - e$
   (b) $n-1$
   (c) solve $\binom{n}{2} - (n-1) = n-1$
   (d)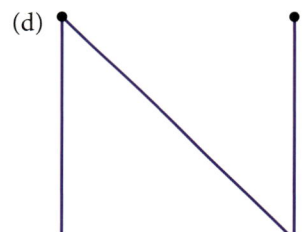

7. (c) (i) $(n, d) = (1, 6), (2, 5), (3, 4), (5, 2)$ or $(6, 1)$
   Note: $(n, d) = (4, 3)$ not possible
   (ii) $n=1, d=6$ $n=2, d=5$

   $n=3, d=4$ $n=5, d=2$
    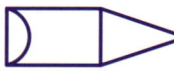

   $n=6, d=1$

8. (c) Yes; all vertices have degree 4, which is even.

9. (b) $v - e + f = 3$

Chapter 7

Exercise 7A

1. (a) (i)

	A	B	C	D	E
A	-	7	8	-	12
B	7	-	-	-	13
C	8	-	-	-	8
D	-	-	-	-	4
E	12	13	8	4	-

   (ii)

	A	B	C	D	E
A	-	5	-	7	5
B	5	-	5	-	7
C	-	5	-	5	7
D	7	-	5	-	5
E	5	7	7	5	-

   (b) (i)

	A	B	C	D	E	F
A	-	3	4	-	-	6
B	3	-	-	1	-	6
C	4	-	-	-	2	7
D	-	1	-	-	-	4
E	-	-	2	-	-	-
F	6	6	7	4	-	-

   (ii)

	A	B	C	D	E	F
A	-	4	5	4	-	-
B	4	-	-	-	-	-
C	5	-	-	-	4	3
D	4	-	-	-	-	3
E	-	-	4	-	-	-
F	-	-	3	3	-	-

2. (a) (i)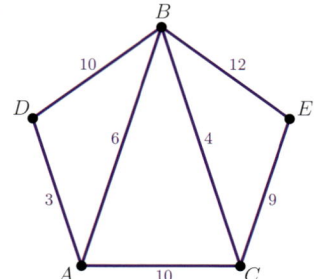

(ii)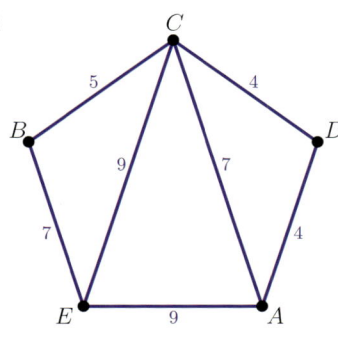

(b) (i)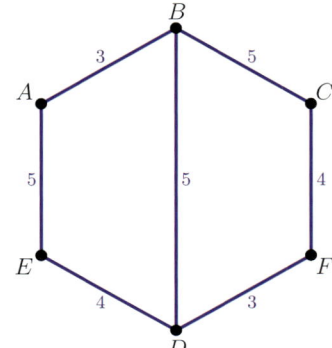

(ii)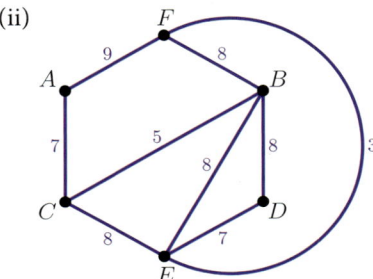

3. (a)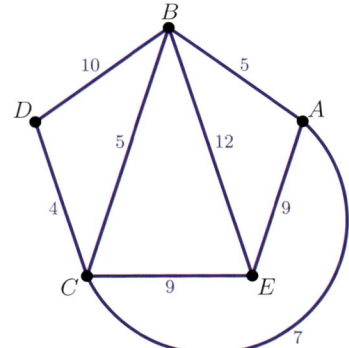

(b)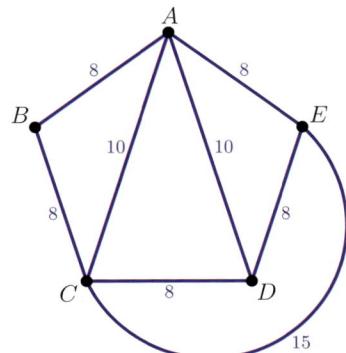

4. (a) ABCDEA, ADCBEA, AEBCDA, AEDCBA

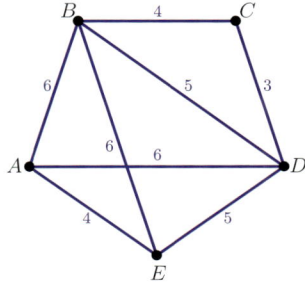

(b) ABCDEA

5. Length = 76

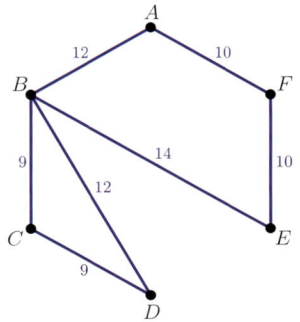

6. All vertices are even; 31

7. (a) B and F have odd degree.
   (b) (i) BF   (ii) 59

Exercise 7B

1. (a) (i) AB, BC, AD, BE (or CE); weight = 41
      (ii) AD, AC, BC, AE; weight = 28
   (b) (i) BG, EH, CD, ED, BH, AB, FG; weight = 141
      (ii) AG, BC, ED, BG, GD, AF; weight = 30
   (c) (i) RS, RP (or PS), SK, SL, LM, RQ, PN; weight = 47
      (ii) PW, PU, PY, PT, PV, PS (or WS), TX, YZ; weight = 91

2. (a) (i) BD, BC, AD, ED; weight = 24
      (ii) AD, AB, BC, AE; weight = 52
   (b) (i) ED, FG, DG (or EF), CG, AC, BD; weight = 120
      (ii) EF, ED, AB, EG, AC, BD; weight = 155
   (c) (i) EF, AB, CF, BC (or BE), AD; weight = 21
      (ii) DF, FC, CE, AB, BE (or DE); weight = 19

3. (a) BD, CD, CE, AB, AF (or EF)
   (b) Add CF first, then start Kruskal's algorithm.

4. (a) Tree of least weight which includes every vertex.
   (b) BD, AC, AE, AF, BE; weight = 45

5. (a) $n - 1$
   (b) It has to be at least $8 + 9 + \cdots + 18 = 143$

6. (a) 49
   (b) 58

7. $x \geq 18$

Answers **167**

Exercise 7C

1. (a) (i)

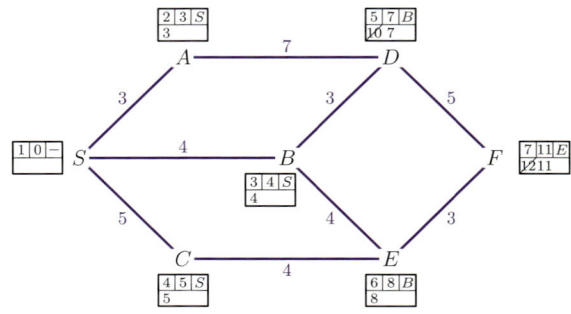

SCEF; 7, 8, 11

(ii)

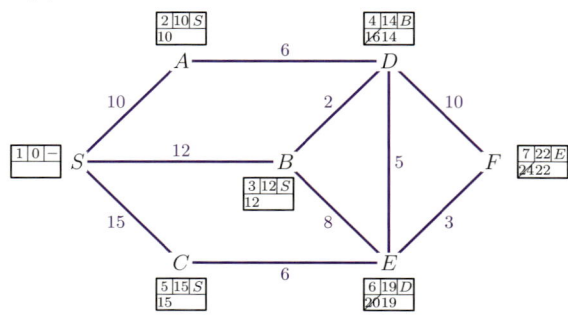

SBDEF; 14, 19, 22

(b) (i)

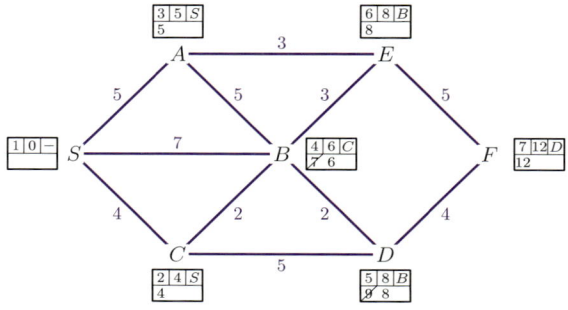

SCBDF; 8, 8, 12

(ii)

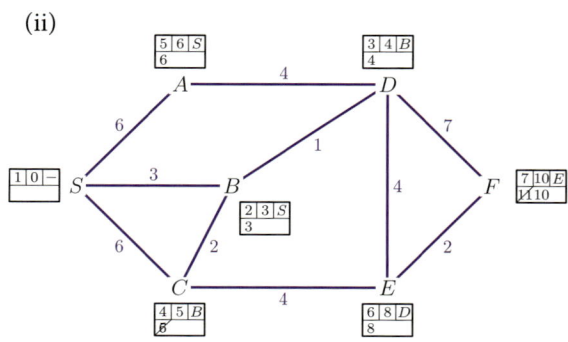

SBDEF; 4, 8, 10

(c) (i)

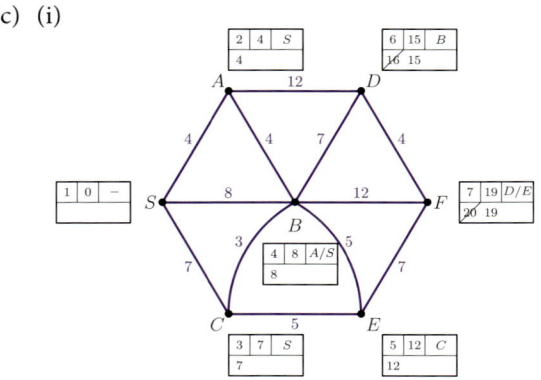

SBDF or SCEF; 15, 12, 19

(ii)

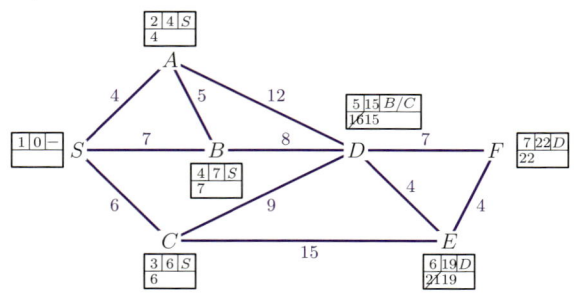

SBDF or SCDF; 15, 19, 22

2. (a) (i) SCET   (ii) SBDET
   (b) (i) SVQT   (ii) SBDT or SABDT

3. (a) (i) SCF   (ii) SCF
   (b) (i) SBGJF or SBCDGJF   (ii) SQBEF

4. (a) SCQRHKM or SBQRHKM or SBPRHKM; cost = 21
   (b) 17

5. (a) 21 (ABEFG)
   (b) ACDEFG

6. $x = 1$

Exercise 7D

1. (b) (i) 50   (ii) 32
   (c) (i) e.g. CDEFABDAEBC
       (ii) e.g. CDEFAECABC

2. (a) (i) Vertices D and F have odd degrees
       (ii) Vertices D and G have odd degrees
   (b) (i) e.g. ABDEFBEGCDEFGA; 70
       (ii) e.g. ABCEHGFDFGEBDA; 40

3. (a) (i) A, B, E, G
       (ii) B, D, F, G
   (b) (i) 78, repeat AB and EG
       (ii) 107, repeat BE, EF and DG

4. (a) O, C
   (b) 9
   (c) 87

5. e.g. CBDFDBAJIHGFHJCFEDC (length 9.1)
6. (a) 99
   (b) 131
7. (a) e.g. AFGAEGBHEDHDCBA, length = 208
   (b) 230
8. (a) C and F have odd degrees
   (b) CEF (15)
   (c) e.g. CEFECDEBACFDBC, length = 180
   (d) (i) 156   (ii) C and F

Exercise 7E

1. (a) (i) 36   (ii) 85
   (b) (i) 63   (ii) 99
   (c) (i) 103   (ii) 110
2. (a) (i) 32   (ii) 77
   (b) (i) 56   (ii) 82
   (c) (i) 95   (ii) 104
3. (a) ABCDA, ABDCA, ACBDA, ACDBA, ADBCA, ADCBA
   (b) $L = 45$
4. (a) The cycle ACBEDA has length 29.
   (b) 28
   (c) 26
5. (a) 40
   (b) 40
   (c) Upper and lower bounds are equal.

Mixed examination practice 7

1. (a) A tree of minimum length which contains every vertex
   (b) BH, NF, HN, HA, BE, CN (weight = 48)
2. (a) Add edges in order of increasing length, skipping any that would create a cycle. Stop when all the vertices are connected.
   (b) EF, BC, CG, IJ, BJ, AB, EG, CH, DE (weight = 117.5)
3. (a) There are several possible answers: the length of any cycle, e.g. ABCDEA gives 73; doubling the weight of the minimum spanning tree gives 92; 5 × the maximum weight of the edges gives 95.
   (b) (i)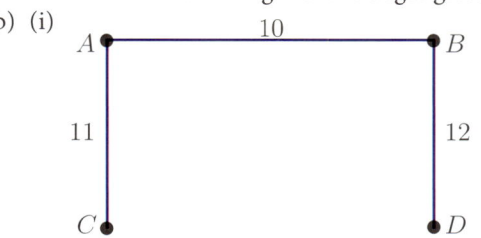
       (ii) weight = 33; LB = 60
4. (a) 114
   (b) 89
   (c) $89 \leq L \leq 114$
5. (a) ACGJ, length = 55

(b) 84 (ACFIJ)
(c) ACFIJ (84)
6. 276
7. (a)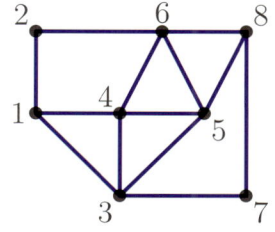
   (b) 1 and 8 have odd degrees
   (c) 1-3-5-8 (length = 12)
   (d) 66
8. (a) A, B, C, D
   (b) length = 92, repeat AE, EB, CG, GD
9. (a) There are vertices of odd degree.
   (b) 890 (repeat AE, ED)
   (c) A and D
10. (a) (i) There are vertices of odd degree.
        (ii) No; there are more than two vertices of odd degree.
    (b) (i) We add one edge between each pair of adjacent vertices, so now all vertices have even degrees.
        (ii) 306 km
11. (a) 33
    (b) The edges included in the lower bound form a cycle.

Chapter 8

Exercise 8A

1. (a) 1, 5, 21, 85, 341
   (b) 3, 1, 3, 1, 3
   (c) 1, 2, 2, 4, 8
   (d) 2, 4, 12, 48, 240

Exercise 8B

1. (a) (i) $2^n + 1$ (ii) $2^{n+1} - 3$
   (b) (i) $-\frac{1}{6}(-3)^n + \frac{1}{2}$
       (ii) $\frac{13}{12}(-3)^n + \frac{5}{4}$
   (c) (i) $\frac{9}{2}\left(\frac{1}{3}\right)^n + \frac{3}{2}$
       (ii) $33\left(\frac{1}{3}\right)^n - 3$
2. $u_n = \left(\frac{u_1}{r}\right)r^n = u_1 r^{n-1}$
3. It gives $d = 0$
4. (a) 8, 48, 248
   (b) $u_n = 2 \times 5^n - 2$

5. (a) $u_n = c \times 2^n + 1$
   (b) $u_n = 1$

Exercise 8C

1. (a) $u_n = 2^n + 3^n$
   (b) $u_n = 2^n - (-2)^n$
   (c) $u_n = 5 + 2^{n+1}$
2. (a) $u_n = (n+1)2^n$
   (b) $u_n = 3 + 2n$
3. (a) $u_n = -3(1+i)^n - 3(1-i)^n$
   (b) $u_n = (1+2i)(1+3i)^n + (1-2i)(1-3i)^n$
4. (a) $u_n = 2\cos\left(\dfrac{n\pi}{3}\right)$
   (b) $u_1 = -6, u_2 = -12$
   $u_n = -6\left(\sqrt{2}\right)^n \sin\left(\dfrac{n\pi}{4}\right)$
5. $u_n = \dfrac{1}{4}\left(2+\sqrt{2}\right)^n + \dfrac{1}{4}\left(2-\sqrt{2}\right)^n$
6. (a) 12
   (c) $a_n = 4^n - (-2)^n$
   (d) $b_n = 4^n + (-2)^n$

Exercise 8D

1. $u_{n+1} = 1.04 u_n$, $u_1 = 1000$,
   $u_{15} = 1800$
2. $u_n = 40\,000(1.05^n - 1)$
3. (b) $u_n = 35\,000 - 18\,812(1.01^n)$
   (c) 62 months
4. (b) $u_1 = 1, u_2 = 2$
   (c) 233
5. (a) $t_{n+2} = \dfrac{1}{2}(t_{n+1} + t_n)$
   (b) $t_n = 23 + 16\left(-\dfrac{1}{2}\right)^n$
   (c) t_n approaches 23, being alternately above and below that value.
6. (b) 1
7. (b) $u_1 = 2, u_2 = 3$
   (c) 2584
8. (a) $H_1 = 1, H_2 = 3$
   (c) $H_n = 2^n - 1$, 1023
9. (b) 130
   (c) 1288
   (d) $R > 50$

Mixed examination practice 8

1. $u_n = \dfrac{1}{4}(5^{n-1} - 1)$
2. (a) $u_n = 0.92 u_{n-1}$
   (b) 11 years
3. $u_n = 3^{n-1}$
4. $u_n = (3-n)(-2)^n$
5. $u_n = (2-i)(3i)^n + (2+i)(-3i)^n$
6. $u_n = 3 + 4\left(-\dfrac{1}{2}\right)^n$
7. (a) (i) u_{n-1}, u_{n-2}
       (ii) $u_{n-1} - u_{n-2}$
       (iii) $9u_{n-2} + (u_{n-1} - u_{n-2})$
   (b) (i) 4
       (ii) $\dfrac{1}{3}\left(4^n - (-2)^n\right)$
8. $a_n = \dfrac{b}{2}(1 - 3^{n-2})$

Chapter 9
Mixed examination practice 9

2. (a) 2 and 4
   (b) (i)

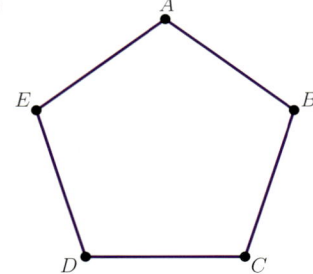

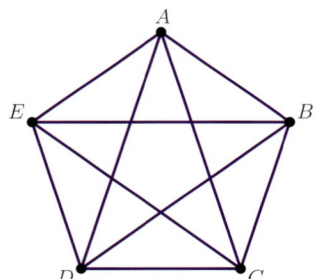

   (ii) Both are Eulerian; $ABCDEA$, $ABCDEACEBDA$
   (c) $ABCDE$
3. (b) $a_k - a_{k-1} + a_{k-2} - a_{k-3} + \ldots$ is divisible by 11
   (c) 22, 55, 88
4. (a) 122
   (b) $x \equiv 2 \pmod{5}$
5. (a) It is a graph containing all the edges which are not in the original graph.
   (b) 9
6. (a) (i) A graph with two sets of vertices such that the vertices from the same set are not adjacent.
       (ii) The number of edges starting from that vertex.
   (b) K is bipartite
   (c) $EDCABC$

7. (b) $x \equiv 14 \pmod{17}$
   (c) $x \equiv 31 \pmod{187}$
8. (b) (i) 9   (ii) 9
9. (b) *ABCDA*, *ABDCA*, *ACBDA*
   (c) $L = 37$ (*ABDCA* or *ACBDA*)
10. (b) *RS*   (c) e.g. *PQRSUV*
11. (a) $m = -1, n = 2$
    (b) (i) $x = -104 + 8k, y = 208 - 15k$
    (c) $x \equiv 3, 18, 33, 48, 63, 78 \pmod{90}$
12. (a) (10 vertices so 9 choices)

Choice	Edge	Weight
1	HP	1
= 2	KQ	2
= 2	QF	2
= 4	FE	3
= 4	PB	3
6	ER	4
= 7	PQ	5
= 7	BC	5
9	CD	6

Total weight = 31

    (b) 48
    (d) 1 814 400
13. (a) Vertices *S* and *T* have odd degree.
    (b) 13 (*SBEGT*)
    (c) 61; *ASBSCEBEGTG EDTFDBA*
14. (a)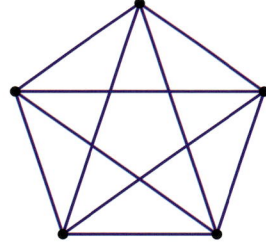

15. (a) All four vertices have odd degree
    (b) 34
16. (a) 6
    (b) 66 and 42 are even, 9 is not
    (c) m divisible by 6
    (d) $x = 6 - 7k, y = -9 + 11k$
17. (c) 281 502 (take $n = 100$)
18. (b) (i) $\binom{n}{2} - e$
19. (a) *AB*, *BC*, *AI*, *DE*, *DG*, *DF*, (or *EF* or *EG*), *BD*, *IH*; weight = 84
    (b) 3
20. (a) $x \equiv 2 \pmod 5$
    (b) 10; there is a unique solution (mod 55)
21. (a) −1, 17, 11, 113, 179
    (b) $u_n = 3^n + 2(-2)^n$
22. (a) *CF*, *EF*, *BC*, *CD*, *AB*
    (b) (i) $v - 1$ (use $v + f = e + 2$ with $f = 1$)
        (ii) $v - c$
23. (b) (i) *AB*, *AD*, *DE*, *BC*
        (ii) 12 m
    (c) (i) Each vertex has degree 4, which is even.
        (ii) *ABCDEACEBDA*, 46
24. (a) *CD*, *AB*, *BC*, *BF*, *CE*
    (b) (i) 213
        (ii) 239
        (iii) 239
    (c) $239 \leq L \leq 253$
25. (b) $u_n = 2100 - 1000 \times 1.05^n$
    (c) 16 years

Answers   **171**

Glossary

Words that appear in **bold** in the definitions of other terms are also defined in this glossary. The abstract nature of this option means that some defined terms can realistically only be explained in terms of other, more simple concepts.

Term	Definition	Example
adjacency table	A table showing which vertices in a **graph** are joined by **edges**.	The following table shows that the edges of the graph are AB and BC: |	A	B	C
---	---	---	---
A	0	1	0
B	1	0	1
C	0	1	0	
adjacent	(of **vertices** or **edges** in a **graph**) joined to each other.	Two vertices are adjacent if they are joined by an edge; two edges are adjacent if they are joined by a vertex.
algorithm	A specified sequence of steps guaranteed to answer a certain question.	Kruskal's algorithm is a sequence of steps guaranteed to find the minimum spanning tree of a graph.
auxiliary equation	A quadratic equation used in solving a **second order linear recurrence relation**.	The recurrence relation $u_{n+2} = u_{n+1} + 2u_n$ has auxiliary equation $k^2 = k + 2$.
base 10	A system for writing numbers using ten digits, 0 to 9, where moving a digit a place value to the left increases its value ten times.	In base ten, the '3' in 438 has value $3 \times 10 = 30$.
base cases	Initial cases that need to be tested in order to start a **proof by induction**.	
bipartite graph	A graph whose vertices can be split into two groups such that only vertices from different groups are joined.	
Chinese postman problem	To find the route of shortest length which includes every edge of a graph and returns to the starting point.	In an **Eulerian graph**, every **Eulerian circuit** is a solution of the Chinese postman problem.
Chinese remainder theorem	A result about the existence of solutions of a system of **linear congruences**.	According to the Chinese remainder theorem, the system of congruence $3x \equiv 5 \pmod{7}$, $2x \equiv 1 \pmod{9}$ has a unique solution modulo 63.
circuit	A closed **trail**.	
complement (of a graph)	A graph consisting of all the edges that were not in the original graph.	If a graph has 4 vertices and 2 edges, its complement has 4 edges.
complete bipartite graph	A bipartite graph where every vertex in one group is joined to every vertex from the other group.	The complete bipartite graph $\kappa_{3,3}$ is not **planar**.
complete graph	A graph in which every pair of vertices is joined by an edge.	A complete graph with 4 vertices has 6 edges.

Term	Definition	Example
composite	An integer that is not prime.	15 is a composite number because $15 = 3 \times 5$.
congruent modulo 12	When two numbers give the same remainder when divided by 12.	5 and 29 are congruent modulo 12.
connected graph	A graph in which it is possible to find a path from any vertex to any other vertex.	
constant coefficients (equation with)	An equation in which coefficients do not depend on n.	The recurrence relation $u_{n+1} = nu_n$ does not have constant coefficients.
cycle	A closed **path**.	
degree (of a **vertex**)	The number of **edges** coming out of the vertex.	
degree sequence	The list of **degrees** of all the **vertices** in a graph.	The degree sequence is important in determining whether a graph is **Eulerian**.
Dijkstra's algorithm	An algorithm for finding the shortest path between two vertices in a graph.	
Diophantine equation	An equation where we are only looking for integer solutions.	Some Diophantine equations can be solved by looking at factors and divisibility. For example, the equation $2n^2 + 4n = 5$ has no integer solutions because the left side is even and the right side is odd.
direct proof	A proof where a new fact is derived by calculation or reasoning directly from previously known facts.	We can prove that $(a-b)(a+b) = a^2 - b^2$ directly by expanding brackets and simplifying.
directed graph (or digraph)	A **graph** in which each **edge** has a specified direction.	A directed graph could be used to represent a network of one-way roads.
divisibility test	A test for determining whether one integer is divisible by another without carrying out the division.	We know that 475 is divisible by 5 because the units digit is 5.
division algorithm	The process of finding the **quotient** and **remainder** when dividing two integers.	We can write $23 = 4 \times 5 + 3$.
edges	'Lines' connecting **vertices** in a graph.	
Euclid's lemma	A statement about prime numbers, saying that if a prime divides a product then it must divide both factors.	We often use Euclid's lemma in proofs involving factorising.
Euclidean algorithm	A method for finding the **greatest common divisor** of two integers without explicitly finding all their prime factors.	We can use Euclidean algorithm in to find a **particular solution** of a **Diophantine equation**.
Euler's relation	A rule giving a relationship between the number of edges, vertices and number of regions of a planar graph.	A **complete graph** with three vertices has $v = 3, e = 3, f = 2$, and satisfies $v - e + f = 2$.

Glossary

Term	Definition	Example
Eulerian circuit	A closed **trail** around a graph which uses each edge exactly once.	Every Eulerian circuit is a solution to the **Chinese postman problem**.
Eulerian graph	A graph that has an **Eulerian circuit**.	An Eulerian graph can be drawn without picking up the pen and without repeating any edges.
Eulerian trail	A **trail** which uses each edge exactly once, but does not return to the starting point.	A graph which has an Eulerian trail is called **semi-Eulerian**.
Fermat's little theorem	A result allowing us to find the smallest power of a number which gives remainder 1 when divided by a prime.	$15^{12} \equiv 1 \pmod{13}$
first order recurrence	A recurrence relation in which each term in a sequence depends on one previous term.	A geometric sequence can be described by a first order recurrence relation.
Fundamental Theorem of Arithmetic	The result stating that every positive integer can be written as a product of prime factors in exactly one way.	$30 = 2 \times 3 \times 5$ and there is no other way to write 30 as a product of prime numbers.
general solution	An expression describing all possible solutions of an equation.	The general solution of the **Diophantine equation** $x + y = 5$ is $x = t, y = 5 - t$ ($t \in \mathbb{Z}$).
graph	A set of points connected by lines.	
greatest common divisor (gcd)	The largest integer which divides two given integers.	The greatest common divisor of 12 and 42 is 6.
greedy algorithm	An algorithm in which the best possible option is chosen at every stage.	Kruskal's algorithm is an example of a greedy algorithm, whereas Dijkstra's algorithm is not.
Hamiltonian cycle	A closed path which includes every vertex of a graph.	The **travelling salesman problem** is to find the shortest Hamiltonian cycle in a graph.
Hamiltonian graph	A graph which has a **Hamiltonian cycle**.	Every **complete graph** is Hamiltonian.
Hamiltonian path	A path which includes every vertex of a graph.	
homogeneous equation	A **linear recurrence relation** with no constant term.	The recurrence relation $u_{n+1} = u_n + 2$ is not homogeneous.
indirect proof	A proof where a new fact is derived using previously known facts, but not in a direct way.	**Proof by contradiction** is one example of indirect proof.
inductive step	A part of **proof by induction** where we show how, if we have already proved the statement up to a certain value of n, we can use this to prove it for the next value of n.	
Kruskal's algorithm	An algorithm for finding the minimum spanning tree of a graph.	
least common multiple	The smallest integer which is divisible by two given integers.	The least common multiple of 6 and 9 is 18.
linear congruences	Equations in which we are only interested in remainders, rather than the actual numbers.	The linear congruence $3x \equiv 6 \pmod{7}$ is satisfied by all integers which give remainder 2 when divided by 7.

Term	Definition	Example
linear recurrence relations	A recurrence relation in which the terms of the sequence appear as linear terms.	The recurrence relation $u_{n+1} = u_n^2$ is not linear.
loop	(in a graph) An edge connecting a vertex to itself.	
lower bound	A number which is known to be smaller than (or equal to) the desired solution.	A lower bound for the **travelling salesman problem** can be found by removing one vertex from the graph.
minimum connector problem	To find the shortest tree containing all the vertices of a graph.	The minimum connector is the same as the minimum spanning tree.
minimum spanning tree	The tree of smallest length which contains all the vertices of a graph.	Minimum spanning tree can be found using **Kruskal's algorithm**.
modular arithmetic	Rules for calculating with remainders.	If x gives remainder 2 when divided by 6 and y gives remainder 3, then $x + y$ gives remainder 5.
multigraph	A graph where some edges are connected by more than one vertex.	
particular solution	One possible solution of an equation.	$x = 2, y = 3$ is one particular solution of $x + y = 5$.
path	A **walk** with no repeated vertices.	
permanent labels	(in **Dijkstra's algorithm**) A number assigned to a vertex showing the shortest possible distance from the starting vertex.	
pigeonhole principle	A principle stating that if $n + 1$ objects are divided into n groups, then there must be a group containing at least two objects.	We can use the pigeonhole principle to show that every graph contains two vertices with the same **degree**.
planar graph	A graph that can be drawn without edges intersecting.	The **complete graph** K_5 is not planar.
prime factorisation	Writing a number as a product of its prime factors.	$50 = 2 \times 5^2$
prime number	An integer that has exactly two factors – 1 and itself.	5 is a prime number, but 1 is not.
proof by contradiction	A method of proving a statement by showing that assuming its opposite leads to impossible consequences.	It can be proved by contradiction that $\sqrt{2}$ is an irrational number.
proof by induction	A 'step by step' method of proving that a statement is true for all natural numbers.	You used proof by induction in the Core syllabus to prove De Moivre's Theorem.
quotient	The (integer part of the) result of dividing two integers.	The quotient when 23 is divided by 5 is 4.
recurrence relation	A relationship showing how a term in a sequence depends on previous terms.	$u_{n+2} = u_{n+1} u_n$ is an example of a recurrence relation.
relatively prime (or coprime)	Two integers whose **greatest common divisor** is 1.	12 and 35 are relatively prime.
remainder	The amount left over when we try to divide one integer by another.	The remainder when 23 is divided by 5 is 3.
Route inspection	Same as **Chinese postman problem**.	

Glossary

Term	Definition	Example
Route inspection algorithm	An algorithm for solving the **Chinese postman problem**.	
second order recurrence	A recurrence relation in which each term in a sequence depends on two previous terms.	The Fibonacci sequence can be described by a second order recurrence relation.
semi-Eulerian graph	A graph that has an **Eulerian trail**.	In a semi-Eulerian graph we can solve the variant of the **Chinese postman problem** where we do not need to return to the starting vertex; the solution is any Eulerian trail.
simple graph	A graph which has no **loops** or multiple edges between vertices.	Many theorems in this course apply only to simple graphs.
strong induction	A variant on **proof by induction** where we need to use more than one previous value of n in the **inductive step**.	In this Option we use strong induction to prove Euler's relation for planar graphs.
subgraph	A graph which is a part of another graph.	The **minimum spanning tree** is a subgraph.
temporary label	(in **Dijkstra's algorithm**) A number assigned to a vertex showing the shortest distance from the starting vertex found so far.	
The Handshaking lemma	The result stating that the sum of **degrees** of all the vertices in a graph is equal to twice the number of edges.	The Handshaking lemma implies that the number of odd vertices in a graph has to be even. This is important in the **Route inspection algorithm**.
trail	A **walk** with no repeated edges.	
travelling salesman problem	To find the route of shortest length which includes every vertex of the graph and returns to the starting point.	Visiting every town in a region in the shortest possible time is an example of a travelling salesman problem.
tree	A graph with no **cycles**.	A tree with 10 vertices has 9 edges.
upper bound	A number which is known to be larger than (or equal to) the desired solution.	An upper bound for the **travelling salesman problem** can be found using the nearest neighbour algorithm.
vertices (vertex)	'Points' in a graph.	
walk	Any sequence of adjacent edges.	
weight	A number associated with an edge in a graph.	The weight of an edge could represent the cost of travelling between two vertices.
weighted graph	A graph in which each edge has an associated weight.	A weighted graph could represent a road network with weights being the lengths of the roads.

Index

adjacency tables, 70, 74–75, 95, 98–99, 172
adjacent (of vertices), 69, 172
algorithm, defined, 172
arithmetic
    in different bases, 36–39
    Fundamental Theorem of, 27–28
    see also modular arithmetic
auxiliary equation, 140–42, 172

base 10, 33–35, 40, 172
base cases, 10, 11, 172
    strong induction, 73–74
bases, 33–35
    arithmetic in different, 36–39
    changing between different, 35–36
    exercises, 34–35
    mixed exam practice, 41
    summary, 40
binary numbers, 33, 34
bipartite graph, 72, 95, 172

Cantor's diagonal proof, 5
Chinese postman algorithm, 113
Chinese postman problem, 112–14, 125, 172
    exercises, 115–18
Chinese remainder theorem, 59–61, 65, 172
    exercises, 61–62
circuit, 87, 95, 172
    Eulerian, 90, 112
complement (of a graph), 85, 95, 172
    exercises, 85–87, 97
complete bipartite graph, 72, 172
complete graph, 72, 95, 172
    and Hamiltonian cycle, 93, 118–19
    planar graph proof, 82–83
    subgraph of, 85
complex roots, recurrence relations, 141
composite numbers, 26, 28, 173
    divisibility by, 63–64
congruences
    linear, 57–59
    simultaneous, 59–62
congruent modulo 12, 51, 173
congruent modulo m rule, 53–54
connected graphs, 71, 95, 173
    exercises, 78, 85
    planar graph proofs, 81, 83–84
    trees as, 73–74
constant coefficients, linear recurrences, 136, 139, 173
constraints, solutions subject to, 47–48
contradiction, proof by, 3, 4–6, 7, 28, 29, 175
coprime (relatively prime) numbers, 20, 21, 23, 26, 175
    Chinese remainder theorem, 60, 61, 63
    division rule, 56
cost adjacency matrix, 98, 101, 109, 130
cycle, 73, 95, 173
    Hamiltonian, 93, 118–21

decimal (base 10) system, 33–34
degree (of a vertex), 70, 95, 173
    and Chinese postman problem, 112–14
    Eulerian graphs, 89–91
    theorems, 79–80
degree sequence of a graph, 70–71, 173
digraph, 69, 95, 173
Dijkstra's algorithm, 106–12, 173
    fill-in diagrams, 131–33
Diophantine equations, 1, 42–43, 49, 173
    finding number of solutions for, 44–46
    general solution, 46–47
    solutions subject to constraints, 47–48
direct proof, 3, 173
directed graph, 69, 173
Dirichlet's principle, 6
divisibility tests, 14–17, 38–39, 40, 173
division algorithm, 14, 31, 173
division/divisibility
    by a composite number, 63–64
    and linear congruences, 56–59
    and remainders, 51–52
    of whole numbers, 13–19
duodecimal (base 12) system, 34

edges, graphs, 69, 70, 95, 173
    theorems involving, 79–85
equations with integer solutions, 42–43
Euclidean algorithm, 23–25, 31, 173
Euclid's lemma, 26, 28, 173
Eulerian circuit, 90, 95, 112, 174
Eulerian graphs, 89–92, 95, 174
Eulerian trail, 90–91, 95, 174
Euler's relation, 80–82, 83, 95, 173

factors, 13–18
Fermat numbers, 12
Fermat's Last Theorem, 2, 43
Fermat's Little Theorem, 62–64, 65, 174
Fibonacci sequence
    example of a second order recurrence, 134
    formula for the nth term, 140
    for modelling population growth, 144–45
    proof by strong induction, 9
first order linear recurrence relations, 136–39, 174
    modelling a savings accounts, 143–44
Fundamental Theorem of Arithmetic, 27–28, 31, 174

general solution, 46–47, 48, 49, 174
    recurrence relation, 137, 140
graph algorithms, 98
    Chinese postman algorithm, 112–18
    Dijkstra's algorithm, 106–12
    Kruskal's algorithm, 102–6
    minimum spanning tree, 102–6
    mixed exam practice, 126–30
    Route inspection problem, 112–18

shortest path, 106–12
summary, 124–25
travelling salesman problem, 118–24
visiting all the vertices, 118–24
weighted graphs, 98–102
graph theory, 2, 67–69
Eulerian graphs, 89–92
Hamiltonian graphs, 93–94
important theorems, 79–85
mixed exam practice, 96–97
moving around a graph, 87–89
subgraphs and complements, 85–87
summary, 95
terminology, 69–78
greatest common divisor (gcd), 19–23, 31, 174
exercises, 23, 25
method for finding, 23–25
greedy algorithm, 102, 174
Green-Tao theorem, 29

Hamiltonian cycle, 93, 95, 174
exercises, 94, 96, 99, 101
travelling salesman problem, 118–21
Hamiltonian graphs, 93–94, 174
Hamiltonian path, 93, 174
Handshaking lemma, 79, 176
homogeneous (recurrence relations), 139, 174
solving second order, 142

indirect proof, 3, 174
inductive proofs, 3, 9–12, 18, 73–74, 135
inductive step, 10, 174
integers
divisibility of, 13–18, 63–64
representation in different bases, 33–39
solutions of equations, 42–44
see also prime numbers
introductory problem, 1, 149
irrational numbers, proof by contradiction, 3, 4

Kruskal's algorithm, 102–4, 124, 174
exercises, 104–6, 126–27

labelling, Dijkstra's algorithm, 107–9
law of excluded middle, 4
least common multiple (lcm), 21–23, 31, 174
linear congruences, 57–59, 174
linear Diophantine equations, 42–44, 49, 173
determining if solutions exist, 44–46
finding the general solution, 46–47
mixed exam practice, 50
solutions subject to constraints, 47–48
linear recurrence relations, 136–39, 143–44, 175
logic, 2
logistic maps, 136
loop (in a graph), 70, 175
lower bound, 119–22, 125, 175

methods of proof, 3
pigeonhole principle, 6–8
proof by contradiction, 4–6
strong induction, 9–12
minimum connector problem, 102, 175

minimum spanning tree, 102–6, 175
mixed exam practice, 151–57
algorithms on graphs, 126–30
Diophantine equations, 50
divisibility and prime numbers, 32
graph theory, 96–97
modular arithmetic, 66
recurrence relations, 148
representing integers in different bases, 41
modular arithmetic, 51–52, 149, 175
Chinese remainder theorem, 59–62
division and linear congruences, 56–59
Fermat's little theorem, 62–65
rules of, 53–56
summary, 65
multigraphs, 70, 175
multiples, 13–18

nearest neighbour algorithm, 119, 120, 121
exercises, 123–24, 127
network modelling see graph algorithms; graph theory
non-constructive existence proof, 8
number systems, 33–34
number theory, 1–2
Euclidean algorithm, 23–25
factors, multiples and remainders, 13–18
greatest common divisor, 19–21
least common multiple, 21–23
prime numbers, 26–29

Occam's razor, 137
optimisation problems, graphs, 2, 67–68
minimum spanning tree, 102–6
shortest path between two vertices, 106–12
shortest route around a graph, 112–18
shortest route visiting all the vertices, 118–24

particular solution, 46, 48, 49, 175
path, 87, 88, 95, 175
closed path (cycle), 73, 74, 75
Hamiltonian path, 93
permanent label, 107, 108, 109, 124–25, 176
pigeonhole principle, 6–8, 175
simple graph proof, 71
planar graphs, 74–75, 80–85, 95, 175
population growth, modelling, 144–45
powers
factors of integer, 16, 31
modular arithmetic, 55, 62–63, 64
prime factorisation, 26–27, 28, 175
prime factors, 21–22
Prime Number Theorem, 28
prime numbers, 26–30, 175
relatively prime, 20, 21, 23
proof by contradiction, 3, 4–6, 7, 28, 29, 175
proof by induction, 3
divisibility example, 18
recurrence relations, 135
strong induction, 9–12
Pythagorean triples, 43

quadratic equation see auxiliary equation
quotient, 14, 175

Ramsey's theorem, 8
recurrence relations, 2, 134, 147, 175
    applications of, 143–47
    defining sequences, 134–36
    first order linear, 136–39
    mixed exam practice, 149
    second order quadratic, 139–43
    summary, 148
recursive definitions of sequences, 134–36
reductio ad absurdum, 4
relatively prime (coprime) numbers, 20, 21, 23, 26, 175
    division rule, 56
    and Fermat's little theorem, 63
remainders, 13–18, 175
    Fermat's little theorem, 62–64
    see also modular arithmetic
repeated roots, recurrence relations, 141–42
Route inspection algorithm, 125, 176
    Chinese postman problem, 112–18
route optimisation *see* optimisation problems, graphs

second order recurrence, 134, 176
second order recurrence relations, 139–43, 147
    modelling population growth, 144–45
semi-Eulerian graph, 90–91, 95, 176
sequences
    defining recursively, 134–36
    degree sequence of a graph, 70–71
    proofs by induction, 9–12
    see also recurrence relations
shortest route problems, graphs, 106–24
simple graphs, 70, 95, 176
    complement of, 85
    degree sequence of, 71
simultaneous congruences, 59–62
strong induction, 9–12, 176
    prime numbers proof, 27
    recurrence relations proof, 135
    tree proof, 73–74
subgraphs, 85–87, 95, 176
    minimum spanning tree, 102–6

temporary label, 107, 108, 109, 124–25, 176
trail, 87, 95, 176
    Eulerian, 90–91
travelling along the edges, 112–24
travelling salesman problem, 118–24, 176
tree, 73–74, 95, 176
    minimum spanning tree, 102–6

upper bound, 119–22, 125, 176

vertex/vertices, 95, 176
    labelling of, Dijkstra's algorithm, 107–9
    theorems involving, 79–85
    visiting all: travelling salesman problem, 118–24
visiting all the vertices, 118–24

walks (around a graph), 87, 95, 176
    closed, 89–90
weight (of an edge), 98, 124, 176
    minimum spanning trees, 102–4
weighted graphs, 98–102, 124, 176